Land, Labor, and Rural Poverty

Land, Labor, and Rural Poverty
Essays in Development Economics

Pranab K. Bardhan

DELHI
OXFORD UNIVERSITY PRESS
BOMBAY   CALCUTTA   MADRAS
1984

Columbia University Press
New York Guildford, Surrey
Copyright © 1984 Columbia University Press

HD
2072
.B29
1982

338.10954
B235

Library of Congress Cataloging in Publication Data
Bardhan, Pranab K.
Land, labor, and rural poverty.

Bibliography: p.
Includes indexes.
1. Agriculture—Economic aspects—India. 2. India—
Rural conditions. 3. Agricultural laborers—India.
4. Land tenure—India. 5. Rural poor—India. I. Title.
HD2072.B29   1982   338.1'0954   83–10082
ISBN 0-231-05388-6
ISBN 0-231-05389-4 (pbk.)

Printed in the United States of America

app 1/14/85

Contents

Preface

Over the years I have taught several courses on economic development at Delhi, Cambridge (Massachusetts), and Berkeley. But I always have a nagging sense of unease at the amorphousness of the material I am supposed to cover in such a course. The subject matter is often loosely defined, its boundaries unmarked, and a compact structure almost nonexistent, even unwanted. There is a permissive atmosphere of "anything goes" and the students cannot be blamed for considering the subject as one of the soft options. This is particularly the case when one deals with the issues of agrarian relations and rural development. Everybody recognizes that these issues are of fundamental importance. But the model-builders of development economics largely ignore them, relegating them to the black box of "institutional" issues, and the institutional economists in their turn often fail to apply rigorous analytical method in discerning meaningful patterns in their largely descriptive materials. As a result preconceived cliches and anecdotal anarchy prevail in the literature.

This book was born out of this sense of frustration, even though it is clearly inadequate in relieving it. It attempts to provide some balance, however tenuous, between formal theoretical analysis and statistical testing (on large sets of data collected from both secondary household survey materials and primary village investigations in India, in the conducting of which I myself participated) and also between rigorous quantitative analysis and a more qualitative probing into the nuances of agrarian relations and their sociological-institutional background. Such acts of balancing opposites usually leave purists on all sides highly dissatisfied, and I do not expect mine to have a different reception. It is also in the nature of this exercise to cross the boundaries of several disciplines. While some of the theoretical analysis in subsequent chapters draws upon ideas and tools forged at the very frontier of current economic theory (for example, those relating to implicit contracts or principal-agent games), quite often our institutional probes take us deep into the territory of social anthropology, cultural geography, or demography. Such "essays in trespassing" (to use the phrase of that distinguished poacher, Albert Hirschman) are bound to be shot at by the border guards of all the disciplines concerned.

Another boundary that the book in its foolhardiness attempts to straddle is that between Marxists and the so-called neoclassicals, the vicious barbed-wire fence that usually divides them. The book shamelessly uses neoclassical-looking tools to analyze problems of traditional Marxist concern. Some explanatory comments on this brand of heretical eclecticism are provided in the introductory chapter. I intend to return to this general theme in more detail elsewhere. Let me only note here that among some Marxist philosophers and social scientists there is growing recognition of the methodological necessity of tracing the microfoundations of class analysis in postulates of individual behavior and the usefulness of rational choice theory in understanding the mechanism of change, relating to the key questions of historical materialism (see, for example, the symposium on "Marxism, Functionalism, and Game Theory" in *Theory and Society*, July 1982).

Economists and development administrators will also note in the subsequent pages the conspicuous absence of policy suggestions. This is somewhat deliberate, arising partly out of my belief that policy discussion without a well-developed theory of the state is largely vacuous. My major purpose in this book is to try to understand the genesis of particular economic institutions in a localized rural context and also the changes in those institutions. I intend to address myself to state-theoretic questions on a separate occasion. Nevertheless, I note at least two recurrent propositions in the subsequent chapters, which may have important policy implications: one relates to how the absence of credit or insurance markets leads to contractual interlinking of land, labor, and credit relations—piecemeal reformist measures which tinker with one part of these transactions without taking care of the interconnections may even worsen the lot of the poor tenant-laborer-borrower; the other underlines the importance of channeling organizational resources toward the building of viable local community institutions, cooperative water management, and provision of alternate sources of credit and social insurance.

This book, like the proverbial Indian peasant, is born heavily in debt. The primary village surveys reported in chapter 9 and elsewhere in the book as well as their empirical analysis were jointly conducted with Ashok Rudra. Chapters 7 and 8 grew out of joint work with Nirvikar Singh, and chapter 6 with Michael Riordan. At various times during the process of writing this book, research and salary support has been provided by fellowships or grants from the J.S. Guggenheim Foundation, the Social Science Research Council, and the National Science Foundation. In the intricate task of managing and analyzing several large data tapes, I received very competent assistance from Karl Iorio, Tom Paynter, and Brian Newton. Dilip Dutta helped in the computation of the appendix data tables, as well as in the preparation of the author index; the subject index was prepared by Dan Hagen. V.M. Dandekar helped me gain access to the data tapes of the National Sample Survey in India, and Sudhir Bhattacharyya of the N.S.S. office was patient in answering all my queries about the data. I have benefited from comments on an earlier draft of this book by Irma Adelman, Bent Hansen, and T.N. Srinivasan; the remaining errors and blemishes are no doubt because of my laxity in following up on all their suggestions for improvement.

Some of the subsequent chapters draw upon revised versions of excerpts from my articles published in the *American Economic Review, American Journal of Agricultural Economics, Economic and Political Weekly, Journal of Development Economics, Journal of Development Studies, Journal of Peasant Studies, Journal of Political Economy, Oxford Economic Papers,* and *Quarterly Journal of Economics.* I am also grateful to Cornell University Press and Longman Group Limited for permitting me to reproduce our figure 15-1 from David E. Sopher, "The Geographic Patterning of Culture in India" in *An Exploration of India: Geographical Perspectives on Society and Culture,* edited by David E. Sopher, 1980. Finally, my thanks are due to the staff in the department of economics and the Institute of International Studies at the University of California, Berkeley, for cheerfully carrying out the typing chores on several drafts.

Introduction

Until very recently much of the analytical attention in development economics has been devoted to macro issues: choice between import substitution and more liberal trade regimes, investment criteria and optimal economic planning, intersectoral transfer and allocation of resources in dual-economy models, and so on. But the microfoundations of these development models are usually rather shaky. For example, they either implicitly assume smooth operation of the various individual commodity and factor markets involved or, more often, distinguish themselves from the models relating to industrially advanced countries by throwing in rigid and mechanical assumptions like that of the "institutionally given" wage rate in the labor market. Apart from the fact that the market is a historical category which may not be fully applicable in some social formations, in the case of factor markets in particular (as opposed to commodity markets) we are in, what Hicks (1969) calls "relatively refractory territory." The macro development literature ignores, for example, the various special (often personalized) ties between individual agents in economic transactions, the kinds of implicit future contracts they often enter into, the moral boundaries of their economic community, and the nature of segmentation of markets all this involves. Even in the micro development literature these issues have been overshadowed by the long and tedious arguments and counterarguments on the "surplus labor" hypothesis or the sterile statistical exercises of fitting production functions.

There are, of course, some who have always been critical of the glib "neoclassical" assumption of smoothly operating market mechanisms or well-behaved production functions. But more often than not, they in their own analysis have not gone beyond a kind of murky institutionalism: economic analysis has got lost in the thick fog of smug statements of it-all-depends-on-institutions-and-the-class-structure variety. While I also believe in the crucial importance of institutional factors and the class structure, a ritual reference to them cannot serve as a substitute for rigorous analysis. In particular, although the behavior of economic agents is seriously constrained by institutions, the latter themselves are constantly shaped by economic, demographic, and technological factors, and the economist cannot shirk the responsibility of analyzing this process of shaping. Institutions in the factor markets of an agrarian economy, like that of labor-tying, sharecropping, and interlocking of land or labor contracts with credit, cannot just be taken as "frozen" data from history; it is important to understand the rationale of the formation of these institutions, how one form was "selected" over another, and how in the historical-evolutionary process the underlying rationale changes and the institutional forms adapt and mutate in response to the changed circumstances.

To take one important example, Marxist economists and sociologists often emphasize how given exploitative "relations of production" (like sharecropping) act as a "fetter" on the development of the "forces of production" and cite that as an institutional obstacle to development. The neoclassical property-rights school, on the other hand, emphasizes how, given well-defined property rights, efficient resource allocation is independent of the choice of land tenure. The latter school often ignores the serious cases of market failures, incomplete markets, and information asymmetry (which falsify the presumption of efficiency of resource allocation) that give rise to sharecropping as an imperfect economic response. But the Marxists often ignore the origin and nature of this economic response: under a set of constraints (like market failure), sharecropping does serve a real economic function, and its simple abolition without taking care of the factors that gave rise to this institution in the first place may not necessarily improve the conditions of the intended beneficiaries of the abolition program. Marxists have also a tendency to equate sharecropping tenancy with a particular ("feudal") mode of production, thus ignoring how in the real world the same institution adapts itself to the development of the forces of production. All this suggests that, while institutions, property structure, and production relations seriously circumscribe the development of technology, one must not forget that over time the former get shaped in important ways by the material base itself. That some Marxists need to be reminded of this is somewhat ironic, since it is usually a part of Marxist orthodoxy to assign "primacy" to the material base. Of course, in my judgment, the "primacy thesis" is much too narrow,[1] and it overlooks the two-way feedback process between "forces of production" and "relations of production" in the laws of motion of history.

Land, labor, credit, production relations, and rural poverty are some of the central issues discussed in this book. The frame of reference for the application of our ideas is the agrarian economy of India in recent years. The subsequent chapters of the book are divided into three parts. Part A consists of essays dealing with agricultural labor. Part B consists of essays dealing with land lease contracts. Part C is a collection of essays on different aspects of production relations in agriculture and the complexities of relationships between growth and poverty, and poverty and

---

[1] For a recent critique of the "primacy thesis" from a Marxist point of view, see the review article on Cohen (1978) by Levine and Wright (1980).

mortality. An introductory essay to each Part gives a brief summary of the individual chapters within that Part.

II

Most of the issues discussed in the subsequent chapters are usually bypassed in economists' aggregative models of development and planning or relegated to the periphery of "institutional" details. Some of them, like labor-tying, sharecropping, multiplex relations, clientelization, and class formation, play a central role in the concerns of social and economic anthropologists. But the latter often show a certain preoccupation with stockpiling richly detailed field evidence rather than deciphering meaningful patterns and causal or explanatory mechanisms. (Geertz 1978 describes this as "inductivism gone berserk.") In particular, the idiosyncrasies of social transactions and what are usually attributed to customary practice can often be shown to have a core of economic and, more generally, material interpretation overlooked by the anthropologists, even if one does not believe in crude economic reductionism in all social phenomena.

Anthropologists are also highly skeptical of the use of large data systems and the application of statistical techniques in hypothesis testing like those employed in many of the subsequent chapters. It is true that the intricacies of social relations are often too delicate to be handled by the blunt instruments at the statistician's disposal, and there is much to be said for the anthropologist's material—"produced by long-term, mainly qualitative, highly participative, and almost obsessively fine-comb field study in confined contexts," to use the description by Geertz (1973)—over the statistical artifacts churned out by bureaucratically operated large-scale surveys. But the critical problem with the ethnographic materials of the anthropologist is that their microscopic nature inhibits wider generalization. As Geertz, an ethnographic practitioner himself, comments:

> The problem of how to get from a collection of ethnographic miniatures...—an assortment of remarks and anecdotes—to wall-sized culturescapes of the nation, the epoch, the continent, or the civilization is not so easily passed over with vague allusions to the virtues of concreteness and the down-to-earth mind. For a science born in (American) Indian tribes, Pacific islands, and African lineages and subsequently seized with grander ambitions, this has come to be a major methodological problem, and for the most part, a badly handled one. (1973:21)

In particular, when it comes to assessing the empirical importance of conflicting alternative findings in these microscopic studies, the evidence in "my" village gets pitted against "yours," that in "my" tribe against "yours," and one ends up in rather chaotic inconclusiveness. Yet on issues central to public policy and political programs, generalizability, with all its sweeping crudity, is an important necessity. Thus even if one is not seized with grander ambitions of describing an epoch or a civilization and confines oneself to the kind of mundane problems of political economy that an economist has to grapple with, some resort to social statistics is inevitable. While using them one can only try to remain highly aware of the limitations of aggregative data sets, particularly in capturing the nuances of relational problems, try not to let oneself be carried away by the occasional goodness of the statistical fit, and also try to supplement secondary data by primary field surveys wherever feasible. The reader may note that in some chapters I shall be using empirical data collected in two primary field surveys in which I myself participated.

Apart from the nature of data used, one general presumption in almost all of the theoretical analysis in the subsequent pages that some anthropologists and other social scientists may object to is that farmers are rational and that they maximize subject to a set of constraints. It may be claimed that in a traditional society their behavior is so deeply embedded in the sociocultural context that it may be beyond the reach of economists' explanatory tools of maximizing calculus. This is a matter ultimately of empirical judgment, but in many of these societies (including those in India) the traditional transactional mode of obligatory payments and custom-determined rewards are being eroded by the steady penetration of market forces. A very large literature has now accumulated on the question of peasant rationality (particularly taking into account the insurance motivation under the pervasive uncertainty in the physical and social environment). In much of this empirical literature rationality has often been interpreted in the very narrow sense of price responsiveness, but even where a farmer is not very sensitive to market prices or the markets themselves are inadequately formed, the evidence is still clear that there is a consistent pattern in his behavior which indicates his attempt, by and large, to improve his condition under the given constraints, and that transactions can no longer be described as mere expressions of social obligations. Even patron–client relations, which are often cited as a mark of traditional social systems, may sometimes be viewed as a form of rational response to a situation of desperate need of subsistence insurance and protection on the part of the client, and that of ready availability of cheap labor services, on emergency as well as regular occasions, for the patron. It is also easy sometimes to be misled by villagers' articulate protestations of their "moral responsibilities" and customary obligations, which may in fact mask their sensitivity to market stimuli or may be nothing more than forms of calculated strategic behavior under certain social constraints. Cultural materialists like Harris (1979) have cited many examples of this and made, for this reason, an important distinction between what they call "emic" and "etic" structures of knowledge.

Besides, the presumption of rationality may be a good starting hypothesis to work with, even if one ends up by finding it to be violated in many particular cases. As Elster comments:

This presumption is a "principle of charity" similar to the one often used in textual interpretation. One should never take textual contradictions at their face value, but consider whether the context might not give a clue to consistency. Similarly, one should always look very closely at apparently irrational behavior to see whether there could not be some pattern there after all. (1979:116–17)

Economics is full of examples of how apparently irrational behavior may be successfully explained as an outcome of more complex exercises in rationality, particularly with deeper probes into the nature of the feasibility constraints or the preference patterns. This includes cases in which costs of information and transaction make the global maximum unattainable, and one may have to be satisfied with bounded rationality.

Structuralists deny the significance (as opposed to attainability or existence) of rational choice and emphasize the overwhelming importance of structural constraints which define a feasible set that is so small that formal freedom of choice within the set really does not amount to much. As Elster (1979) illustrates, while the behaviorist would study the activity of the cattle within the bounds of the fence, the structuralist asserts that the cattle have very little freedom of movement within the fence. This kind of structuralism is popular with some Marxists. While it is true that in many cases the constellation of constraints is such as to exclude all but a very small subset of possible actions, as a general theory of action it is indefensible: as Elster comments, ruling classes in most societies have tried to consolidate their rule by reducing the set of opportunities open to the oppressed classes, but this very statement implies that the ruling classes themselves were acting freely and rationally in their own interest. In the theoretical framework of our subsequent chapters I have usually allowed for larger degrees of freedom for maximizing landlords or employers than for their tenants or employees. As I have noted, it is also my intention in the subsequent analysis to look into the origin and constantly evolving nature of the institutions which are often rigidly taken as a given part of the structural constraints.

Apart from maximizing calculus, I have also, occasionally, used in my models a production function or a utility function, concepts which are anathema to many non-neoclassical economists. I personally think that the most objectionable elements in the economics of some (though certainly not all) neoclassicals have to do more with their ahistorical categories, institutionally aseptic assumptions, and the presumption of (and overemphasis on) the efficiency of market allocation. If in one's analytical framework one is aware of and careful about these basic problems, the simplifying devices of a production function (a particular way of summarizing technological possibilities) here or a utility function (a particular notional form of representing preferences) there may not pose problems any more serious than those involved in the various abstractions of Marxian or neo-Ricardian model building. In addition, the production function in none of the subsequent chapters where I have used it involves capital as an input, the heterogeneity of which raises knotty problems for the neoclassical theories of value and distribution (just as heterogeneity of labor, as some Marxists now recognize, plays havoc with the usefulness of the labor theory of value). My use of the utility function in some subsequent chapters has been largely to explore the implications of some risk-aversion properties[2] of peasant behavior (even though it may not always be the best way of capturing those properties, it is among the simplest).

When the late Stephen Hymer once asked Samuelson's opinion about what he thought was valid in Marxian thinking but not included in the MIT economics curriculum, Samuelson's cryptic answer was reportedly in two words: class struggle. While I do not share Samuelson's general underappreciation of Marx, it is certainly true that most models in economics do not incorporate class struggle in any serious way. The theoretical models in this book share this deficiency, even though in chapter 13 I go into agrarian class formation in some detail. In particular, many Marxists regard the wage rate as politically determined (by the balance of class forces) and may find the demand–supply framework of determination of agricultural wages in chapter 4 deficient in that respect. But, as chapter 13 indicates, class formation (particularly in the sense of what Marx called class-for-itself) is yet in its infancy in the overwhelming majority of Indian villages (as in the countryside of many other poor parts of the world), where the agricultural laborers are as yet highly unorganized. In such a situation the determination of agricultural wage in terms of an essentially demand–supply framework, with the landlord-employer having some degree of monopsony power, may not be widely off the mark, *if* there is an adequately formed labor market. (One may also note that in my model of chapter 4 the landlord's use of his influence on the village unemployment rate to keep down the peak recruitment costs has some family resemblance to Kalecki's (1943) idea of a political business cycle in rich countries.) Cases of labor market segmentation on the basis of credit and other personalized ties between the employer and the employee are extensively discussed in chapters 4, 5, 6, and 12. Even where the agricultural laborers are somewhat organized and there is some formal or informal collective bargaining, the demand–supply framework provides indispensable clues in understanding the "disagreement payoffs" in any bargaining game and in delimiting the range of wage indeterminacy. One deficiency of our wage model on which future research work, both theoretical and empirical, will be important relates to the logic of interaction among employers which is not captured in a model of monopsony. In some villages I have observed the phenomenon of "wage

[2] See Binswanger (1981) for a test of utility-based models of behavior under risk on the basis of large-scale experimental evidence in rural India. He also shows that predicting behavior with the alternative safety-based rules of thumb is often not straightforward; besides, the predictions derived from these rules are seen to be inconsistent with the experimental behavior reported.

leadership": at the beginning of each season (or crop operation), an "influential" farmer sets the current wage rate at which he hires laborers, and then other employers follow his leadership. One would like to know more of this or any other wage-setting mechanism in agriculture.

III

One hazard of hypothesis testing on the basis of oversimplified theoretical models and an inadequate data base is that the relationship between the theory and the evidence turns out to be rather tenuous at times. Yet if one wants to go beyond armchair theorizing on the one hand and descriptive stockpiling of data or anecdotes on the other (there is a surfeit of both of these alternatives in the development economics literature), one has to face this hazard squarely and can only try to improve the odds. In the econometric exercises in many of the subsequent chapters I did not have requisite data on some of the obviously important variables; for some others, in the absence of data on the most appropriate form of the variables, I had to make do with proxy variables. In some other cases, even though I had data on some variables, the level of aggregation was not right; for example, in the case of a model of farm-level decision making, the State-level data on the variables (as in chapter 11) are much too aggregative. Of course, in a majority of cases I have tried to use alternative data sources at varying levels of aggregation, and my use of very large sets of household- and farm-level data has been at a much more disaggregated level than has hitherto been the practice in the analysis of the problems of the rural economy of India. Although in the regression equations the explained proportion of total variance in the dependent variable has not always been very high (particularly for the data sets for which we have a very large number of observations), the signs of most of the regression coefficients have been in the direction expected from the theoretical framework, and their levels of statistical significance have been remarkably high in general. I should also note that in the regression equations I have mostly used linear functional forms, even though the underlying theoretical model suggests nonlinear relations. I have done so primarily because, given the nature of the data base, I did not want to erect on it too sophisticated a structure of estimation methods and because in some cases my attempts to use nonlinear estimation methods did not yield any strikingly different qualitative results (about the direction of signs as well as the levels of significance of most of the coefficients) as compared with the linear approximation. For some cases I have presented the results of the use of the LOGIT and the TOBIT estimation procedures.

Finally, let me give an account of the alternative data sources I have used. My largest data sets relate to the household-level data drawn from individual field schedules of the Employment and Unemployment Survey carried out in India by the National Sample Survey (NSS) Organization of the government of India, once in 1972–73 (the Twenty-Seventh Round) and again in 1977–78 (the Thirty-Second Round). I acquired access to the raw data for rural West Bengal in both of these Rounds. I thus have detailed data for rural workers belonging to nearly 4,900 sample households drawn from about 500 sample villages in the year 1972–73, and to about 6,500 sample households from about 550 sample villages in the year 1977–78. The sampling design for both surveys was stratified two-stage, with villages being the first stage units and households at the second stage. The survey period of one year was divided into four subrounds of three months each. One-fourth of sample villages were surveyed in each subround, and each sample village was visited only once in the year. The sample units were so staggered over four subrounds that valid estimates could be built up for each of the subrounds separately; subround comparisons can thus capture the seasonality effects of agriculture to some extent. The data collected in either survey for each household are of three kinds: (a) those relating to characteristics of the household as a whole and also to those of each individual member of the household, whether a worker or not; (b) day-to-day time disposition particulars on each day of the seven days preceding the date of survey (along with wage and salary earnings reported for the week) for those who are currently in the labor force; (c) response to various probing (and sometimes hypothetical) questions about the long-term work pattern, job search, minimum acceptable wage/salary rates, etc.

In terms of detailed micro-level data from secondary surveys, I have also used, particularly in chapter 3, farm-level data from the Farm Management Surveys in several districts in India. These surveys, sponsored by the Ministry of Food and Agriculture of the government of India, followed the method of multi-stage, stratified random sampling. For each district the sample size was 100 to 150 farms from 10 to 15 villages. The data collection of these surveys was based on a detailed record of the activities of each sample farm involving periodic visits to the same farm by the field investigators throughout the agricultural year.

From household-or farm-level data we now go to the next level of aggregation, that of NSS agroclimatic regions. The whole of India has been divided by the NSS for this purpose into 66 (the number has gone up more recently) regions by grouping districts having similar population density and crop pattern; on an average, a cluster of 4 or 5 homogeneous districts forms a region. Appendix tables A-D present the regionwise data relating to the early 1970s and describes how I have put together Land Holdings Survey data from the NSS, demographic data from the Census, agricultural data from various Season and Crop Reports, and assets and investment data from the All-India Debt and Investment Survey of the Reserve Bank of India. I have used State-level data in chapters 10, 11, 14, and 15. These data are presented and their sources described in tables 10.4, 11.1, 14.1, and 15.1.

All these data at the household, farm, region, and State-level are from secondary surveys, Census, or other official sources. In addition I have utilized two large-scale primary surveys conducted by myself in collaboration with Ashok Rudra. The first survey was carried out in 1975–76 in 334 randomly chosen villages in four states in north and east India: West Bengal, Bihar, Uttar Pradesh, and Orissa. A description of the survey design is given at the beginning of chapter 9, where some of the results of the survey relating to the terms and conditions of sharecropping contracts are presented; for some of the other detailed results of the survey relating to labor and credit contracts, one may refer to Bardhan and Rudra (1978). The second survey was carried out in 1979 in 110 randomly selected villages in West Bengal, with the major purpose of an even more intensive inquiry into the terms and conditions of agricultural labor contracts. The sample design for this survey was similar to that of the 1975–76 survey. Within each village a questionnaire was canvassed with six different types of laborers; there was in addition a general village questionnaire to be filled out on the basis of information obtained from all these six or more respondents and the latter cross-checked with other people living in the village. The village questionnaire contained questions on the general economic, demographic, and agricultural conditions of the village as well as questions on types of labor contracts prevailing in the village (and the particulars of these contracts). For detailed results of the survey, see Bardhan and Rudra (1981).

These two primary field surveys were designed to focus on the terms and conditions of various formal or informal contracts involved in land-lease, wage labor and credit relations in agriculture and to bring out the nature of interlinkages among these relations. I felt the need for this particularly because the existing large-scale surveys in India do not capture the intricacies of these interlinkages or even the important qualitative properties of contractual variations. For example, the NSS Land Holdings Surveys give us aggregative estimates on the distribution of ownership and operational holdings or on the proportion of area that is leased in. But we learn from them very little about the nature of the lease contracts, not to speak of the linkages of landownership or land-lease patterns with wage labor or credit contracts. The Rural Labor Enquiries of the Labor Bureau in India give us information on wages, unemployment, indebtedness, and living standards of agricultural labor households. They tell us very little about the forms of segmentation in the labor market, not to speak of the interrelationships between indebtedness and various forms of labor tying with the employer. The Rural Credit (or Debt and Investment) Surveys of the Reserve Bank of India give us estimates of borrowings of different agricultural groups by source and purpose of borrowing, but they do not indicate how the terms of borrowing interact with the terms in land or labor contracts. It is with these information gaps in mind that we carried out our primary field surveys. As intensive and yet fairly large-scale surveys of contractual relationships in rural India, they may have been the first of their kind in India.

PART A

AGRICULTURAL LABOR

Part A starts with separate analyses of supply and demand sides in the agricultural labor market, then focuses on the determination of equilibrium wage and level of unemployment, with some special discussion of two-tiered labor markets where some part of the labor force enters into voluntary labor-tying arrangements with the employers. Chapter 1 is primarily an econometric analysis of the social, demographic, and economic determinants of market supply of farm labor by peasant households. Part of chapter 1 and chapter 2 concentrates on determinants of usual labor force participation by women in these households, on the pattern of their seasonal withdrawal from the labor force, and how, in view of this, the standard measures underestimate their underemployment. In chapter 3 there is an econometric analysis of the farm-level determinants of the use of hired labor. Chapter 4 empirically shows how the agricultural wage rate is sensitive to the demand and supply factors contrary to the implications of the popular theories of determination of wages by biological (subsistence or nutrition-determined efficiency) factors or by custom. In the same chapter there is also developed a theoretical model incorporating involuntary unemployment, some degree of monopsony power on the part of the employer, and the high premium he places on quick and ready availability of labour during some peak operations. This model generates some comparative-static variations in wage rates and unemployment which seem to be consistent with Indian data at different levels of aggregation. Chapters 4, 5, and 6 intensively probe cases of labor-tying arrangements cemented with credit from the employer, which reduce the latter's recruitment costs of casual labor in the peak season, or act as a risk-sharing device against the uncertainties of peak wage rates facing the laborers or as an intertemporal barter transaction in the case of a double coincidence of wants between employer-creditors and laborer-borrowers arising out of irregularities of the agricultural crop cycle.

CHAPTER 1

Peasant Labor Supply: A Statistical Analysis

I

In the literature on models of economic development one frequently encounters standardized assumptions about rural labor supply behavior. One popular assumption is that of a horizontal or perfectly elastic supply curve at a given wage rate. Although this has been mostly used in positing an "unlimited" supply of labor migrating to the industrial sector at a given industrial market wage in dual-economy models devised for describing a certain stage of the development process or for prescribing shadow prices, its use for agricultural wage determination in the rural sector itself is also not uncommon. Yet there have been very few systematic empirical studies of labor supply and labor market participation behavior of peasant households.[1] In this chapter I shall analyze cross-section variations in labor supply from peasant households and focus on their social, demographic, and economic determinants. The main data set used is from the NSS household survey on employment and unemployment in rural West Bengal in 1977–78. Section I discusses the market supply of farm labor from peasant families. Section II analyzes the wage rates quoted as "acceptable" by farm labor respondents in the survey in response to hypothetical questions of wage employment to give us some idea of the supply prices of labor. Section III concentrates on the special social and economic constraints on the female rate of participation in the labor force, ending with a brief summary of this chapter.

In estimating labor supply functions the first serious, though familiar, problem is that of finding an appropriate wage as an independent variable. If the daily wage rate is derived as wage earnings divided by days worked and if the days worked also appear as the dependent variable, there is the well-known measurement error problem (errors in reporting days worked are transmitted inversely to the measured market wage rate, biasing down directly estimated effects of the wage rate on labor supplied) and also a "simultaneity" problem because labor supplied and the wage may be jointly determined by other variables. On top of this, one has the practical problem that those who did not work at all in the reference period did not have a wage to report even though the wage rate in the market may have been positive. The familiar procedure in such a case of replacing the

---

[1] The few exceptions include Bardhan (1979), Barnum and Squire (1979), and Rosenzweig (1980).

observed wage rate with an instrumental variable estimator inferred from
the sample of workers for whom market wages are observed has been
known to give rise to the "selectivity bias" from sample censoring.[2]

In our analysis we have adopted an alternative wage variable. On the
basis of the data on wage earnings and days of wage employment for each
worker in a village, we have worked out an aggregate weighted-average
wage rate for agricultural work for the village as a whole. Let us call this
village wage variable VWAGE. Presumably, to the individual workér the
VWAGE variable is more exogenous and less amenable to individual
control than the actual individual wage rate as derived from the
individual's reported wage earnings. The measurement error in any
individual's reported days of work is also likely to be diluted in the
aggregation process for the whole sample of workers in the village. In
addition, VWAGE is quite often positive even though an individual may
not have reported any wage work. Since agricultural work in different
farms for workers in one village during roughly the same fortnight when
the village is surveyed is likely to be fairly homogeneous, and since there is
independent evidence (see chapter 4 footnote 11) that the agricultural wage
rate in a village is remarkably uniform for workers of a given sex and for a
given agricultural operation, any bias resulting from our use of the
aggregate wage rate VWAGE as an independent variable in the labor
supply equations is not likely to be large.

The dependent variable here is the number of agricultural labor days[3]
supplied against daily wage payment in the reference week: we shall call
this variable HOUI ($I = M$ for males, and $I = F$ for females, both in the 15–
60 age group). We should note here that HOUI includes hired-out farm
labor days and days unemployed: the days in the week when the laborer did
not work but was either seeking work or reported being available for work
(presumably at the going market wage rate) should obviously be added to
the days actually worked to constitute labor supply from the point of view
of the supplier.[4]

Since the decisions on labor supply in rural families are quite often made
on the household level rather than by each individual separately, we have
computed HOUI as a total household labor supply variable (aggregating
the labor supply of all the working members of the household belonging to
a given age-sex group). The HOUI equations in tables 1.1 to 1.4 refer to the
agricultural labor households (i.e., those whose primary source of earning
is from agricultural wage labor), constituting nearly half of our total

[2] For a comprehensive discussion of these problems, particularly in estimating female
labor supply, see the articles in Smith (1980).

[3] Intensity of work in any activity on each day was measured in binary codes of "full" and
"half". Since work in agriculture cannot easily be reduced to a standard hourly pattern and
since the rural respondents find it rather difficult to report hourly disposition of their time,
intensity of work by "full" or "half" day has been adopted as a better measure.

[4] We have assumed that, when cultivators or agricultural laborers report that they were
seeking work or were available for work in the reference week, it is agricultural work they were
after. This is not necessarily so, but it is likely to be so in most cases.

sample of agricultural households. Since TOBIT estimation procedure is often regarded as more appropriate than ordinary least squares regression for limited dependent variables like days worked, in tables 1.1 to 1.4 I have

TABLE 1.1

Linear regression analysis of determinants of person-days in the reference week hired out on farm work (or reported unemployed) for men in the 15-60 age group belonging to agricultural wage labor households, in rural West Bengal, 1977-78

	Dependent Variable:	HOUM (number of days in the reference week hired out on farm work, or reported seeking or being available for work, for such men)
	Mean:	6.77 days
	Standard Deviation:	4.82 days

Explanatory Variables	Regression Coefficient	Standard Error	Significant at Percent Level
LABFORM (no. of adult men currently in labor force)	5.0999	0.0926	0.0
CULTIVAT (area cultivated by the household in acres)	−1.7783	0.1320	0.0
DEP (no. of dependents as proportion of household size)	0.6251	0.3006	3.8
EDM (no. of men with above-primary education level in 15–60 age group)	−0.4420	0.2465	7.3
VWAGEM (average daily wage rate in Rs. for male agricultural labor in village in reference week)	−0.0753	0.0578	19.3
PUBWORKM (dummy for male wage employment in public works in or near village)	−1.5981	0.3220	0.0
RAIN (normal annual rainfall in district in meters)	0.2003	0.0972	4.0
RAINDEF (percentage deficit in actual rainfall in 1977 from normal in district)	−0.4902	0.2425	4.3
SBRND 3 (dummy for January–March quarter)	−0.4300	0.1841	2.0
SBRND 4 (dummy for April–June quarter)	−0.6989	0.1861	0.0
Constant term	0.6314	0.3747	9.2

$R^2 = 0.5785$; $F = 258.8$; no. of observations = 2,276

SOURCE: The source of the data used, as in all the subsequent tables in this chapter, is NSS, 32d Round, 1977–78, except for RAIN and RAINDEF, which are from the *Statistical Abstract of West Bengal*. VWAGEM has been computed by taking the total wage earnings on casual farm male labor by all the sample households in the village divided by the corresponding total number of casual farm male labor days.

alternatively tried both procedures for HOUM and HOUF.

In the 2,276 agricultural labor households in a sample of 511 villages (where a male agricultural wage rate, VWAGEM, was reported), on an average a male worker in the 15–60 age group worked for farm wage employment (or was unemployed) for 5.32 days in the reference week and worked on his own farm for 0.91 days (in many cases, of course, the household did not have a farm). It may be noted that in neither the OLS nor the TOBIT equation for HOUM is the village wage variable VWAGEM significant, although in both cases it is negative.[5] It seems in this sample that the ("uncompensated") effect of the wage rate on market labor supply is not significantly different from zero.[6]

TABLE 1.2

TOBIT analysis of determinants of person-days in the reference week hired out on farm work (or reported unemployed) for men in the 15–60 age group belonging to agricultural wage labor households, rural West Bengal, 1977–78

	Dependent Variable:	HOUM[†]
	Mean:	6.77 days
	Standard Deviation:	4.82 days
Explanatory Variables†	Estimated Coefficient	Asymptotic Standard Error
LABFORM*	5.6398	0.0894
CULTIVAT*	−2.1376	0.1273
DEP*	1.2849	0.3815
EDM*	−0.5666	0.2431
VWAGEM	−0.0917	0.0671
PUBWORKM*	−1.6848	0.2895
RAIN*	0.2338	0.1254
RAINDEF	−0.4779	0.2858
SBRND 3*	−0.4789	0.2266
SBRND 4	−0.6422	0.2242
Constant term	0.7556	0.4509
Value of log likelihood function = −5,511.8		

SOURCE: See table 1.1.
† See table 1.1 or Glossary of Variables
*Denotes a variable significant at 5 percent level

[5] The regression coefficient for VWAGEM is also insignificant in an equation for HOUM that we have tried for primarily cultivator households with agricultural wage labor as a subsidiary occupation.

[6] In Bardhan (1979), using an alternative data set based on the NSS household survey on employment and unemployment in rural West Bengal in 1972–73, we found a better fit of a quadratic equation for HOUM for the set of all agricultural households cultivating less than 2.5 acres of land: the regression coefficient for VWAGEM was significantly positive, but the

The effect of assets (for which CULTIVAT, the size of land cultivated by the household, is a proxy) on market labor supply is more strongly negative. The larger the size of own farm, the smaller the extent of hiring out of family labor. Similarly, the higher the level of schooling of the male members of the household, the lower the extent of hiring out on farm work: the coefficient of EDM, the number of household males in the 15–60

TABLE 1.3

Linear regression analysis of determinants of person-days in the reference week hired out on farm work (or reported unemployed) for women in the 15–60 age group belonging to agricultural wage labor households, rural West Bengal, 1977–78

Dependent Variable:	HOUF (number of days in reference week hired out on farm work, or reported unemployed, for women in 15–60 age group)
Mean:	2.98 days
Standard Deviation:	4.16 days

Explanatory Variables†	Regression Coefficient	Standard Error	Significant at Percent Level
LABFORF (no. of adult women currently in labor force)	4.6003	0.1249	0.0
UNEMPM (rate of unemployment of male members in household)	−0.5932	0.3513	9.2
CULTIVAT	−0.4261	0.1474	0.4
RAIN	0.2856	0.1087	0.9
RAINDEF	−0.5778	0.2824	4.1
HMUNOWN (dummy for unowned homestead)	0.4815	0.2648	6.9
SCHTRIBE (dummy for scheduled tribe)	0.7305	0.2186	0.1
SCHCASTE (dummy for scheduled caste)	0.2446	0.1987	21.9
PUBWORKF	−1.6753	0.5825	0.4
VWAGEF (average daily wage rate in Rs. for female agricultural labor in village in reference week)	0.0337	0.0835	68.6
Constant term	−0.2020	0.2256	37.1

$R^2 = 0.6869$; $F = 189.4$; no. of observations $= 787$

SOURCE: See table 1.1.
† See table 1.1 or Glossary of Variables.

quadratic term had a significantly negative coefficient, implying a backward-bending supply curve. When we ran the same regression separately for landless wage labor households and for landed cultivator households, the regression coefficient for VWAGEM was positive and significant for the former group of households, but negative for the latter. This result is in sharp contrast to a result in Rosenzweig (1980), derived from a competitive neoclassical model of peasant labor supply, that the own labor supply response to a wage change in landed households will be algebraically *greater* than that in landless households.

age group with above-primary education level, is significantly negative.[7] The coefficient of PUBWORKM, a dummy variable indicating the existence of male wage employment on public works projects in or near the village, is negative, possibly due to income effect from this source of supplementary income.

The elasticity of HOUM with respect to LABFORM, the number of males in the household (in the 15–60 age group) currently in the labor force, is 0.96 (from the OLS equation), suggesting that an increase in the number of such males leads to a slight decline in their average extent of hiring out on farm work.[8] The number of dependents per household size,

TABLE 1.4

TOBIT analysis of determinants of person-days in the reference week hired out on farm work (or reported unemployed) for women in the 15–60 age group belonging to agricultural wage labor households, rural West Bengal, 1977–78

	Dependent Variable:	HOUF†
	Mean:	2.48 days
	Standard Deviation:	4.16 days

Explanatory Variables†	Estimated Coefficient	Asymptotic Standard Error
LABFORF*	7.7282	0.3663
UNEMPM*	−2.0436	0.8414
CULTIVAT*	−1.8798	0.3752
RAIN*	0.6045	0.2364
RAINDEF*	1.6940	0.6704
HMUNOWN	0.9383	0.5847
SCHTRIBE*	1.4045	0.5392
SCHCASTE	−0.4996	0.4759
PUBWORKF*	−3.6148	1.1845
VWAGEF	−0.0658	0.2020
Constant term	−3.9814	0.8584
Value of log likelihood function = −1,030.8		

SOURCE: See table 1.1
† See tables 1.1–1.3 or Glossary of Variables.
* Denotes a variable significant at 5 percent level.

---

[7] When we ran the regression separately for landless wage labor households and for landed cultivator households in the exercise referred to in footnote 6, the coefficient for EDM was significantly negative for the former group of households, but not significantly different from zero for the latter group of households. Again, this is in contrast to a result in Rosenzweig (1980), derived from the assumption of education improving managerial efficiency on own farm, that the response of market labor supply to educational levels in landed households will be algebraically *less* than that in landless households.

[8] This elasticity is lower (0.77) in an equation for HOUM that I have tried for primarily cultivator households with agricultural wage labor as a subsidiary occupation.

DEP, increases the extent of hiring out, probably because of the income effect, the larger number of dependents reducing the per capita consumption equivalent of the same wage income.

The coefficients for the dummy variables representing slack agricultural seasons, the January–March quarter (SBRND 3) and the April–June quarter (SBRND 4), are significantly negative. This means there is less willingness to hire out on *farm* work in relatively slack seasons, the income effect possibly outweighed by the general job search discouragement effect. A similar interpretation may be given to the positive coefficient for the level of normal annual rainfall (RAIN) in the district where the household is located and the negative coefficient for the percentage deficit (RAINDEF) in actual rainfall (in 1977) from normal in the district. A lower normal level of rainfall and a higher current deficit in the rainfall both discourage the prospective job seeker for farm work in the locality; he presumably goes more for nonfarm and nonmarket work.[9]

All the nonwage independent variables are significant at less than the 5 percent level (except for EDM in the OLS equation, which is significant at the 7 percent level and RAINDEF in the TOBIT equation, which is not significant).

Let us now turn to HOUF, the corresponding variable for labor days hired out (or unemployed) by female members (in the 15–60 age group) of agricultural labor households in sample villages where a female agricultural wage rate, VWAGEF, was reported. In these villages on an average each woman (in the 15–60 age group) who is in the current labor force worked for farm wage employment (or was unemployed) for 4.94 days in the reference week. Again, as can be seen from tables 1.3 and 1.4, in neither the OLS nor the TOBIT equation for HOUF is the village wage variable VWAGEF significant.

The asset effect (through CULTIVAT) and the supplementary income effect (through PUBWORKF, the dummy variable indicating the existence of female wage employment on public works projects in or near the village) are negative. Since VWAGEM and VWAGEF are highly correlated, I have not tried the wage rate earned by male members of the family as a separate independent variable.

The elasticity of HOUF with respect to LABFORF, the number of females in the household (in the 15 60 age group) currently in the labor force, is 0.93 (from the OLS equation), slightly less than that for corresponding males (possibly indicating that the social constraint on women's working on wage employment on other's farms is stronger than that for males, even for agricultural labor households). This social constraint is least applicable to women belonging to tribal and low-caste

[9] Presumably, this discouragement effect is stronger than any positive effect of lower on-farm productivity in lower-rainfall areas or years on hiring out of family labor. The latter effect is, however, stronger in cultivator households: the regression coefficient for the variable RAIN is significantly negative in an equation for HOUM that we have tried for primarily cultivator households with agricultural wage labor as a subsidiary occupation.

households at the bottom of the social hierarchy in the village. Consistent with this, the coefficients for the dummy variables for "scheduled" tribe households (SCHTRIBE) and for "scheduled" caste households (SCHCASTE) are positive (highly significant for the former and not as significant for the latter variable), in both the OLS and the TOBIT equations for HOUF.

The coefficient for HMUNOWN, a dummy variable to represent cases where the household does not own its homestead, is positive (significant in the OLS equation, not so in the TOBIT equation). This may indicate cases where members of a household give commitment to wage labor for an employer who provides the homestead.

The interpretation of the significant coefficients for RAIN and RAINDEF (in both the OLS and the TOBIT equations) is similar to that already offered in the case of male workers, in terms of farm job search discouragement effect. An additional factor in the same direction to be noted here is that the coefficient for the variable UNEMPM, the rate of unemployment of male members in the household,[10] is significantly negative in both the OLS and the TOBIT equations for HOUF. This indicates that the job search discouragement effect is stronger for women in households where the unemployment (or underemployment) rate for men in the household is higher. ("It's no use being in the *farm* labor force when even the men in the household do not have enough farm work."[11]) The discouragement effect clearly outweighs the income effect, which should have encouraged more women to seek work.[12] I shall come back to this question of labor supply depending on its own demand in the next chapter.

II

Apart from reporting wage and salary earnings actually received in the reference week, the respondents in our data set also answered hypothetical questions about an *acceptable* wage rate (in case they were looking for wage employment) inside and outside the village. It would be interesting to

[10] The rate of unemployment is defined as the number of days reportedly seeking (or being available for) work as a percentage of the total number of days spent in the labor force over the reference work.

[11] This, of course, assumes that men and women are looking for similar jobs. Except for plowing (which is usually regarded as a "male job" in this region), for the other tasks like harvesting and transplanting, for which the major part of wage labor is hired, demand conditions in the labor market will have closely similar effects on the job opportunities of males and females. For most of these tasks caste segregation of the labor market is more acute than sexual segregation. The latter is more important on the prior issue of participation versus nonparticipation in the labor force.

[12] In industrially advanced countries also this has been noted. See, for example, Layard, Barton, and Zabalza (1980) for evidence of the negative effect of husband's unemployment on wife's labor supply in Britain, explained less by the working of the Supplementary Unemployment Benefit system and more by the discouragement effect of local labor market conditions.

analyze this information on what might be considered as *ex ante* supply prices on the part of workers. Take the set of casual agricultural laborers. About half of them reported they were available for work (or additional work). For the laborers who reported both a current farm wage received and an acceptable wage for a hypothetical wage employment *inside* the village which they are prepared to take, the value of the ratio of the acceptable to the actual wage is, on an average, about 1.67; thus 67 percent seems to be the average desired margin of wage on a hypothetical job (or additional work) inside the village over their current one. This margin is higher in the busy season than in the lean (75 percent in the October–December quarter and 58 percent in the April–June quarter). Similarly, 57 percent is estimated to be the desired margin of wage on a hypothetical job *outside* the village over that *inside* the village, for those who reported preparedness to accept jobs outside the village. This margin is 134 percent

TABLE 1.5

Linear regression analysis of the acceptable wage rate inside the village reported by casual agricultural laborers, rural West Bengal, 1977–78

Dependent Variable:	WAGEACPT (acceptable daily wage rate for hypothetical wage employment inside village)		
Mean: Rs. 5.92			
Standard Deviation: Rs. 2.01			

Explanatory Variables	Regression Coefficient	Standard Error	Significant at Percent Level
FWAGE (daily farm wage rate in Rs. currently received by laborer in reference week)	0.2987	0.0357	0.0
UR (current rate of underemployment of laborer in reference week)†	−0.5540	0.2245	1.4
DUR (duration for which the laborer has been available for work or additional work)†	0.5471	0.0535	0.0
AGE (age of laborer in years)	0.0842	0.0231	0.0
$(AGE)^2$	−0.0011	0.0003	0.1
SEXF (dumy to represent women)	−0.3404	0.1817	6.1
MECHSKILL (dummy for laborers with special mechanical skills)†	2.0012	1.0650	6.1
Constant term	1.9275	0.4630	0.0
$R^2=0.1660$; $F=34.1$; no. of observations$=1,207$			

SOURCE: See table 1.1

†UR: the proportion of days in the reference week spent in seeking (or being available for) work.

†DUR: four lengths of period of unemployment: up to 3 months, 3–6 months, 6–12 months, and above 12 months.

†MECHSKILL: skills of machineman, molder, fitter, diemaker, welder, electrician, and motor vehicle driver.

in the busy October–December quarter and 29 percent in the slack April June quarter.

Let us call WAGEACPT the acceptable wage rate reported by casual agricultural laborers for hypothetical wage employment inside the village. For those who report it, its mean value is Rs. 5.92 with a standard deviation of 2.01. Let us now try to identify the factors that may explain the variations in the level of WAGEACPT. Table 1.5 presents the results of the relevant regression equation. Clearly, the current farm wage rate received by the laborer; FWAGE, has a significantly positive effect on the level of the wage asked for the hypothetical job. The individual labor respondent's current rate of underemployment, UR, has, as expected, a significantly negative coefficient. But the coefficient of DUR, the variable representing duration of unemployment, is significantly positive, possibly indicating that those who can afford to wait longer have a higher reservation wage. The coefficient of AGE, the age of the worker, is positive, but that of the quadratic term is negative, indicating that the acceptable wage rate increases with productivity-enhancing experience only up to a certain age, after which the effect of advancing age on energy and stamina tends to dominate. Other things remaining the same, women have a lower acceptable wage. Those with special mechanical skills (MECHSKILL) have a higher acceptable wage compared with what they currently get for farm labor.

III

At the end of section I we considered the factors influencing the number of labor days hired out on farm work in the reference week by women in primarily agricultural wage labor households. But a prior and a more substantive question is that of the participation of rural women in general in the labor force over a long period. In many African countries that Boserup (1970) refers to (and even in some hilly areas in India) the agricultural system is one of shifting cultivation in which the role of female farming is dominant; similarly, in some Latin American countries many able-bodied males have recently migrated to the nonagricultural sector, leaving small-scale farming largely to women in the family. But our data set relates to a region of settled agriculture where the agriculturists are primarily men, and except for some dispossessed groups at the bottom of the social hierarchy, women's role in field work on farms is not extensive. The dominant culture ascribes low status to women's extramural activities, particularly on manual work, and upwardly mobile social groups and households often withdraw their women from the labor force. In our rural West Bengal sample, on an average only one out of ten adult (strictly speaking, 15–60 age group) women in the primarily cultivator households and only three out of ten adult women in the primarily agricultural wage labor households participated in the labor force by "usual status" (defined as the status which prevailed over the major part of the last year).

No doubt this is an underestimate of the extent of female participation on account of the restrictive nature of the standard definition of "gainful" work. In particular it excludes, apart from household chores, various collection activities from village common property (like collecting fish, small game, wild fruits and vegetables, firewood, and cow dung for fuel). If a woman harvests grains on the family farm and brings them home for consumption, she is part of the labor force, but if she catches fish in a nearby pond and brings it home for consumption or picks up firewood from the village bushes and brings it home for fuel, she is not. In our data set, out of all adult women classified as housewives and hence out of the labor force by usual status, about 50 percent reported that, along with their domestic duties, they regularly carry out these collection activities or work

TABLE 1.6

Linear regression analysis of determinants of usual labor force participation by women in the 15–60 age group in agricultural wage labor households, rural West Bengal, 1977–78

	Dependent Variable:	UALABFORF (number of such women in each household participating in labor force by usual status)
	Mean:	0.41
	Standard Deviation:	0.65

Explanatory Variables†	Regression Coefficient	Standard Error	Significant at Percent Level
ADWOMEN (no. of adult women in household)	0.3986	0.0176	0.0
LABFORM	−0.1680	0.0168	0.0
BAB (no. of children in 0–4 age group in household)	−0.0756	0.0150	0.0
VWAGEM	−0.0710	0.0098	0.0
HMUNOWN	0.2267	0.0359	0.0
SCHTRIBE	0.3983	0.0380	0.0
SCHCASTE	0.2269	0.0249	0.0
VILPOP (village size in thousands of population, 1971)	0.0054	0.0029	6.2
AWAYM (dummy for some male member of household gone away for work)	0.1052	0.0686	12.5
CULTIVAT	−0.0119	0.0230	60.5
CHDOM (no. of children in household in 5–14 age group currently in domestic work)	0.0348	0.0260	18.1
EDM	−0.0127	0.0436	77.1
Constant term	0.4740	0.0516	0.0

$R^2 = 0.3078$; F = 100.7; no. of observations = 2,276

SOURCE: See table 1.1. VILPOP is from 1971 census.

† See table 1.1–1.5 or Glossary of Variables.

TABLE 1.7

Linear regression analysis of determinants of usual labor force participation by women in the 15–60 age group in Primarily Cultivator Households, Rural West Bengal, 1977–78

	Dependent Variable:	UALABFORF†
	Mean:	0.17
	Standard Deviation:	0.46

Explanatory Variables†	Regression Coefficient	Standard Error	Significant at Percent Level
ADWOMEN	0.1553	0.0118	0.0
LABFORM	−0.0864	0.0105	0.0
BAB	−0.0500	0.0102	0.0
SCHTRIBE	0.4186	0.0406	0.0
SCHCASTE	0.0447	0.0223	4.6
EDF	0.0711	0.0245	0.4
EDM	−0.0426	0.0124	0.1
CHDOM	0.0513	0.0244	3.6
SCHOOLCH	−0.0194	0.0081	1.6
AWAYM	0.0920	0.0804	25.3
VLIPOP	0.0023	0.0021	27.5
CULTIVAT	−0.0030	0.0032	34.6
Constant term	0.1149	0.0271	0.0

$R^2 = 0.1521$; $F = 38.0$; no. of observations = 2,341

SOURCE: See table 1.1.
† See tables 1.1–1.6 or Glossary of Variables.

on sewing, tailoring, and weaving for household use or on household poultry and dairy, and so on. Even in crop production, most of the post-harvest operations like threshing, winnowing, parboiling, and processing rice for home consumption is mostly done by women often classified out of the labor force.

In spite of all these glaring sources of underenumeration, it is probably correct to say that the extent of labor force participation by women in West Bengal is significantly below that of men and that there are interesting patterns in the household-to-household variations in the participation rates even by the restrictive definition of standard usage. In tables 1.6 and 1.7 we report the results of a linear regression analysis of the determinants of the variations in UALABFORF (the number of adult women in the household participating in the labor force by usual status) in agricultural wage labor households and cultivator households (i.e., those whose primary source of earning is cultivating their own farm), respectively. Since female labor force participation is often a dichotomous decision, with women in the majority of our sample households taking the decision not to participate, a LOGIT analysis is often regarded as more appropriate than

TABLE 1.8

LOGIT analysis of the probability of usual labor force participation by women in the 15-60 age group in agricultural wage labor households, rural West Bengal, 1977-78

Explanatory Variables†	Estimated Coefficient	Standard Error
ADWOMEN*	0.9801	0.0859
LABFORM*	−0.7367	0.0867
BAB*	−0.2445	0.0689
WVAGEM*	−0.3764	0.0496
HMUNOWN*	0.8655	0.1561
SCHTRIBE*	1.3948	0.1653
SCHCASTE*	1.0013	0.1127
VILPOP*	0.0023	0.0012
AWAYM	0.3685	0.3094
CULTIVAT*	−0.2329	0.1082
CHDOM*	0.2452	0.1154
EDM*	−0.6384	0.2470
Likelihood ratio Index=0.2614; no. of observations=2,276		

SOURCE: See table 1.1.   † See table 1.1-1.6 or Glossary of Variables.
*Denotes a variable significant at 5 percent level.

OLS; hence tables 1.8 and 1.9 provide the LOGIT equations for UALABFORF (i.e., the probability that UALABFORF is positive). Let us first take the agricultural wage labor households and refer to tables 1.6 and 1.8. The coefficient for VWAGEM is significantly negative in both the OLS and LOGIT equations. Apart from the usual cross-wage effect of husband's wage earning on a wife's labor force participation, this coefficient also indirectly captures the own wage effect, since we have not included VWAGEF as a separate variable on account of colinearity with VWAGEM.

Also, the larger the number of adult men in the family who are in the current labor force, the lower the female participation rate, presumably due to income effect: hence, LABFORM has a significantly negative coefficient in both equations for UALABFORF.

Similarly, AWAYM, the dummy variable for some male member in the family gone away for work or in search of work, has a positive (though not very significant) coefficient.

The asset effect through CULTIVAT is negative (and significantly so in the LOGIT equation): the usual wealth effect is presumably mixed here with the status effect of the upwardly mobile in immuring women. The coefficient of EDM, the number of adult men in the household with above-primary education level, is negative (significantly so in the LOGIT equation): again, the income effect and the status effect following from a

TABLE 1.9

LOGIT analysis of the probability of usual labor force participation by women in the 15–60 age group in primarily cultivator households, rural West Bengal, 1977–78

Explanatory Variables†	Estimated Coefficient	Standard Error
ADWOMEN*	0.8009	0.0859
LABFORM*	−0.7845	0.0965
BAB*	−0.3947	0.0868
SCHTRIBE*	1.8582	0.2354
SCHCASTE	0.1568	0.1728
EDF*	0.4808	0.1643
EDM*	0.3748	0.1255
CHDOM	0.2490	0.1732
SCHOOLCH*	−0.1346	0.0683
AWAYM*	1.0877	0.5259
VILPOP	0.0019	0.0014
CULTIVAT	−0.0183	0.0278
Likelihood ratio index=0.5167; no. of observations=2,341		

SOURCE: See table 1.1.

†See tables 1.1–1.6 or Glossary of Variables.

*Denotes a variable significant at 5 percent level.

higher schooling level of males in the household are operating jointly. The dummy variables for tribal (SCHTRIBE) and low-caste (SCHCASTE) households have significantly positive coefficients in both equations, confirming the higher female participation from these socially disadvantaged groups. It may also be noted that the coefficient for SCHTRIBE is significantly higher than that for SCHCASTE in both equations, again confirming the common observation in this area that the participation of tribal (Santhals, etc.) women in the labor force is especially high.

The number of babies and small children (in the 0–4 age group) in the household, represented by our variable BAB, has a significantly negative coefficient, indicating the usual child-care constraint on women's participation in the labor force. (I am, of course, assuming that women's labor force participation behavior itself does not affect their reproductive behavior.) The number of children (in the 5-14 age group) who are currently in domestic work, represented by our variable CHDOM, has a positive coefficient (and a significant one in the LOGIT equation), suggesting how children (particularly female) doing domestic work ease the constraint on adult women in these families for work outside. The elasticity of UALABFORF with respect to ADWOMEN, the number of adult women in the family, is larger than unity in both equations, suggesting that the proportion of women participating in the labor force from a given household improves when there are more adult women in it (presumably sharing in the household chores and thereby easing the constraint on participation).

The coefficient for HMUNOWN, the dummy variable for cases where the household does not own its homestead, is significantly positive in both equations, possibly indicating work commitment to an employer who provided the homestead. VILPOP, the population size of the village has a significant positive coefficient in both equations, possibly suggesting that larger size of a village with its attendant commercialization may provide more opportunities for (particularly nonfarm) work and less rigid taboos on female participation.

Let us now turn to primarily cultivator households, where female participation rate is even lower than in agricultural wage labor households. Most of the variables that had significant coefficients in the earlier equations for agricultural labor households are again significant and have similar signs to be interpreted in a similar way, as may be seen from tables 1.7 and 1.9: female participation is higher for households with larger number of adult women (ADWOMEN), for tribal households (SCHTRIBE), for low-caste households (SCHCASTE, significant only in the OLS equation), and for households with larger number of children in domestic work (CHDOM, significant only in the OLS equation); participation is lower for households with a larger number of adult males in the current labor force (LABFORM), with a larger number of adult males with above-primary education (EDM), and with a larger number of babies and small children (BAB). Three variables which were not significant in the earlier equations for agricultural labor households now have significant coefficients: female participation is lower for households with a larger number of school-going children (SCHOOLCH), and higher for households with some male member gone away for work or in search of work (AWAYM, significant only in the LOGIT equation) and also higher for households with a larger number of adult females with primary education (EDF). These women with above-primary education may be going to nonfarm nonmanual jobs for which the taboo against women's working outside is weaker. Unlike in the earlier equations, the asset effect through the variable CULTIVAT is now insignificant[13] (though still negative), and the effect of commercialization of village size VILPOP is also insignificant (though still positive).

With a relatively small proportion of adult women participating in the usual labor force, it is to be noted that both for agricultural wage labor households and for cultivator households the OLS and LOGIT coefficients

---

[13] One possible reason is that for cultivator households, more than for agricultural wage labor households, CULTIVAT is significantly correlated with LABFORM and EDM, all three variables having a depressing effect on UALABFORF.

are significantly different in value (although similar in sign), with almost all coefficients increasing in absolute value in the LOGIT equation.

Let us now summarize main conclusions of this chapter on peasant labor supply. The wage response to market labor supply seems to be insignificant for both men and women in agricultural labor households. The asset effect and the status effect following from variables like farm size and level of schooling of male members of the family on market labor supply is expectedly negative. Similar is the income effect following from supplementary income on public works or fewer dependents to share the same wage income. Women from tribal and low-caste households are likely to hire themselves out more often, as are women from households with unowned homestead, possibly obligated to work for the employer who provides the homestead. In addition to these social and economic factors, demand conditions in the local labor market strongly influence the labor supply behavior both of men and women: market labor supply (including days seeking work) is significantly less for households located in districts with lower normal rainfall, larger deficit in last year's actual rainfall from the normal level, or in slack agricultural seasons, or, in the case of women, even a higher rate of unemployment of the male members of the household. In all these cases the job search discouragement effect outweighs the usual income effect on market labor supply.

Market agricultural labor supply seems to be primarily determined by other economic, social, and demographic constraints, not by the wage rate. The labor supply function looks more like a vertical line than the horizontal one commonly assumed in the development literature. The size of the desired margin of wage reported by casual agricultural labor respondents for (hypothetical) additional work inside the village over their current wage rate also suggests a low elasticity in the labor supply function. It is possible, however, that the presumed horizontal supply curve of labor in the literature is not an *ex ante* supply curve as in our estimates but more like a locus of equilibrium points (as in the case of the Keynesian aggregate supply curve), suggesting constancy of the equilibrium wage rate. Our critical comments on the latter position are presented in chapter 4.

It should also be emphasized that our labor supply estimates are in terms of *person-days* of wage work on farm during the reference week and not in terms of *persons*. It is quite possible that market supply of farm labor days is wage-inelastic and yet if *nonfarm* employment opportunities open up many more persons may be available for work at only a slightly higher wage. Even if *farm* employment opportunities expand, more persons may be available for work at the same wage rate, as my results about the effects of general demand conditions in the farm labor market on labor supply have suggested. At times when or in areas where labor demand conditions are depressed, instead of the market wage rate bearing the full brunt, the labor supply function itself may be shifting leftward.

As for usual participation of women in the (farm and nonfarm) labor force, its likelihood decreases with asset and status effects of farm size and income effects from variables like the number of male members of the family currently in the labor force, their level of schooling, and the village wage rate for males. Participation is higher for more educated women (possibly in nonmanual work), for women in larger and more commercialized villages, for women whose child-care and other household chores are eased by the presence of a larger number of other adult women and children in the family in domestic work, and in households with fewer babies and school-going children to take care of. In addition, women in tribal and low-caste households or in households obligated to work for unowned homestead participate more in the usual labor force.

CHAPTER 2

Seasonal Withdrawals from Female Labor Force and Measurement of Unemployment

1

In section III of the preceding chapter, we focused on the determinants of usual labor force participation by adult women in agricultural households. But quite often a woman in the *usual* labor force may not be in the *current* labor force. Unlike in much of the organized industrial sector, in the rural economy the major economic activities are often irregular and sporadic with pronounced seasonal fluctuations leading to periodic entry and withdrawal from the labor force, especially on the part of marginal laborers, often women, who shift back and forth between what is reported as "domestic" work and "gainful" work. According to my estimates from the NSS rural West Bengal survey data for 1977–78, on an average about 28 percent of adult women who are in the usual labor force withdraw into domestic work in the current reference period, and there are clear seasonal patterns in such withdrawals. For example, out of the adult women in the sample who are casual wage laborers in agriculture by their usual status, 12.1 percent are currently outside the labor force and into domestic work in the agriculturally relatively busy quarter of June–September; this percentage is 11.0 in the busiest (harvesting) quarter of October–December, and 23.0 and 22.8 in the relatively slack quarters of Jaunary–March and April–June, respectively. Such an extent of variation in the participation of these women in domestic work cannot be explained by fluctuations in necessary household chores.[1] Of course, there is some seasonality in social and ceremonial activities, which are part of domestic work, but in most areas in this region they are bunched more in the October–December quarter, when many of the more important festivals take place; in any case, they cannot fully explain the significant rise in the incidence of domestic work in the lean seasons. It may have more to do with fluctuations in opportunities for gainful work leading to periodic entries and involuntary withdrawals from the labor force.

Table 2.1 gives the results of a linear regression analysis of the variations in the current labor force participation by adult women who are in the usual labor force in the NSS 1977–78 rural West Bengal sample. The

[1] For additional evidence of such seasonal variations in the intensity of domestic work from NSS data relating to poor households in all major states in India, see Bardhan (1978).

dependent variable is the number of person-days (CLFDAYS) each adult woman in the usual labor force spent in the current labor force in the reference week. First of all, these usual working women tend to withdraw from the current labor force more with unemployment of male members of the family (judging by the highly significant negative coefficient of the variable for the current unemployment rate of the latter, UNEMPM), more with the slack quarter of April–June (SBRND 4 has a negative, though not significant, coefficient), more in areas where the percentage deficit in actual rainfall in the last year from the normal level has been larger (RAINDEF has a significant negative coefficient), and more in areas where the normal annual rainfall or the level of fertilizer use or the village irrigation level is lower (RAIN and NHA have significant positive coefficients, and VILIRR has a positive, though not significant, coefficient). All of this confirms the strong discouragement effect of current demand conditions in the local labor market on the current participation behavior of adult women who are in the usual labor force.

These households with larger family farms have more work of one kind

TABLE 2.1

Linear regression analysis of determinants of current labor force participation for individual women in the 15-60 age group who are in the usual labor force, rural West Bengal, 1977-78

	Dependent Variable:	CLFDAYS (number of person-days each such woman spent in current labor force in reference week)
	Mean:	4.33 days
	Standard Deviation:	3.2

Explanatory Variables	Regression Coefficient	Standard Error	Significant at Percent Level
AGE (age of laborer in years)	0.8165	0.0276	0.3
$(AGE)^2$	−0.0009	0.0004	1.4
WID (dummy for widowed, divorced, and separated women)	0.8032	0.1772	0.0
NMAR (dummy for women who never married)	0.7432	0.2255	0.1
SCHTRIBE (dummy for scheduled tribe)	0.6916	0.1773	0.0
SCHCASTE (dummy for scheduled caste)	0.3601	0.1465	1.4
EARNERM (number of male earners in household)	−0.2948	0.0702	0.0
UNEMPM (rate of unemployment of male members in household)	−0.8281	0.2253	0.0
BAB (number of children in 0–4 age group in household)	−0.2536	0.0861	0.3
CULTIVAT (area cultivated by household in acres)	0.1167	0.0343	0.1

Agricultural Labor

Table 2.1 (continued)

RAIN (normal annual rainfall in district in meters)	0.9425	0.0896	0.0
RAINDEF (percentage deficit in actual rainfall in 1977 from normal in district)	−0.9962	0.2509	0.0
NHA (nitrogenous fertilizer, in kg., used per hectare of area under foodgrains in district)	0.0236	0.0087	0.7
VILIRR (village irrigation level)	0.0892	0.0598	13.6
SBRND 4 (dummy for April–June quarter)	−0.1209	0.1405	39.0
UNSKILL (dummy for unskilled women) †	−0.4444	0.2148	3.9
PRIMED (dummy for education up to primary level)	−0.7965	0.2320	0.1
ABPRIMED (dummy for education beyond primary level)	−0.7689	0.3177	1.6
REG (dummy for women having regular wage employment)	2.6358	0.1954	0.0
NFFE (dummy for women employed in nonfarm family enterprise)	2.0262	0.1964	0.0
Constant term	1.1730	0.6105	5.5

$R^2 = 0.2345$; $F = 34.4$; no. of observations = 2,156

SOURCE: NSS, 32d Round, 1977-78. For RAIN, RAINDEF, and NHA: *Statistical Abstract of West Bengal.*

NOTE: The percentage rate of unemployment is defined as the number of person-days a laborer reported seeking (or being available for) work as a proportion of the days spent in the labor force in the reference week. VILIRR represents four percentage levels of cultivated area irrigated in the village: zero; positive but not over 10 percent; between 10 and 25 percent; and over 25 percent.

† Refers to lack of various skills (29 specified in survey questionnaire), mostly in the areas of artisans, craftsmen, social services, etc.

or another the year round, so that CULTIVAT has a significant positive coefficient. To the extent the family farm shares the local characteristics of higher normal rainfall, fertilizer use and irrigation level, and smaller deficit in actual rainfall in the last year, the positive coefficients of RAIN, NHA, and VILLIRR and the negative coefficient of RAINDEF that we have already referred to may also indicate more current work opportunity on own farm for households with a farm. The income effect on current participation of usually active women in the labor force works through the significantly negative coefficients of the number of male earners in the household (EARNERM) and the education levels of women (PRIMED, the dummy variable for education up to primary level and ABPRIMED, for education beyond primary level).[2] Similarly, those women who have to

[2] In tables 1.7 and 1.9, the education level of women has a positive effect on their usual labor force participation, whereas here in table 2.1 it seems to have a negative effect on their current labor force participation. The explanation might be that in the latter equation the effect of education is net of the effects of regular salaried employment (farm and nonfarm) and of nonfarm self-employment, so that it is negative for farm (casual and self-employed) work alone. But in the earlier tables no such controls were there, and the positive effect indicated the opportunity of more nonfarm and regular (particularly nonmanual) work for educated women.

ΓABLE 2.2

Linear regression analysis of determinants of current labor force participation for women in the 15–60 age group who are in the usual labor force and belonging to primarily agricultural wage labor households, rural West Bengal, 1977–78

	Dependent Variable:	CURPCPF (proportion of all usually active women in the household in current labor force)
	Mean:	0.66
	Standard Deviation:	0.47

Explanatory Variables†	Regression Coefficient	Standard Error	Significant at Percent Level
EARNERM	−0.0536	0.0215	1.3
UNEMPM	−0.2533	0.0569	0.0
BAB	−0.0526	0.0199	0.8
SCHOOLCH	−0.0755	0.0300	1.3
SCHTRIBE	0.1430	0.0369	0.0
SCHCASTE	0.0734	0.0360	4.2
RAIN	0.0682	0.0160	0.0
RAINDEF	−0.0880	0.0540	10.4
REGP (percentage of women in usual labor force who have regular wage employment)	0.3803	0.0508	0.0
NFFP (percentage of women in usual labor force who are in nonfarm casual labor or family enterprise)	0.3607	0.0481	0.0
SBRND 3 (dummy for January–March quarter)	−0.0864	0.0358	1.6
AWAYM	−0.2107	0.0958	2.8
Constant term	0.6193	0.0442	0.0
$R^2 = 0.2227$; F = 18.8; no. of observations = 799			

† See table 2.1 or Glossary of Variables.

depend on themselves more, like widows and spinsters, participate more in the current labor force, so that the dummy variables WID and NMAR in table 2.1 have significant positive coefficients. The current participation rate is obviously higher for those women who have regular salaried employment (farm or nonfarm) or who are employed in nonfarm family enterprise, so that REG and NFFE in table 2.1 have significant positive coefficients. Unskilled women have fewer, particularly nonfarm, work opportunities, so that their current participation rate is lower (significant negative coefficient for the dummy variable UNSKILL).

Women with more small children withdraw from the current labor force more often so that BAB has a significant negative coefficient. AGE has a significant positive coefficient, but the quadratic term has a significantly negative coefficient, suggesting that productivity-enhancing experience

TABLE 2.3

Linear regression analysis of determinants of current labor force participation for women in the 15–60 age group who are in the usual labor force and belonging to primarily cultivator households, rural West Bengal, 1977–78

	Dependent Variable:	CURPCPF⁺	
	Mean:	0.70	
	Standard Deviation:	0.48	

Explanatory Variables†	Regression Coefficient	Standard Error	Significant at Percent Level
EARNERM	−0.1005	0.0291	0.1
UNEMPM	−0.3882	0.1863	1.3
CULTIVAT	0.0247	0.0099	1.3
DEP	−0.1623	0.1029	11.6
SCHTRIBE	0.1478	0.0665	2.7
RAIN	0.1567	0.0401	0.0
RAINDEF	−0.2378	0.1100	3.1
REGP	0.3953	0.1073	0.0
NFFP	0.4142	0.0968	0.0
AWAYM	−0.4261	0.1915	2.6
NHA	0.0038	0.0030	20.9
SBRND 3	−0.0766	0.0678	25.9
SBRND 4	−0.0655	0.0577	25.7
Constant term	0.4764	0.1160	0.0

$R^2 = 0.2190$; $F = 6.5$; no. of observations $= 317$

† See tables 2.1 and 2.2 or Glossary of Variables.

brings more current work opportunities, but after a point more advanced age is a liability on participation. Women belonging to tribal and low-caste households have more need and fewer social constraints for current participation, so that the dummy variables SCHTRIBE and SCHCASTE in table 2.1 have significant positive coefficients.

In table 2.1 my analysis is for all individual adult women in the usual labor force. In tables 2.2 and 2.3 I have carried out a similar exercise at the household level, separately for primarily agricultural wage labor and primarily cultivator households. The dependent variable now is the proportion of all usually active working women in the household who are in the current labor force. The mean value of this variable, CURPCPF, is 0.66 for agricultural wage labor households and 0.70 for cultivator households. In other words, on an average between 30 and 34 percent of usually active adult women in these households withdraw from the current labor force. The social, economic, and demographic determinants of this withdrawal, as shown in the regression results in tables 2.2 and 2.3, are very similar to those in table 2.1. In particular, the discouragement effect of bleak job prospects inducing involuntary withdrawal from the current labor force, as is to be observed from the estimated coefficients of UNEMPM, slack seasons (like SBRND 3), RAIN, and RAINDEF, is again remarkably clear.

II

This discouraged drop-out effect from the current labor force for usual members of the labor force suggests a source of serious underestimation in the standard procedures of measuring unemployment or under-employment in the rural sector. In several attempts that have been made at measuring rural unemployment,[3] the most common factor is that of finding the *intersection* of two basic sets of workers: those who are fully or partially idle in terms of working days or hours in the reference period; and those who report willingness to work (presumably at the going market rate). In cases where day-to-day time disposition data for the reference period (usually a week) are available and where different households are surveyed in different weeks staggered over the year, as in our NSS data set, one constructs from the averages of different weekly situations an aggregate *time rate* of unemployment, computed as the ratio of the total number of (idle) person-days seeking or being available for work to the total number of person-days reported to be in the labor force. In the preceding chapter we have called this unemployment rate for an individual UR. Apart from open unemployment, UR clearly takes into account underemployment in a time sense,[4] but it overlooks the phenomenon of discouraged drop-outs and that of involuntary unemployment that takes the form of withdrawal from the current labor force, often into domestic work.

We have, therefore, devised an alternative measure which may go toward correcting this underestimation bias. This measure starts with the presumption that if a person is in the labor force by usual status, any withdrawal from the labor force in the reference week is more due to the perceived lack of opportunities, and that days actually spent by her in domestic work in the reference week should more properly be counted as unemployed days, even though she may not have explicitly reported her availability for work to the survey investigator. So our alternative measure of (potential) underemployment, called PUR is defined as:

---

[3] For a survey of the various concepts used in the literature, see Krishna (1976); see also Sen (1975), Hauser (1974), and ILO (1974).

[4] UR, of course, does not take into account underemployment in the sense of low earnings or unsuitable occupations. The latter involve the specification of arbitrary norms (or cut-off points) of income, productivity, or consumption or of some matching of skills and occupations that introduce issues qualitatively different from those involved in a time measure. Here we shall confine our attention to the problem of time measures of unemployment.

$$PUR = \frac{S+D+d}{G+S+D+d}$$

where G = number of days in the reference week spent in all kinds of gainful activities

S = number of days spent in the reference week in seeking work or in being available for work

D = number of days spent in domestic work by a person who was in the labor force in the reference week

d = number of days spent (assumed to be seven per person) in domestic work by a person who was in the usual labor force but in the reference week was in domestic work (and hence outside the current labor force).

The admissible set over which PUR is defined is that of all persons in the labor force by *usual* status. Contrast this to the standard measure of $UR = S/(G+S)$, defined over the set of persons in the *current* labor force in the reference week. In our NSS sample of rural West Bengal 1977-78, taking all women in the usual labor force, UR is estimated to be 10.02 percent, whereas PUR is four times as large at 40.20 percent. Taking different groups of female workers separately, for women in casual wage labor, UR is 13.76 percent and PUR 34.17 percent; for women self-employed on own farm, UR is 0.73 percent and PUR is 19.59 percent; for women who are farm helpers on family farm, UR is 0.98 percent and PUR is 26.81 percent.

That the withdrawal by a usual laborer into domestic work in the reference week is not entirely voluntary has already been corroborated by the strong evidence of discouragement effects of local labor market conditions cited in the regression analysis earlier in the chapter. The significant extent of withdrawal into domestic work even by women in very poor households (whose propensity to substitute leisure for income is not likely to be very strong) also suggests that for them it may be more due to a lack of work opportunities. Take, for example, the three poorest size classes of households by household per capita monthly expenditure at current prices in 1977-78: (a) those with per capita expenditure equal to or below Rs. 20 per month; (b) those with per capita expenditure between Rs. 20 and Rs. 30 per month; and (c) those with per capita expenditure between Rs. 30 and Rs. 40 per month. These three groups of households together constitute the bottom one-third of rural households in our sample. Yet for group (a) UR for women in usual labor force is 10.82 percent and PUR is 42.61 percent, for group (b) UR for these women is 13.16 percent and PUR is 50.66 percent, and for group (c) UR for these women is 8.58 percent and PUR is 36 percent. So the substantial difference in the two unemployment rates is relevant even for the poorest working women who cannot afford the luxury of voluntary withdrawal from the current labor force.

It is quite possible that not all the days spent in domestic work in the reference week by a person in the usual labor force should strictly be counted as involuntary unemployment, and as such PUR may in some cases overestimate such unemployment. On the other hand, to ignore the phenomenon altogether, as in the case of the standard UR measure, is to underestimate unemployment seriously. Besides, PUR itself may be an underestimate to the extent that discouraged drop-outs withdraw not merely from the current labor force but also from the usual labor force. A woman facing bleak job opportunities may have opted for being a housewife by usual status and will be counted out of the admissible set for our measure of PUR. Another related reason why PUR may give an underestimate (so does UR, a fortiori) is the way in which the survey investigator's question about "seeking work or being available for work" is usually interpreted. Quite often the respondent interprets this question as one of availability for *wage* employment outside. There are large numbers of self-employed or family workers (particularly women) who may be available for extra work at home or on their own farm but do not report availability for wage employment outside. In this way a woman may be classified as a housewife (and hence outside the usual labor force because of her negative answer to the question), even though she would have really been available for gainful work at home. In our NSS data set one of the probing questions to women in domestic work was: "In spite of your preoccupation in domestic duties, are you willing to accept work if work is made available at your household?" In our sample for rural West Bengal about 30 percent of adult women in domestic work answered "yes" to this question. It is also interesting to note that even out of those adult women in domestic work who report *not* being available for additional work, in response to a separate, prior question in general about additional work, 24 percent answered "yes" to this specific question about availability if work is brought to the household. This points to the need for policy focus on employment expansion particularly on ancillary activities in and around the household; rural works program is not a remedy for this aspect of the unemployment problem of rural women.

Finally, both UR and PUR as measures of unemployment are subject to the varying limitations of time disposition data for different groups of workers. For hired casual laborers, time disposition data in terms of standardized days or hours are more meaningful. But for the self-employed even the most precise count of time spent in different activities may at times be misleading. In particular, neither of the two measures can take account of underemployment disguised in the form of work spreading. When there is not much work, self-employed workers may reduce the intensity of work effort but spread it over the whole day or week—the survey investigator will count it as a full day or week worked. This is a difficult problem to handle in large-scale surveys. In serious cases of this sort, time measures of unemployment fail, and we may have to resort to more indirect measures with prespecified norms of productivity or consumption.

CHAPTER 3

Demand for Hired Farm Labor

I

Given the large inequalities in the distribution of cultivated land, variations in demographic composition of farm families, and status-determined aversion to manual work, it is not surprising that in most parts of South Asia hiring of farm labor is quite significant, contrary to the image of self-sufficient family farms assumed in much of the theoretical development literature. This chapter focuses on the determinants of variations in farm labor hiring on the basis of detailed farm-level Farm Management Survey data collected in three predominantly paddy-growing districts in east and south India and also data collected by the National Sample Survey in 1972–73 for the whole of rural West Bengal.

Obviously the problems of data availability at the disaggregated level of farms and households limit our choice of the form and number of variables representing those determinants, and the ones actually chosen here should be regarded as crude proxies for more appropriate variables. The dependent variable is hired farm labor days per acre of cultivated area. The farm-level independent variables are of different kinds—economic, demographic, technological, and institutional. Other things remaining the same, one would expect an inverse cross-section relationship between the market wage rate and the use of hired labor per acre. Among demographic variables, one obviously expects that dependence on hired labor is less, the larger the number of adult workers in the farmer family. Technological yield-increasing or land improvement factors, like irrigation, fertilization, improved varieties of seeds, and double cropping, are likely to increase the use of hired labor by shifting out the labor productivity function.

Of course, such productivity shifts can be labor-using or labor-saving depending on their specific types. For example, lift irrigation is normally much more labor-using than gravity-flow irrigation. Farm-yard manure is more labor-using than chemical fertilizers (so that an increase in the value of fertilizers applied per acre may sometimes actually mean a substitution of chemical for farmyard fertilizers and hence may result in a decline in labor intensity per acre), although all fertilizers, apart from increasing yields, also increase the growth of weeds, thereby increasing the need for weeding as well as harvesting and other labor per acre. Productivity shifts brought about by engineering (as opposed to biological-chemical) innovations such as tractors, transplanters, mechanical weeders, and threshers are, of course, more often expected to be labor-displacing. There is a large and controversial literature on this,[1] and we need not get into the issue here, since the data set in this chapter relates to areas and time periods in which mechanization of farm operations is rather insignificant.

By shortening the duration of the crop cycle and increasing the importance of timeliness of each operation, the new technology in agriculture may also heighten the acuteness of the demographic bottleneck on a farm with fewer family workers and increase its dependence on hired labor. It may also increase the need for hiring workers with specialized skills for special operations.

One usually expects a positive relationship between the size of farm and the use of hired labor per acre. Smaller farms are more dependent on family labor. It has been widely noted in the literature on farm size and productivity that for the smaller farms the imputed cost of labor is likely to be less than that for larger farms hiring labor at the market wage rate.[2] This is largely due to the various social and economic constraints on the family laborers (particularly for women and children) offering themselves on the wage labor market. Farm size is also usually a good proxy for the household's asset situation and access to resources. The latter clearly conditions the introduction of yield-increasing practices and crop patterns, involving an increased use of labor.

One social institution which has a very important bearing on the use of hired labor is the caste status of the family. Almost all of the manual work, even in small farms, is usually done by hired (low-caste or tribal) labor if the family belongs to an upper caste. In some areas there is a caste taboo against plowing, which dictates the need for delegating the tillage operation to hired plowmen who bring their bullocks, even when other farm operations are largely in the hands of family workers.

II

The first district we shall take up is that of West Godavari in Andhra Pradesh. We have access to detailed data for 97 farms (selected by the method of multi-stage stratified random sampling for the Farm Management Survey of the Ministry of Food and Agriculture) in this district for the year 1958–59. West Godavari is agriculturally one of the most advanced districts in the state, with a very high percentage of irrigated area. The predominant crop is paddy, which is raised in the fertile alluvial soil of the delta, watered by the canals flowing from the Godavari River. In 1958–59 the methods of paddy cultivation in the selected villages in the sample were traditional, with local seeds, mostly farmyard manure (rather than chemical), wooden plows and bullock power. In the selection of the villages for the sample the district has been divided into two zones: a

---

[1] For a good survey of the issues arising from tractorization in Indian agriculture, see Binswanger (1977).

[2] See, for example, Sen (1962), Mazumdar (1965), and Bardhan (1973a).

TABLE 3.1

Linear regression analysis of determinants of hired labor intensity in farm production, west Godavari, 1958–59

Dependent Variable:	HLDA (hired man-days per year per acre of cultivated area)	
Mean:	61 days	
Standard Deviation:	61 days	

Explanatory Variables †	Regression Coefficient	Standard Error	Significant at Percent Level
CULTIVAT (area cultivated by household in acres)	1.4558	0.5275	1.0
MCI (multiple cropping index)†	20.6322	2.2888	0.0
IRRCULT (percentage of cultivated area irrigated)	58.8945	16.8807	0.1
VWAGE (average farm wage rate in village)†	−53.4965	16.5877	0.2
ADA (number of adult family workers per acre)	−8.4279	5.0710	10.0
Constant term	28.0222	28.0553	32.0
$R^2 = 0.825$; F=41.6; no. of observations=60			

†MCI: calculated by dividing gross cropped area by sown area.
†VWAGE: the average farm wage rate per man-day in the village, calculated from the figures of total wage costs and hired labor days for all sample farms in a village taken together.

paddy zone and a tobacco zone. My subsequent analysis will be carried out only for the 60 farms in the paddy zone. Paddy accounts for nearly 80 percent of the cropped area in the paddy-zone farms.

In this sample of 60 farms the average number of farm labor days (in terms of standardized 8-hour person-days) used per acre of cultivated area is about 102 days in the year. Sixty-two percent (a high figure even in comparison with other ares in South Asia) of this labor is hired. Table 3.1 presents the results of a linear regression analysis of the determinants of hired man-days per year per acre of cultivated area (what we call HLDA) in terms of the farm-level data available to us from the Farm Management Survey. It seems, consistent with my discussion earlier in the chapter, hired labor intensity is positively associated with land quality or improvement factors like irrigation or multiple cropping and negatively associated with the village wage rate (VWAGE). We should note, however, that the proportion of area irrigated (IRRCULT) that we have taken as an explanatory variable is a very crude proxy for the effect of irrigation and does not take into account farmwise variations in the number of times and frequency intervals of irrigation or the effectiveness of particular types of irrigation facilities, etc., on which we do not have data. The size of net sown area (CULTIVAT) is significantly positive in explaining HLDA: obviously, larger farms depend more on hired labor. Similarly, a farm with

TABLE 3.2

Linear regression analysis of determinants of hired labor intensity in farm production, Tanjore, 1967–68

Dependent Variable:	HLDA†		
Mean:	56.6 days		
Standard Deviation:	34.6 days		

Explanatory Variables†	Regression Coefficient	Standard Error	Significant at Percent Level
MCI	34.7282	3.7241	0.0
VWAGE	−19.0107	6.2229	0.3
ADA	−9.2765	5.3067	8.0
FMA (value of fertilizers and manure per acre)	0.1281	0.1020	21.0
Constant term	55.7926	19.2080	0.4
$R^2 = 0.394$; $F = 23.6$; no. of observations $= 150$			

†See table 3.1.

a larger number of adult workers in the family (ADA) depends less on hired labor.

Table 3.2 presents similar results for Tanjore District, 1967–68 in Tamil Nadu, again agriculturally one of the most advanced districts in the State, reputed to be its "rice bowl". Most of the cultivated land is irrigated, normally with canal water, and the predominant crop is paddy (grown three times in the year). In 1967–68 the farmers had already substantially adopted high-yielding varieties of seeds (particularly what is called ADT-27 rice) and chemical fertilizers.

In our sample of 150 farms in Tanjore, as high as 68 percent of farm labor days are hired. Table 3.2 suggests that, consistent with our earlier discussion, hired labor intensity is positively associated with the multiple cropping index (MCI) and negatively with the village wage rate (VWAGE). As expected, the number of adult workers in the family (ADA) is negatively associated with hired labor intensity. Fertilizer and manure per acre (FMA) seem to have a weak positive influence on hired labor use.

Hooghly is the only predominantly paddy-producing district in India to be surveyed under the Farm Management Survey scheme in the middle 1950s and resurveyed toward the end of the 1960s. Between the two periods of survey in this district there was substantial progress: the irrigated proportion rose from about 15 percent to 55 percent of sown area of the surveyed farms, the multiple cropping index went up from 1.23 to 1.53, and farm business income per acre rose from Rs. 161 in 1956–57 to Rs. 665 in 1970–71 at current prices. Hired labor days per year per acre of cultivated area rose from 21 days on an average (for our sample of 83 farms in 1956–57) to 54 days (for our sample of 115 primarily cultivator households in 1970–71).

Table 3.3 presents the results on determinants of hired labor intensity in Hooghly in 1956—57. The importance of labor hiring on farms varies negatively with the number of adult workers in the family and positively with size of farm and incidence of bullock labor hiring (represented by hired bullock labor days per acre, HBKDA). As we have noted before, hired bullock service and hired plowmen are joint inputs; one cannot get the one without the other, and sometimes caste considerations dictate the need for hired plowmen who bring their bullocks.

Table 3.4 uses the data for Hooghly 1970-71 for a sample of 115 primarily cultivator households. As before, hired labor is positively associated with size of cultivated land, bullock labor hiring, and fertilizers and manures used and negatively with the village wage rate and the number of adult farm workers in the family.

At this point we may note some results on seasonal fluctuations in labor use. In all of the preceding discussion, labor day figures are annual and do not capture season-wise or operation-wise variations. On the basis of monthly labor use data from the primary schedules for Hooghly 1970-71, we have been able to compute for each farm the (seasonal) coefficient of variation in total (hired plus family) labor days used on farm—what we have called SCVTLDF—taking a mean value of 0.7576. In table 3.5 we have tried to explain variations in this value across farms. It seems that larger farms have a lower seasonal coefficient of variation of labor use, possibly indicating their better ability to muster resources like groundwater irrigation during the winter and early summer months and credit (major constraints for raising high-yielding varieties of summer paddy, wheat, and potato) and thereby to sustain labor use in all seasons. Similarly, the

TABLE 3.3

Linear regression analysis of determinants of hired labor intensity in farm production, Hooghly, 1956–57

	Dependent Variable:	HLDA†	
	Mean:	21.2 days	
	Standard Deviation:	17.5 days	

Explanatory Variables†	Regression Coefficient	Standard Error	Significant at Percent Level
CULTIVAT	1.3927	0.7976	9.0
MCI	8.6400	6.6200	20.0
ADA	−2.4776	1.0786	2.0
FMA	0.2942	0.1221	2.0
HBKDA (hired bullock labor days per acre)	1.2156	0.2668	0.0
Constant term	−0.5860	8.5444	95.0
$R^2 = 0.316$; $F = 7.1$; no. of observations $= 83$			

† See tables 3.1 and 3.2 or Glossary of Variables.

seasonal coefficient of variation of labor use is negatively associated with the multiple cropping index (MCI) and percentage of area irrigated from canals and tubewells (CTIRRP), which are more dependable, all-weather sources of irrigation, and also with the proportion of cropped area harvested (HARVPROP)—if the latter is low on account of crop damage. labor use in plowing, sowing, and transplantation seasons is not matched by labor use in the harvesting season.

TABLE 3.4

Linear regression analysis of determinants of hired labor intensity in farm production, Hooghly, 1970–71

	Dependent Variable:	HLDA†		
	Mean:	54.3 days		
	Standard Deviation:	46.7 days		

Explanatory Variables†	Regression Coefficient	Standard Error	Significant at Percent Level
CULTIVAT	2.2789	1.2811	8.0
VWAGE	−16.2001	7.7346	4.0
ADA††	−11.5220	5.4030	4.0
FMA	0.2043	0.0311	0.0
HBKDA	2.2349	0.5727	0.0
Constant term	76.1412	26.9649	0.6

$R^2 = 0.383$; $F = 11.2$; no. of observations = 115.

NOTE: In the Hooghly 1970–71 sample of 150 farms, about 35 are primarily noncultivator households (occupied mostly in agricultural wage labor or trade and services). Since our purpose is to analyze labor use patterns on farm, we have excluded these 35 households from the relevant sample.

† See tables 3.1 and 3.2 or Glossary of Variables.

†† In earlier tables, ADA means the number of adult workers in the family, while in this table it refers to such adults who are engaged in cultivation as their main occupation.

III

The preceding section analyzed labor use patterns on the basis of small-scale farm management data for some predominantly paddy-producing districts. This section is based on the large-scale sample survey of labor use behavior of households in rural West Bengal as a whole, collected by the National Sample Survey in 1972–73. In all, we have data for about 4,900 sample households drawn from about 500 sample villages. Out of this set we shall confine my attention primarily to agricultural households cultivating more than 0.1 acres of land. Apart from information on various economic and demographic characteristics of the households, details of

TABLE 3.5

Linear regression analysis of seasonal variation in farm labor use, Hooghly, 1970–71

	Dependent Variable:	SCVTLDF † (seasonal coefficient of variation in total labor days used on farm)		
	Mean:	0.7576		

Explanatory Variables†	Regression Coefficient	Standard Error	Significant at Percent Level
CULTIVAT	−0.0261	0.0076	0.1
MCI	−0.1500	0.0435	0.1
HARVPROP (proportion of paddy cropped area harvested)	−0.1712	0.0595	0.5
CTIRRP (percentage of area irrigated from canals and tubewells)	−0.1083	0.0722	14.0
Constant term	1.2643	0.0987	0.0
$R^2 = 0.226$; $F = 8.0$; no. of observations = 115			

NOTE: SCVTLDF has been calculated from monthly data over the whole year as obtained from the primary schedules of the Hooghly Farm Management Survey made available by A. Rudra.

†See tables 3.1 and 3.2 or Glossary of Variables.

both hired and family labor use *in the reference week* are available. Table 3.6 presents the results of my analysis of the determinants of hired farm labor use for rural West Bengal.

The average number of hired farm labor days per acre in the reference week (HLDAR) for a household is 1.1 days. As expected from my earlier discussion, it is positively associated with the size of cultivated land (CULTIVAT), percentage of cultivated area irrigated (IRRCULT), and also an educational variable, ADED, the number of adults in the household having more than primary education. (Households with more educated adults obviously depend more on hired labor for farm work.) HLDAR is negatively associated with the village wage rate (VWAGE), the number of adult farm workers in the household (ADF), the slack season dummies for the January–March and April–June subrounds, and the scheduled caste or tribe dummy (implying that, if the household members do not belong to the scheduled castes or tribes, they are more likely to depend on hired labor, other things remaining the same).

One major limitation of these NSS data for my present purpose is that the survey investigation visited each household only once a year; the detailed labor use data relate only to the reference week of the survey and do not sufficiently capture variations over the agricultural crop cycle, in spite of our subround dummies. A subround of three months is too long a period to coincide with the duration of particular agricultural activities or slack intervals.

TABLE 3.6

Linear regression analysis of determinants of hired labor intensity in farm production, rural West Bengal, 1972–73

Dependent variable:	HLDAR (hired person-days per acre in reference week of farm)		
Mean:	1.1 days		
Standard deviation:	2.3 days		

Explanatory Variables†	Regression Coefficient	Standard Error	Significant at Percent Level
CULTIVAT	0.1251	0.0155	0.0
IRRCULT	0.4841	0.1368	0.0
VWAGE	−0.0289	0.0128	2.0
ADF (number of adult workers in family)	−0.1083	0.0418	1.0
ADED (number of adults in household having more than primary education)	0.5118	0.0480	0.0
SBRND 3 (dummy for January–March quarter)	−0.6637	0.1061	0.0
SBRND 4 (dummy for April–June quarter)	−0.4476	0.1083	0.0
CASTRIB (scheduled caste or tribe)	−0.6061	0.0914	0.0
Constant term	1.1670	0.1197	0.0

$R^2 = 0.166$; F = 57.7; no. of observations = 2,326

NOTE: Out of the total of about 4,900 NSS sample households for rural West Bengal, table 3.6 relates only to primarily agricultural households cultivating more than 0.1 acres of land. While in the preceding tables on the basis of Farm Management Surveys person-days refer to standardized 8-hour days for the year as a whole, in table 3.6 person-days relate to the reference week of NSS investigation, and the intensity of work on each days has been measured in binary codes of "full" and "half".
† See table 3.1 or Glossary of Variables.

But the major limitation of both the Farm Management Survey data used in section II as well as the NSS household survey data as used here is that they do not contain sufficient information to enable one to analyze labor use patterns in the detailed context of various institutional and contractual constraints on the farmer or the laborer. For example, these data do not tell us how constraints on the farmer's access to credit inhibit the adoption of labor-using land improvements or how the employer-creditor, by giving consumption credit in the lean season or allotting a tiny plot of land to the laborer for residential or cultivation purposes, ensures the availability of hired labor often at a below-market wage rate. In chapters 5 and 6 we shall comment on various aspects of such labor-tying and labor market segmentation.

The cross-section survey data also do not capture the farm-level impact of significant institutional changes like tenant eviction on the use of hired labor. In recent years, "protective" tenancy legislation as well as the increased profitability of self-cultivation by the landowner over large parts of India have caused large-scale tenant eviction, which has led to a significant rise in the use of hired labor. Apart from a decline in tenancy, the composition of the tenant farmer group is changing significantly, in turn changing the pattern of hired labor use. The increased costliness and credit intensity of the new agricultural technology dependent on privately controlled irrigation (pumps and tubewells) and purchased inputs (like fertilizers and pesticides) have driven many small farmers out of cultivation, particularly in agriculturally more progressive areas, and land is gradually passing on to a new class of large farmer-entrepreneurs, who account for an increasing share in the total leased-in area.[3] This change is evident in a comparison of the NSS Land Holdings Surveys for 1970–71 and 1960–61, particularly in the agriculturally advanced region of Punjab and Haryana. In 1970–71 in Punjab (including Haryana), even though only 9 percent of the rural households did not *own* any land, as much as 54 percent did not *cultivate* any land. The corresponding percentages in 1960–61 were 12 and 39, respectively. A comparison of the Lorenz curves of distribution of operated area (see figure 3.1) in Punjab (including Haryana) shows that inequality in this distribution increased unambiguously between 1960–61 and 1970–71. This kind of change clearly increases the hired proportion of labor use on farm.

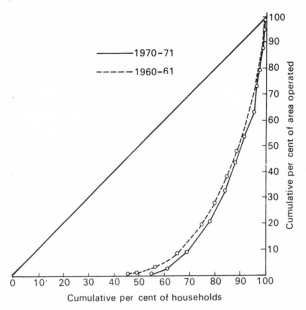

Figure 3.1 Lorenz Curves for Distribution of Operated Area
in Punjab (Including Haryana) in 1960-61 and 1970-71

[3] Cross-sectionally, taking the NSS data for 55 regions in India in 1970–71, the correlation coefficient between the percentage of area irrigated and the proportion of rural households owning but not operating land is 0.52, possibly suggesting that in better irrigated areas cost of cultivation has driven many small landowners away from farming.

CHAPTER 4

Wages and Unemployment

I

Most of the standard theories of agricultural wage determination used in the development literature do not have much empirical foundation. Yet by constant repetition they have now become part of the development orthodoxy. This chapter starts with some evidence from large-scale surveys of rural West Bengal and other regions in India to show that the agricultural wage rate (either for casual or long-term attached laborers) is sensitive to demand and productivity conditions, contrary to the implications of the popular theories of determination of wages by biological (subsistence or nutrition-determined efficiency) factors or by custom. The competitive wage-equals-marginal-productivity theory, on the other hand, cannot take into account, as noted in section III, the observed persistence of involuntary unemployment (even with some wage flexibility); it also pays insufficient attention to frequent cases of monopsony power that the employer comes to exert in the village labor market and, in particular, to the high premium the employer places on quick and ready availability of labor during some peak operations, leading him to various formal or informal labor-tying arrangements.

In section IV we develop some simple theoretical models to incorporate these factors ignored in the standard theories and generate comparative-static hypotheses about variations in wage rates and unemployment which seem to be consistent with the data. For example, we are able to explain the positive association of the wage rate not only with demand expansion factors (through agricultural development or across seasons) but also with the dependency ratio in the labor household and the negative association with women, lower-caste workers, and landed workers. In one variation of the model, considered in section V, we analyze interseason adjustments in labor hiring, with tied labor being paid more than its marginal product in the lean season to ensure the employer a dependable supply of labor in the peak season, and the amplitude of interseason wage variation is less than that in productivity. In terms of the same model we are also able to explain the observed positive association between the importance of permanent labor contracts and the tightness of the peak-season labor market. Finally, we comment briefly on the mode of wage payment, differential abilities of workers, and the territorial domain of the wage determination process.

One class of wage theories veers around an essentially biological determination of agricultural wages in the context of a very poor country. There is first the age-old, still popular, subsistence theory of wages. Apart

TABLE 4.1

Percentage distribution of villages by ranges of the village average daily male farm wage rates,
rural West Bengal, 1972–73

Wage Range (Rs.)	Oct.–Dec Quarter	Jan.–March Quarter	April–June Quarter	July–Sept. Quarter	Himalayan Region (1)	Eastern Plains (2)	Central Plains (3)	Western Plains (4)
0.1–2.0	14.4	21.5	22.6	6.7	7.0	28.0	6.6	23.6
2.01–2.5	22.1	29.0	20.8	15.1	16.2	33.6	15.5	21.7
2.51–3.0	27.9	32.7	33.0	29.2	34.9	29.0	36.5	21.7
3.01–3.5	22.1	11.2	9.4	24.5	23.3	7.5	22.8	14.2
Above 3.5	13.5	5.6	14.2	24.5	18.6	1.9	18.6	18.8
All	100	100	100	100	100	100	100	100

SOURCE: NSS, 27th Round data.
NOTE: The total number of sample villages reporting some hiring out of male farm labor is 423. For each quarter all the regions have been put together; similarly, for each region all the quarters have been put together.

from the fact that there is no one subsistence level (even assuming the same basal metabolic rate of the body and the same level of external temperature), there is the dismal fact that in poor countries (certainly in India) the majority of agricultural laborers have a level of living or a daily calorie intake significantly below even the barest minimum recommended by most nutritionists, and yet they survive (at what level of vitality, body weight, and morbidity is another matter). More important for the present purpose, the subsistence theory of wages should imply, for a fairly homogeneous region, a roughly constant level of real wage invariant to changes in demand or in productivity conditions.

Let us pause here for a look at the agricultural wage data from the large-scale survey of rural households in West Bengal in 1972–73 carried out by

TABLE 4.2

Linear regression analysis of determinants of daily farm wage rate, rural West Bengal, 1972–73

	Dependent Variable:	FWAGE (average daily wage received by casual laborers in farm work in reference week)		
	Mean:	Rs. 2.64		
	Standard Deviation:	Rs. 0.98		

Explanatory Variables	Regression Coefficient	Standard Error	Significant at Percent Level
PCULTIVAT (per capita land cultivated by the household to which the laborer belongs)	−0.3836	0.1185	0.1
AGE (age of laborer in years)	0.0042	0.0014	0.2
DEPE (number of dependents per earner in labor household)	0.0819	0.0128	0.0
AGDEV (composite agricultural development index for district)	0.0056	0.0013	0.0
VUR (unemployment rate in village) †	−0.6085	0.1588	0.0
SEXF (dummy to represent women)	−0.3962	0.0507	0.0
VIRR (dummy for village irrigation) ‡	0.1458	0.0469	0.2
SBRND 1 (dummy for July–Sept. quarter)	0.5247	0.0529	0.0
SBRND 2 (dummy for Oct.–Dec. quarter)	0.2641	0.0537	0.0
SBRND 3 (dummy for Jan.–March quarter)	−0.1310	0.0529	1.4
Constant term	1.7150	0.1268	0.0

$R^2 = 0.1105$; $F = 33.2$; no. of observations $= 2,687$

SOURCE: NSS, 27th Round, except for AGDEV, which is a weighted-average index of a number of agroclimatic and commercialization indices, reported for most districts in India around the middle of the 1960s in *Reserve Bank of India Bulletin* (October 1969).

† VUR: weighted-average unemployment rate (defined in the same way as UR in chapter 2) for the sample households in the village.

† VIRR: dummy variable to indicate whether most of the cultivated land in the village is irrigated (this variable is thus different from VILIRR, defined in table 2.1).

the NSS. As we have mentioned before, we have for this year detailed data for about 8,500 rural workers belonging to nearly 4,900 sample households drawn from about 500 sample villages. In this sample, if we take the villages in which some farm labor was reported to be hired out, we find that the village average wage rate for male casual farm labor VWAGEM has a mean value of Rs. 2.76 per day with a standard deviation of 0.71. Table 4.1 presents the percentage distribution of these villages by different ranges of VWAGEM for the four quarters in the year separately (while aggregating over four regions within West Bengal) and then for the four regions separately (while aggregating over the four quarters). There is quite a bit of dispersion in this distribution, contrary to the hypothesis of wage constancy.[1] Even if we take the mean VWAGEM of Rs. 2.76 and a wide band of 25 percent below and above the mean, we are well within the wage range of Rs. 2.01–Rs. 3.5. In table 4.1 the proportion of villages having VWAGEM outside this range is about 26 percent in region 1, 30 percent in region 2, 25 percent in region 3, and as high as 43 percent in region 4; it is about 28 percent in the October–December quarter, 27 percent in the January–March quarter, 37 percent in the April–June quarter, and 31 percent in the July–September quarter.

Taking the set of all individual casual agricultural laborers in the sample, we have tried to explain the variations in the wage rates received by them in the reference week in terms of the linear regression equation in table 4.2.

All the independent variables in the regression equation in table 4.2 have coefficients which are statistically significant at less than the 1 percent level. It seems that the casual farm wage rate is positively associated with the village irrigation dummy, the district agricultural development index, age

[1] One major problem with the NSS wage data for the present purpose is that we do not have any detailed cost-of-living data to deflate money wages and, after all, the constant wage hypothesis is about real wages. The seasonal differences in cost of living may not be a great problem for our case. Food prices (which constitute the predominant part of the cost of living of rural laborers) are usually assumed to decline around the busy agricultural season of harvesting and rise in the slack season. So this may in fact widen the seasonal wage disparity *more* in real terms than in money terms. Actually, in recent years the increased storage capacity of the grain sellers, price-stabilizing effects of government procurement policy, and the larger number of crops raised in the year have all contributed to a remarkable reduction in interseason price variability of grains. As for regional cost-of-living differences in West Bengal, we have access to some fragmentary data from a published source. The West Bengal State Statistical Bureau publishes the food cost indices for different expenditure groups of families; using data from this source over 10 years, 1957–66, and averaging over the centers in each region, we find that the difference across four regions in our sample is very small: the food cost in the highest-cost region is only 11 percent above that in the lowest-cost region. Another problem for this wage data is that in the survey intensity of work has been measured only in "full-" and "half-" day units, and if in peak seasons workers work for longer than a usual full day, the larger wage earnings will show up in our data as higher wage rates even if the wage rate per standardized day actually remains the same. On this question of seasonal variability in hours of work and its implications for variability in hourly wage rate, see the discussion in Hanson (1971) and Hansen (1971) in the context of rural Egypt.

of the worker (possibly indicating higher productivity of experienced workers), and the relatively busy seasons of October–December and July–September and negatively associated with the relatively slack season of January–March and the current unemployment rate in the village. Thus, contrary to the constant wage hypothesis, the wage rate seems to be quite sensitive to demand and productivity factors. We shall comment later on an interpretation of the negative coefficients in the regression equation for household cultivated land and for the dummy for women and of the positive coefficient for the number of dependents per earner in the labor household.

We have carried out a similar analysis on the more recent set of NSS household-level data for rural West Bengal in 1977–78 utilized in chapters 1 and 2. Table 4.3 presents the results of the first regression equation with this

TABLE 4.3

Linear regression analysis of determinants of daily farm wage rate, rural West Bengal, 1977–78

Dependent Variable:	FWAGE	
Mean:	Rs. 4.05	
Standard Deviation:	Rs. 1.63	

Explanatory Variables†	Regression Coefficient	Standard Error	Significant at Percent Level
AGE	0.0608	0.0111	0.0
(AGE)²	−0.0007	0.0002	0.0
DEP (number of dependents as proportion of household size)	0.7592	0.1445	0.0
SEXF	−0.5136	0.0880	0.0
SBRND 2	0.2714	0.0649	0.0
RAIN (normal annual rainfall in district in meters)	0.3603	0.0491	0.0
RAINDEF (percentage deficit in actual rainfall in 1977 from normal in district)	−0.4722	0.1121	0.0
NHA (nitrogenous fertilizer, in kg, used per hectare of area under foodgrains in district)	0.0299	0.0039	0.0
PRIMED (dummy for education up to primary level)	0.2379	0.0699	0.0
SCHCASTE (dummy for scheduled caste)	−0.1146	0.0612	6.2
FDINDEX (food cost-of-living index in 1977–78 in district center)††	−1.2160	0.2554	0.0
Constant term	5.5192	0.9636	0.0

$R^2 = 0.1287$; F=38.8; no. of observations=2,902

† See table 4.2 or Glossary of Variables.
†† Calculated from the food cost indices for district centres for the lowest expenditure group of families in 1977-78 (with 1960 as 100) published by the West Bengal State Statistical Bureau.

data set for all agricultural laborers. Again the casual farm wage rate is positively associated with productivity-enhancing factors like age (indicating experience), normal rainfall, lower deficit in actual rainfall, use of nitrogenous fertilizers, primary education (as opposed to illiteracy) of the laborer, and the relatively busy season of October–December. It is negatively associated with the quadratic term $(AGE)^2$, indicating that after a certain age of the worker the positive effects of experience are dominated by the effects of advancing age on energy and stamina. As before, the wage rate is lower for women and higher for laborers in households with a larger number of dependents. The wage rate is also lower for low-caste workers. The negative coefficient for FDINDEX, the food cost index, is surprising. One would have thought that, in areas of higher food cost rises, FWAGE would be higher to preserve the same real wage. I suspect that the negative coefficient only reflects the fact that the food cost index is higher in areas of low food productivity, and the latter in turn is associated with low wage rate.

For the same data set for rural West Bengal I have also carried out an analysis of *intervillage* variations in the village weighted-average farm wage rate for casual male laborers, VWAGEM, as reported in table 4.4. In

TABLE 4.4

Linear regression analysis of determinants of daily farm wage rate across villages, rural West Bengal, 1977–78

	Dependent Variable:	VWAGEM (village weighted-average farm wage rate for casual male laborers)
	Mean:	Rs. 4.17
	Standard Deviation:	Rs. 1.21

Explanatory Variables†	Regression Coefficient	Standard Error	Significant at Percent Level
RAIN	0.3085	0.0895	0.1
RAINDEF	−0.7183	0.2024	0.0
NHA	0.0314	0.0064	0.0
SBRND 2	0.1701	0.1201	15.7
VUR	−1.2479	0.4477	0.6
NONAGMP (proportion of nonagricultural male workers in village) ††	1.1877	0.2601	0.0
Constant term	3.0237	0.1078	0.0
$R^2 = 0.12$; F = 10.5; no. of observations = 470			

†See tables 4.2 and 4.3 or Glossary of Variables.
†† From the 1971 Census data I calculated, for each village in the NSS sample, the proportion of all male workers who were neither cultivators nor agricultural laborers to get NONAGMP.

TABLE 4.5

Linear regression analysis of determinants of harvesting wage rate per day for male laborers, rural West Bengal, 1977–78

Dependent Variable:	HARVWAGEM (male daily wage rate for harvesting)		
Mean:	Rs. 4.42		
Standard Deviation:	Rs. 1.26		

Explanatory Variables†	Regression Coefficient	Standard Error	Significant at Percent Level
DEP	1.1787	0.2911	0.0
RAIN	0.5595	0.0940	0.0
RAINDEF	−0.7124	0.2366	0.3
NHA	0.0237	0.0066	0.0
SBRND 2	0.3697	0.1487	1.3
SBRND 3	−0.2409	0.1802	18.2
Constant term	2.2393	0.3448	0.0
$R^2 = 0.1516$; $F = 11.9$; no. of observations = 408			

†See tables 4.2 and 4.3 or Glossary of Variables.

this equation, obviously, many of the disaggregated household-level variables cannot be used. We have, therefore, confined ourselves to the village-level variables available. Again, the wage rate is positively associated with productivity-increasing factors such as normal rainfall, lower deficit in actual rainfall, use of nitrogenous fertilizers, and (weakly with) the relatively busy season of October–December and negatively associated with the village unemployment rate. The significant positive coefficient for NONAGMP, the variable representing the importance of nonagricultural activities in the village, suggests that, in villages where the alternative of nonfarm work is important, the farm wage is driven up, other things remaining the same.

Another use we have made of the NSS data set for rural West Bengal from 1977–78 is to analyze the variations in HARVWAGEM, the male daily wage rate for a single, though crucial, agricultural operation, harvesting, in contrast to the wage rates we have so far considered, which are averages over all agricultural operations. Table 4.5 reports the results. The harvesting wage rate is positively associated with higher normal rainfall and fertilizer use and a lower deficit in actual rainfall, all factors working toward a bigger harvest. Obviously, harvesting is a more important operation in the busy season of October–December and less so in the slack season of January–March. As with the average agricultural wage rate, the harvesting wage rate is also positively associated with the dependency ratio of the labor household (we will provide an interpretation of this in a subsequent section).

TABLE 4.6

Linear regression analysis of determinants of average farm wage per day across 52 regions, rural India, 1970-71

Dependent Variable:	WMR (average rate of earning per man-day of farm wage work for males in 15-59 age group in noncultivating wage-earner households in 1970-71 at 1960-61 prices)
Mean:	Rs. 1.24
Standard Deviation:	Rs. 0.41

Explanatory Variables	Regression Coefficient	Standard Error	Significant at Percent Level
SOIL (index of soil rating of land in region)	0.0142	0.0061	2.5
NRAIN (normal annual rainfall in region in meters)	0.1665	0.0763	3.5
RAINDEF (percentage deficit in actual rainfall in 1970-71 from normal in region)	−0.0044	0.0022	5.2
MONRAIN (proportion of annual normal rainfall concentrated in June-Sept. monsoon)	−0.0084	0.0034	1.8
URR (average rural unemployment rate in region)	−0.0291	0.0106	0.9
ASTPOOR (proportion of rural households that are asset-poor)	−0.0129	0.0054	2.2
FHA (value, in Rs. of fertilizers used per hectare of cropped area)	7.6110	2.5813	0.5
SPARSVIL (proportion of sparsely populated villages in region)	−0.0071	0.0039	7.6
LFARMP (large farmer households as a proportion of total rural households)	0.0081	0.0041	5.5
Constant term	1.0921	0.5351	4.8

$R^2 = 0.5552$; F = 5.8; no. of observations = 52

SOURCE: The dependent variable WMR is the average rate of earning of males in wage-earning households for work on others' farms, as estimated from the NSS, 25th Round, survey of noncultivating wage-earning households in rural India, and deflated by the consumer price index of agricultural laborers (with 1960-61 as base) of the state where the region belongs. The region-level estimates for NRAIN, RAINDEF, and MONRAIN are simple averages of district-level data from *Season and Crop Reports*. FHA has been worked out after taking simple averages of district-level data given in *Fertilizer Statistics* and the cropped acreage data for 19 major crops as given in Bhalla and Alagh (1979). The soil rating index for the region, SOIL, has been similarly worked out after taking averages of the district-level indices prepared by K. B. Shome and S. P. Raychaudhuri and reported in *Reserve Bank of India Bulletin* (October 1969). The percentage unemployment rate, URR, is from NSS 27th Round estimates. SPARSVIL is the proportion of total inhabited villages in each region where the population is less than 200, according to the 1971 Census. ASTPOOR is the proportion of rural households in each region who possess assets of Rs. 1,000 or less as of June 30, 1971, according to the Reserve Bank of India,

All-India Debt and Investment Survey, 1971–72. From the same source we have taken LFARMP, the proportion of total rural households operating land above 7.5 acres.

NOTE: For the actual values of the dependent and independent variables for all of the 52 NSS regions taken here, see appendix tables A–D. Some regions had to be omitted because of lack of data for at least one of the variables.

An alternative source for harvesting wage data has been the Bardhan–Rudra primary field survey of 110 sample villages in West Bengal in 1979. For each village we have estimated the hourly wage rate for daily laborers in harvesting the main paddy crop (*aman*) in terms of rice equivalents from our data on cash wages, kind wages, meals and snacks at work,[2] village price of paddy in the harvesting months, number of hours worked per day, the paddy–rice conversion ratio, etc. This way I have tried to overcome two problems with the NSS wage data referred to in footnote 1 (viz., absence of a suitable deflator for the money wage rate and any possible lack of adjustment for seasonal variability in hours worked). The mean value of this estimated wage rate for male laborers in our sample villages is 469 grams of rice per hour (the corresponding wage for women is 17 percent lower), and the standard deviation is 112 grams. It varied from 471 grams of rice in agriculturally more "advanced"[3] villages in our sample to 451 grams in more "backward" villages. One possible explanation for this relatively small difference is that the advanced villages draw more in-migration of labor (of which there is evidence in the sample), and the consequent wage-depressant effect counteracts the wage-boosting effect of agricultural advance itself. The mean wage rate is strikingly lower in villages with relatively plentiful supply of laborers. If we crudely define two categories of villages from this point of view, one where during the harvest months 100 percent (or almost) of male laborers reportedly get work and the other containing the rest of the villages, we find that the former set of villages has a significantly higher wage rate. The mean harvesting wage rate per hour for male laborers is estimated to be 476 grams of rice in the former set and 378 grams in the latter.

The last data set on cross-section wage rates we are going to use in this section relates not just to West Bengal but to 52 agroclimatic regions across the whole of rural India. For a description of the data on both dependent and independent variables derived from the NSS, Reserve Bank of India Debt and Investment Survey, Census, Season and Crop Reports, etc., see appendix tables A–D. Table 4.6 presents the results of the regression equation explaining regional variations in the farm wage rates deflated by

[2] On an approximation basis, meals only have been assumed to contain the equivalent of 1 kg. of rice, snacks only that of 0.50 kg. of rice, and meals plus snacks that of 1.25 kg. of rice.

[3] We have defined the sample villages as agriculturally more "advanced" if more than half of the cultivated area is irrigated, or is under chemical fertilizers for some season or crop or is under HYV seeds in some season. The rest of the sample villages are relatively "backward"

the consumer price index for agricultural laborers.[4] Again, the farm wage rate is positively associated with productivity-enhancing factors like the use of fertilizers, the soil quality index, and a lower deficit in actual rainfall compared with the normal and (weakly) with the level of normal rainfall. Since rainfall concentrated in a few (usually the monsoon) months of the year may have very different consequences for crop pattern and yields than more evenly distributed rainfall, we have also included another rainfall variable: MONRAIN, the proportion of annual normal rainfall concentrated in the June–September monsoon. As expected, this variable has a significantly negative effect on the wage rate. As in the earlier regressions, the wage rate is negatively associated with a variable indicating excess supply of labor, that is the rural unemployment rate and the proportion of asset-poor households (which provide the main source of agricultural laborers). It is also negatively associated with the proportion of sparsely populated villages in the region, indicating that remote villages not well-connected with commercial centers will have fewer alternative opportunities for the agricultural laborers and hence will have a lower wage rate. Lastly, the wage rate is positively associated with LFARMP, the proportion of large farmer households. Since the major demand for hired labor is provided by large farms, a region with a higher proportional importance of them will tend to have a higher wage rate, other things remaining the same, than a region with more middle-sized, predominantly family farms.

Putting all of the above cases of variations in farm wage rates and their determinants together, it is clear that there is substantial evidence that the wage rate is quite sensitive to demand and productivity factors, contrary to the implications of subsistence or other theories of wage invariance to these factors.

II

A more recent, and somewhat more sophisticated, variation in the biological theory of wages is the nutrition-based efficiency theory of wages.[5] This theory is based on the idea of wages being influenced by an explicit link between productivity and consumption at low levels of nutrition of workers in such a way that competition among workers, even in the face of unemployment, does not reduce the wage rate below an efficiency wage, since a lower wage would not provide workers with enough

[4] We should note that in the absence of region-specific data I had to take the same state-level consumer price index for all regions in the state, and using the price index with 1960–61 as base is overlooking the regional variations in costs of living in the base year itself.

[5] For an exposition of this theory of wages, see Leibenstein (1957), Mazumdar (1959), Mirrlees (1975), and Stiglitz (1976); for a detailed critical analysis as well as a discussion of empirically testable implications of this theory, see Bliss and Stern (1978).

consumption to enable them to work effectively.

It seems that the efficiency theory of wages is consistent with the negative coefficient of PCULTIVAT, per capita land cultivated by the household, in explaining wage variations in our regression equation in table 4.2 and with the positive coefficient for the variable representing the number of dependents per earner in the labor household in the regression equations in tables 4.2, 4.3, and 4.5. Rodgers (1975) also notes a positive association between the wage rate and the dependency ratio for the worker in his survey of some villages in Bihar, and he interprets this, in the light of the efficiency theory, as the employer paying a higher wage to the laborer with a larger number of dependents in order to maintain his minimum nutrition and hence productivity. Bliss and Stern (1978) note that the noncompetitive version of efficiency wage theory is consistent with the possibility of landed laborers being paid a lower wage rate than landless laborers. The efficiency wage theory also implies that permanent laborers (i.e., those with long-term contracts) would have a higher consumption standard, since permanency allows employers to capture the productivity benefits of higher wage and consumption. In our data set for rural West Bengal, the "casual" farm laborers (taking only the landless males) belong to households with an average monthly per capita consumption expenditure of Rs. 26, whereas for the corresponding set of landless male "regular" farm laborers it is Rs. 32. Although later in this chapter we shall try to give an alternative explanation for these observations, let us note here their consistency with the efficiency theory of wages.

Some of the other implications of the efficiency theory of wages are, however, less consistent with our data. In particular, contrary to this theory, our regression equations in the preceding section show that the wage rate for agricultural laborers (even controlling for the size of land cultivated by the labor household) is not invariant with respect to changes in demand or productivity conditions. It may be argued, however, that our equations relate only to casual farm laborers, whereas the efficiency theory may be regarded as applicable more to the case of permanent laborers. But, first, in a situation of widespread malnutrition, the efficiency theory predicts a high incidence of long-term labor contracts, and yet in the NSS 1972–73 sample for rural West Bengal the number of regular farm laborers is, for example, only 18 percent of the total number of farm laborers, even though the overwhelming majority of them suffer from poverty and malnutrition. It is possible, however, that the data collectors may have missed some of the *implicit* contracts for long-term labor. Second and more important, though, in the data sets we note a good deal of variation in the monthly salary of even permanent laborers in spite of their belonging to similar consumption backgrounds. Table 4.7 presents mean values and standard deviations of monthly per capita household expenditure and monthly salary of male regular farm laborers for three poor-expenditure classes of such laborers in the NSS 1972–73 sample for rural West Bengal.

TABLE 4.7

Mean and standard deviation of household per capita consumption and monthly salary of regular male farm laborers in poor expenditure groups, rural West Bengal, 1972–73

Size Class Of Household Per Capita Monthly Expenditure (Rs.)	Household Per Capita Monthly Consumer Expenditure (Rs.)		Monthly Salary (Rs.)	
	Mean	Standard Deviation	Mean	Standard Deviation
0 –15	12.59	1.98	65.35	21.65
16–30	23.55	4.07	68.27	29.24
31–50	38.44	5.78	83.96	29.42

SOURCE: NSS, 27th Round.
NOTE: In this table I have taken only the 3 poorest size classes of household monthly per capita consumption at current prices. Regular male farm laborers belonging to these 3 poorest expenditure groups constitute 71 percent of all regular male farm laborers.

It seems that the standard deviation of monthly salary is quite large even for regular laborers with roughly similar consumption expenditures. In fact, for explaining variations in REGSAL, the monthly salary of regular farm laborers, we have an estimated regression equation in table 4.8. All the independent variables in the regression equation in table 4.8, except for DEPE, are significant at the 2 percent level. It seems the monthly salary of regular farm laborers is positively responsive to demand factors implicit in the village multiple-cropping intensity and the general agricultural development index of the district. Again, the salary is higher with the worker's age[6] and lower for women and lower-caste workers. Land cultivated seems to be positively associated with the salary; if the (noncompetitive version of) efficiency theory of wages were to apply to permanent or regular laborers, its possible implication of lower pay for landed laborers compared with the landless is not borne out by the equation in table 4.8. Also, REGSAL is negatively (if weakly) associated with the number of dependents per earner in the regular laborer's family: this is in contrast to the positive association Rodgers (1975) derives from the efficiency theory of wages.

III

Getting away from biological theories of wage, we should take note of another frequent assumption of wages being fixed by custom, paternalism,

[6] In the Bardhan–Rudra 1979 survey we found that in at least 60 percent of all the villages where we have two or more annual-contract labor respondents in our sample, the laborer with longer years of service with a given employer receives a higher salary. Apart from farm-specific experience (or learning by doing) enhancing a laborer's productivity, long years of service usually imply dependability for the employer, which gets reflected in the higher wage.

TABLE 4.8

Linear regression analysis for determinants of monthly salary of regular farm laborers, rural West Bengal, 1972–73

Dependent Variable:	REGSAL (monthly salary of regular farm laborers)	
Mean:	Rs. 75.15	
Standard Deviation:	Rs. 28.66	

Explanatory Variables†	Regression Coefficient	Standard Error	Significant at Percent Level
PCULTIVAT	0.5907	0.2500	1.8
AGE	0.6889	0.0808	0.0
DEPE	−0.5361	0.8754	54.1
AGDEV	0.3509	0.0656	0.0
SEXF	−19.7767	4.0517	0.0
CASTRIB, (dummy to represent scheduled caste or tribe)	−8.1471	1.9999	0.0
VMULCR (dummy to represent whether most of village land is cropped more than once a year)	5.4643	2.0784	0.9
Constant term	21.4132	7.2837	0.3

$R^2 = 0.2078$; $F = 23.0$; no. of observations $= 709$

SOURCE: NSS, 27th Round.
† See table 4.2 or Glossary of Variables.

or social sanctions. There is, however, hardly any *economic* theory of wages here and, in any case, its implication of wage constancy in the face of demand and productivity variation is not borne out by the data, as we have already seen. As forces of agrarian capitalism and commercialization gather strength and erode traditional patron–client relationships, age-old customs often have a way of adjusting to economic changes. In one respect, the market forces play a fuller (and harsher) role in a poor agrarian economy than in a developed country, as minimum-wage legislation is much less effectively, if at all, implemented, unionization of rural labor is rare, and the state does not pay unemployment benefits. The agricultural labor force is also relatively homogeneous, and most operations are performed by illiterate and unskilled workers.

All these factors quite often prompt some economists to go to the other extreme of regarding agricultural wages and employment as determined by forces of demand and supply in a competitive market. In particular, the role of marginal productivity of labor in determining labor demand and that of wage flexibility in clearing the labor market are emphasized. What this theory—at least the usual simple version of it—is particularly incapable of explaining is the persistence of unemployment among

extremely poor farm laborers whose appetite for voluntary unemployment
(or leisure preference) is not likely to be great. In the data set for rural West
Bengal there is clear evidence that the wage rate, even though it is sensitive
to demand pressures, does not adjust sufficiently to come anywhere near
clearing the labor market. The unemployment rate UR (measured in the
way explained in section II of chapter 2) in our NSS 1972–73 sample for
rural West Bengal is estimated to be 8 and 14 percent even in the relatively
busy seasons of October–December and July–September, respectively, for
male casual agricultural laborers; for the corresponding female laborers it
is 19 and 21 percent, respectively. In 15.4 percent of the sample villages the
weighted-average male unemployment rate for the village as a whole is
more than 5 percent, and yet in these villages the average wage rate for male
agricultural labor (VWAGEM) is above Rs. 3 (whereas the mean for the
whole sample is Rs. 2.76) in roughly the same fortnight. Confining our
attention to those households which (1) have cultivation or agricultural
labor as the principal occupation; (2) have a total household-level average
unemployment rate exceeding 5 percent; and (3) belong to villages where
VWAGEM is above the sample mean of Rs. 2.76, we find that most of these
households are poor, landless (or with very small farms), illiterate, and low-
caste. For example, according to our estimate, about 59 percent of these
households have a per capita consumer expenditure of Rs. 30 per month (a
fairly low "poverty line") or below at 1972–73 prices; 92 percent of these
households are either landless or cultivating land not exceeding 2.5 acres;
82 percent of them have not a single literate (male) member in the family;
and 53 percent belong to the lowest rung of the village social hierarchy—
the "scheduled castes and scheduled tribes"—having none of the aversion
to manual work often noticed in the high-caste families. And yet, there is
significant unemployment in these households, while the prevailing village
wage rate is above the sample mean. We can hardly expect that this
unemployment be voluntary or that the prevailing wage rate be below the
minimum reservation wage of these households.

Apart from its inability to explain the persistence of some obviously
involuntary unemployment, the competitive marginal productivity theory
obviously does not take into account the monopsonistic or oligopsonistic
power[7] (in view of the extremely unequal land distribution, severe
unemployment, low mobility, and lack of alternative opportunities the
village workers often face) that the employer is frequently in a position to
exert in fixing the terms of the labor contract. This dominance may be rein-
forced by the worker's dependence on the employer for consumption credit.

The standard marginal productivity theory also pays insufficient

[7] In the Bardhan–Rudra 1979 survey we found that in about 21 percent of our sample
villages in West Bengal 4 or fewer employers account for most of casual labor employment in
the village, and in about 45 percent of the sample villages 7 or fewer employers account for
most of the casual labor employment in the village. In many villages there is open or tacit
collusion of big employers in the labor market, and in some villages one big employer provides
"leadership" in setting the wage rate, which the others follow.

attention to the high premium the employer places on quick and ready availability of labor. Agricultural production is a long, discontinuous operation with periodic bouts of hectic activities and intervals of relative idleness. Weather dependence not only makes the timing of each individual operation somewhat unpredictable, it also means that when the time comes the job has to be done very quickly, and there are various risks and costs of delay. This implies that the employer is usually keen on entering into some explicit or implicit contracts with workers about a dependable supply of labor at the right time or, at least, is aware of the significant hiring or recruitment costs to be incurred as and when such recruitment needs arise. This recruitment cost plays an important role in the theoretical models further in this chapter. Apart from affecting the determination of wages and unemployment, in our models it also contributes to the employer's incentive to have long-term labor-tying arrangements with the so-called permanent laborers, a phenomenon the efficiency theory of wages attributes to the employer's desire to capture the productivity effects of higher wages and nutrition. In the Indian village labor market the employer clearly puts a high value on his expected recruitment cost, even though the prevailing unemployment of workers should have made recruitment easier than otherwise. Not only does he provide a kind of employment insurance to permanent laborers, but also he often supplies the workers with tiny plots of land to cultivate (occasionally at nominal or zero rent) as an income supplement or to build their mud huts on, with wage advances long before the crop is harvested and with other kinds of consumption credit (often at interest rates below what the professional village moneylenders would have charged),[8] all in return for the workers' assurance of ready availability whenever the need arises.

IV

In view of the discussion in the preceding three sections, we have tried in this and the next section to build some very simple models incorporating the employer's monopsony power, recruitment cost, wage variations (in response to demand and productivity factors), and involuntary unemployment. We then derive some comparative-static propositions from these models which seem to be consistent with the empirical observations in the data set, in particular the regression equations discussed in the sections I and II explaining variations in wages and those discussed subsequently in this section explaining variations in unemployment.

Suppose at any point in time the employer's profits are given by $[BF(L) - WL - c(u, v)R]$. Here, with the size of land and other

[8] Data from Rural Credit Surveys of the Reserve Bank of India show that the interest rates charged by "landlords and agriculturist money lenders" are somewhat lower than those charged by professional money lenders. In the Bardhan–Rudra surveys of West Bengal we got plenty of evidence on the role of loans in the form of wage advances in the labor markets. We shall discuss this matter in more detail in the next two chapters.

complementary factors given, $BF(L)$ represents a strictly concave production function with B, a multiplicative parameter (to be interpreted later); L is the amount of labor used; and W is the wage rate per unit of labor. In order to model the problem of ensuring a ready availability of labor and the wage premium the employer usually is prepared to pay for it, we introduce some recruitment cost for new laborers. For each new recruit R, the employer incurs an average recruitment cost of c. All costs are measured in terms of the homogeneous agricultural output.

In general, recruitment is easier in a slack labor market than in a tight one. So we shall assume that the average recruitment cost is a declining function of the extent of unemployment u in the village. In particular we shall assume that the first derivative of c with respect to u (i.e., c_1) is negative, and the second derivative (c_{11}) is positive (so that the rate of decline in average recruitment cost itself declines with increasing unemployment). The extent of unemployment in the village is given by

$$u = N\,(W) - L \qquad\qquad 4.1$$

where N is the supply of labor in the village that depends on the agricultural wage rate W the employer pays. We shall assume the wage elasticity of labor supply to be a positive constant (denoted by e) less than unity.

In the village labor market the employer has some monopsony power to determine the wage rate and the unemployment level of workers, but this power is not enough for him to eliminate the recruitment-cost problem referred to earlier. At some wage cost to himself, he can only keep the unemployment level high to maintain a low recruitment cost for new labor. (This is akin to Kalecki's idea (1944) of the capitalist's use for worker unemployment over the "political" business cycle in industrial economies.) The average recruitment cost also depends on some other parameters (denoted by v) to be specified later.

The changes in the employer's labor force are given by

$$\dot{L} = R - qL \qquad\qquad 4.2$$

where q is a given quit rate (a given percentage of the existing labor force) that the employer faces.

Let us suppose the employer wants to maximize the discounted value of his stream of profits over a given finite time horizon. His control variables are R and W. The current-value Hamiltonian H of the problem is then given by

$$He^{Pt} = BF(L) - WL - c(u,v)R + \lambda(R - qL), \qquad\qquad 4.3$$

where p is the rate at which the employer discounts his profits and λ is the shadow price of increase in employment. The necessary conditions of interior maximum are:

$$\lambda - c = 0, \qquad\qquad 4.4$$

$$-c_1 N'(W)R - L = 0, \qquad\qquad 4.5$$

$$\lambda = \lambda(p+q) - [BF'(L) - W + Rc_1].\qquad\qquad 4.6$$

Equation 4.4 tells us that the value of a marginal recruit is equal to the marginal (or average) cost of recruiting him; 4.5 tells us that the rise in direct cost of labor following an increase in the wage rate should at the optimum be just equal to the fall in recruitment cost on account of increased unemployment following from the wage-induced entry into the labor force at a given level of unemployment; and 4.6 gives us the time rate of change in the shadow price of additional employment.

Since the primary interest here is to derive some comparative-static propositions from this model, let us confine our attention to the steady state of the two differential equations 4.2 and 4.6 in the system. In long-run equilibrium, equations 4.2, 4.4, 4.5 and 4.6 may be rewritten as

$$-c_1 eNq - W = 0,\qquad\qquad 4.7$$

$$BF' - W + qL c_1 - c(p+q) = 0.\qquad\qquad 4.8$$

These two equations determine the equilibrium values of wage and employment, W and L, and hence from 4.1 the equilibrium volume of unemployment, u. Note from 4.8 that in equilibrium marginal product of labor is higher than the wage rate, implying that the equilibrium level of employment is lower than in the standard case of wage equal to marginal product of labor.

It is easy to check that under these assumptions the Jacobian matrix associated with 4.7 and 4.8 has a positive determinant, J. From 4.1, 4.7, and 4.8,

$$\frac{dW}{dB} = \frac{F'c_{11}}{c_1 J} > 0.\qquad\qquad 4.9$$

$$\frac{du}{dB} = \frac{F'(e-1)}{WJ} < 0,\qquad\qquad 4.10$$

where B is the multiplicative parameter in the production function and, hence, in the demand curve for labor. A rise in B, implying an outward shift in this demand curve, raises the wage rate and lowers unemployment, according to equations 4.9 and 4.10. One may interpret a shift in parameter B as one due to improved practices in agriculture, chemical-biological innovations, better irrigation, better rainfall, a higher cropping intensity, and agricultural development in general, all tending to raise the wage rate and lower unemployment. One may interpret B as also a purely seasonal, shift parameter in the demand for labor, implying a higher wage rate and lower unemployment in the busy agricultural season. The results here are, of course, consistent with the positive association of the wage rate for casual farm laborers with demand factors implicit in variables representing irrigation, fertilizers, rainfall, etc., the district agricultural development index, and the relatively busy seasons (and negatively with the slack season) in our regression equations in section I, contrary to the standard

TABLE 4.9

Linear regression analysis of determinants of unemployment of casual farm laborers, rural West Bengal, 1972–73

Dependent Variable:	UR (unemployment rate in reference week for a casual farm laborer)
Mean:	0.22
Standard Deviation:	0.31

Explanatory Variables	Regression Coefficient	Standard Error	Significant at Percent Level
PCULTIVAT	−0.1238	0.0325	0.0
DEPE	−0.0085	0.0036	2.0
SEXF	0.2065	0.0129	0.0
VIRR	−0.0288	0.0111	1.0
SBRND 1	−0.1262	0.0121	0.0
SBRND 2	−0.1553	0.0124	0.0
CENPL (dummy for central plains region)†	−0.0603	0.0113	0.0
Constant term	0.3052	0.0117	0.0

$R^2 = 0.1556$; F = 85.6; no. of observations = 3,258

†The central plains region of rural West Bengal consists of four districts: Howrah, Hooghly, Bardhaman, and Twenty-four Parganas.

constant wage hypothesis. Our section II also shows a similar positive association between the monthly salary of regular farm laborers and the demand factors implicit in the village multiple-cropping intensity and the district agricultural development index. The regression equation in table 4.9 similarly shows an expected association between such demand factors and the extent of unemployment for farm laborers in rural West Bengal.

Taking the set of all casual farm laborers in the NSS 1972–73 data set, we have tried to explain variations in the unemployment rate in the reference weeks in terms of the regression equation in table 4.9. Unemployment is negatively associated with farm size and dependency ratio of the household and demand expansion factors like irrigation and the busy season and positively associated with women. Unemployment is also less in the Central Plains region (having the largest urban agglomeration in West Bengal), which presumably has more alternative opportunities for casual farm laborers.

Going back to the theoretical model, we can carry out other parametric variations. For example, from 4.7 and 4.8,

$$\frac{\mathrm{d}W}{\mathrm{d}v} = (p+q)c_{11}\ \frac{c_2}{c_1 J},$$

4.11

where c_2 is the derivative of c with respect to parameter v (for simplification we have assumed here that the cross partial of c_1 with respect to v is zero). We have not yet specified the parameter v. Suppose v stands for any factor constraining, and hence raising the average cost of, recruitment on the part of the employer: in that case, c_2 is positive and, hence from equation 4.11 dW/dv is negative. Let us take the case of landed casual farm laborers. Since they have some work on their own land they are more encumbered in their supply of labor services than the landless workers at times when the job needs to be done quickly.[9] For example, in the harvesting or the transplanting season the landed worker would like to complete the job first on his own farm—because there are various risks and costs of delay— before making himself available on the labor market, but the same risks and costs of delay make the employer pay a wage premium to more readily available landless workers. In terms of equation 4.11 v, working as a constraint on recruitment, is higher for the landed worker, and, other things remaining the same, he will be paid less. We have already seen in the regression equation in table 4.2 that landed casual farm laborers are paid at lower rates, an observation which is consistent with the (noncompetitive version of) efficiency theory of wages but for which mine is an alternative explanation.

Similarly, we have noted in several regression equations a positive association between the casual farm wage rate and the number of dependents per earner in the worker's family. Again, the efficiency theory of wages is consistent with it, but the alternative explanation here is that it is easier to recruit a worker burdened with a higher dependency ratio so that his v is lower and from equation 4.11 his wage rate is higher.

The data sets provide clear evidence that women are paid lower wages than men. It is possible that in some agricultural operations (like plowing and land preparation) there is a wage premium for muscle power (in formal terms, our parameter B in the production function may be larger for men), but there are some other operations in paddy production (like transplanting, weeding, and threshing) for which women are quite often preferred. Yet their wage rate is lower.[10] One partial explanation may be that the women are encumbered in their supply of labor services by various social and economic restraints (in particular, their need to coordinate outside work with the rhythms of the household economy) which make them relatively irregular suppliers of labor: in terms of equation 4.11 their v is higher and hence their wage rate is lower.

A larger v, implying a higher average recruitment cost, not only lowers the wage rate but also increases unemployment for the group of workers having that characteristic. From 4.1, 4.7, and 4.8,

[9] In the Bardhan–Rudra 1979 survey of rural West Bengal, 46 percent of landed laborers in our sample report foregoing wage employment opportunities to give priority to own farm work.

[10] In the Bardhan–Rudra 1979 survey, in 60 out of 75 sample villages for which we have comparable wage rates for male and female laborers in transplantation, women got a lower rate.

Agricultural Labor

$$\frac{\mathrm{d}u}{\mathrm{d}v} = \frac{c_2(p+q)(1-e)}{WJ}.$$

With c_2 positive, $\mathrm{d}u/\mathrm{d}v$ is positive. This goes toward explaining the higher unemployment rate of women, as I noted in the regression equation in table 4.9, and similarly the lower unemployment rate for easier-to-recruit workers with higher dependency ratio.

In equations 4.7 and 4.8, if we parametrically vary e, the constant elasticity of labor supply, we get

$$\frac{\mathrm{d}W}{\mathrm{d}e} = \frac{-1}{eJ}[BF''(L)+c_1(p+2q)-qLc_{11}] > 0. \qquad 4.13$$

This implies that laborers with a lower elasticity of supply will get lower wages—a familiar result from the theory of discriminating monopsony. The case of the lowest-caste workers, having a lower wage as in our regression equation in table 4.8, may thus be explained by low elasticity of supply and the consequential low bargaining power in facing a monopsonist employer. In general, the stronger the monopsony power of the employer, the lower the wage rate.

We would like to emphasize that conceptually there is a distinction in the impact of v on the wage rate and that of e. A large value of v, caused by irregularity of supply, is not the same thing as a low value of e, or supply inelasticity. A poor, low-caste worker may have wage-inelastic, but not necessarily irregular (and hence difficult to hire on the part of the employer) labor supply, as may be in the case of landed or women workers. The worker, burdened with a larger number of mouths to feed, may have low supply elasticity (lowering his wage rate), but his easier availability to the employer allows the latter to economize on his search or recruitment costs and to offer a higher wage: the net effect on the wage will depend on which aspect is stronger. The landed worker, on the other hand, may have higher supply elasticity than the landless (in view of his alternative source of income), but because of the constraints described above may be more difficult to hire on the part of the employer.[11]

In equations 4.7 and 4.8, if we parametrically vary q, the quit rate of

$$\frac{\mathrm{d}u}{\mathrm{d}q} = \frac{1}{qJ}[-BF''(L)eN+(1-e)q(c-Lc_1)+2W] > 0 \qquad 4.12$$

[11] One should not, however, overmphasize these cases of wage rates varying with the worker's social background (say, caste), demographic background (say, dependency ratio in the family), or asset background (say, landownership), as suggested by the NSS data. One should keep in mind that the NSS data do not report task-specific wage rates as such, but the average rate of earning of a wage earner per man-day in the reference week. It is quite possible that the wage rate for a specific task does not significantly differ for workers with varying backgrounds, but that they get different tasks in different proportions, affecting their average rate of wage earning. In the Bardhan–Rudra 1979 survey of rural West Bengal we did not observe much evidence of daily wage rates (for a worker of a particular sex and for a given agricultural operation) varying with the worker's social, demographic, or asset background. For similar findings on uniformity of wage rates in semi-arid parts of India, see Binswanger et al. (1981) and, in West Java villages, White and Makali (1979).

workers, the effect on the wage rate is ambiguous without further assumptions, but the effect on umemployment is clear:

Workers characterized by higher quit rates will have more unemployment. Women and other intermittent workers will, therefore, have a larger incidence of unemployment. Workers having a long-term contract (explicit or implicit: in the closed village labor market and with the employer as a major source of credit the costs to the employer of enforcing an implicit contract are low) have a lower quit rate; in contrast, purely casual workers have a higher quit rate and a larger incidence of unemployment, as is commonly observed.

We have tried to work out if the total wage income (WL) varies systematically with the quit rate parameter, q. In the model the sign of $d(WL)/dq$ is, in general, indeterminate. For a very special case, however, we can have a definite sign. If the labor elasticity of output (let us denote it by β) and the (positively defined) elasticity of the average recruitment cost with respect to unemployment (let us denote it by α) are constant, and if [12] $\beta \geqq P/q$ and $1 \geqq \alpha$, then $d(WL)/dq$ is negative. For this special case, the workers having a higher quit rate will have a lower total wage income, which is consistent with my earlier observation in section II that in our NSS 1972–73 data set for rural West Bengal the per capita consumption of regular laborers is higher than that of casual laborers.

V

In the models of the preceding section we have abstracted from the seasonal nature of the agricultural production. In particular, we would now introduce the seasonal complementarity in the agricultural production process and the interseason adjustments in wages and employment associated with labor-tying arrangements. Suppose we have a separable two-stage production function in the form of $BG(L_2)F(L_1)$, where B, as before, is a multiplicative parameter; $F(L_1)$ is the production of seedlings with the use of labor in season 1 on a given land; $G(L_2)$ is the harvesting labor coefficient dependent on the amount of labor used, L_2, in season 2; and $BG(L_2)F(L_1)$ is the total crop harvested. Season 1 is a "lean" season in the labor market, while it is a tight labor market in the harvesting season 2. The employer, in order to save on his recruitment cost in season 2 (i.e., the cost of ensuring quick and ready availability of labor during peak operations), enters into explicit or implicit contracts with a group of laborers in season 1. In a general situation of unemployment in season 1 he offers employment to L_1 of such laborers (who are prepared to enter such long-term contracts), even if they were to be paid a wage rate higher than their marginal product in season 1. In exchange they offer him a dependable supply of labor in season 2. The residual labor need in the

---

[12] In words, these two conditions are: (1) the labor elasticity of output is larger than the interest (on the recruitment cost) over the tenure of a worker, and (2) the rate of decline in recruitment cost on account of unemployment is sufficiently low.

harvesting season $(L_2 - L_1)$ is supplied by short-term casual laborers involving a recruitment cost on the part of the employer. His profits are thus given by: $[BG(L_2)F(L_1) - W_1L_1 - W_2L_2 - kW_2^{-\epsilon}(L_2 - L_1)]$, where W_1 and W_2 are the wage rates in seasons 1 and 2, respectively (to make the wage rates in the two seasons comparable, one should interpret W_1 as incorporating an interest factor on account of its being paid well in advance of the harvesting); $(L_2 - L_1)$ is the new recruits in season 2; $kW_2^{-\epsilon}$ is the average recruitment cost, which, in a slight variation of our earlier model, we assume to be directly a declining function (with a constant elasticity $\epsilon > 0$) of the average rate W_2 (i.e., the higher the wage rate paid the easier it is to recruit in the peak season); and k is a positive constant. Let us assume, for simplicity, that the lean-season wage rate W_1 is a given rock-bottom wage rate determined by the opportunity cost of labor in household or nonfarm work, various collection activities in village common property, or seasonal migration. Maximizing his profits with respect to L_1, L_2 and W_2, he gets:

$$BG(L_2)F'(L_1) - W_1 + kW_2^{-\epsilon} = 0, \qquad\qquad 4.15$$

$$BG'(L_2)F(L_1) - W_2 - kW_2^{-\epsilon} = 0, \qquad\qquad 4.16$$

$$k\epsilon(L_2 - L_1) - W_2^{1+\epsilon}L_2 = 0. \qquad\qquad 4.17$$

Note that the employer hires some labor in the lean season even if the wage rate W_1 is higher than its marginal product in that season. This is because of the saving on peak-season recruitment cost from labor-tying arrangements made in season 1. Similarly, the peak-season wage rate, W_2, is lower than the marginal product of labor in that season. The wage variation between the two seasons is thus less than that warranted by the difference in the marginal products of labor in the two seasons. Interseason adjustment through labor-tying is thus a major contributory factor in reducing the amplitude of seasonal wage fluctuations. This is in contrast to the standard explanation of any observed low-amplitude seasonal wage fluctuations in terms of subsistence or custom determination of wages implying the latter to be relatively invariant to demand changes.

Going back to equations 4.15, 4.16, and 4.17, I have carried out some comparative-static exercises for the special case when the labor elasticities in $G(L_2)$ and $F(L_1)$ functions are constant and add up to a value less than unity. (Diminishing returns to scale are not implausible when land and other complementary factors are being kept constant.) For this case (and assuming that the second-order conditions of maximization are satisfied so that the determinant of the Jacobian matrix is negative), I have checked that (L_1/L_2) goes up as the value of the parameter k goes up. Given the wage rate, k is an index of the difficulty of recruitment; (L_1/L_2) is the ratio of labor employed in season 1—presumably tied or attached labor—to all labor (casual and attached) employed in season 2. The comparative-static result is that there is a positive relation between the difficulty of recruitment (i.e., the tightness of the labor market) and the importance of attached labor in total labor force. In section II of the next chapter I shall cite empirical evidence consistent with this result.

VI

All of the above discussion has assumed a uniform mode of wage payment (for example, in the preceding theoretical models we have assumed that workers are paid in kind per unit of time). Actually there is a whole variety of modes of wage payment. Table 4.10 reports the relative incidence of different modes of payment for daily labor contracts in the Bardhan–Rudra 1979 sample of villages. It seems that the most common mode is for the worker to receive wages in some combination of cash, kind, and perquisites like meals or snacks. This prevails as at least one mode of daily wage payment in 96 percent of our sample villages.

It is commonly observed that in a substantially larger percentage of longer-term contracts than in daily contracts the wage includes meals. The efficiency theory of wages implies a substantial kind payment of wages to permanent laborers, particularly in the form of meals provided by the employer and consumed at the work site so that the employer can ensure that wages are spent more on productivity-enhancing calories for the worker and less on his dependents and on nonfood items of expenditure. An alternative, and probably more relevant, explanation of the practice is the employer's inclination to avoid loss of time in the worker's going home for lunch.

Another explanation of kind payment to workers is related to foodgrain price uncertainty and differential risk aversion on the part of employers and workers. It is interesting to note from table 4.10 that daily wage payment in the form purely of cash applies to only 23 percent of the sample villages and that monetization of wage payments seems to increase with technical advance in agriculture.

A very important factor that affects the mode of wage payment is, of course, the question of incentive payment when the supervision and monitoring of work effort is costly for the employer. Table 4.10 indicates that in 58 percent of sample villages daily wage payment on a piece rate (for a job done, like the plowing of a given plot) or, somewhat less frequently,[13] on a share rate system (payment to the laborer of a fraction of the total number of bundles harvested by him, for example) prevail, along with other forms of wage payment. In general, in operations (like harvesting) where speed of completion of the job is crucial and the possible loss of

---

[13] The share rate system of wage payment, particularly harvest sharing, is much more common in north India than in West Bengal.

TABLE 4.10

Modes of wage payment on daily contracts in major agricultural operations, rural West Bengal

Type of Village	Percentage of Villages of Each Type Where the Following Modes of Payment are Reported									
	Cash only	Cash plus meals	Cash plus meals plus kind	Cash plus kind	Kind only	Kind plus meals	Meals only	Piece rate	Share rate
Advanced	24.7	35.8	13.6	23.4	0.0	5.0	0.0	53.0	12.3
Backward	17.11	65.2	3.4	6.9	6.9	13.7	0.0	17.2	20.0
All	22.7	43.5	10.9	19.1	1.8	7.2	0.0	43.5	14.5

SOURCE: Bardhan–Rudra 1979 survey.
NOTE: Percentages across each row add up to more than 100 percent because the same village may report more than one mode of wage payment.

product quality involved in its faster completion is not likely to be significant, piece rates and harvest sharing are quite common. In other operations time rates are more frequent. But a worker who is paid at a time rate in sowing, land preparation, or weeding may not be slack in his work if he also expects to participate in harvesting for the same employer in the harvesting season and to be paid a share in the harvest at that time.

Apart from uniformity in the mode of wage payment, all of the preceding discussion has also assumed uniform abilities of workers. Clearly abilities vary from worker to worker even on relatively unskilled agricultural jobs, and within the small closed world of a traditional village the employer usually has a fairly good idea of the ability characteristics of the different members of his work force. Yet, with a few exceptions, the wage rate for casual labor (of a given sex, and for a given farm operation) is remarkably uniform within the village, and workers recognized by the employer as belonging to different ability types do not get paid at significantly different wage rates. Even the monopsony power of the employer does not seem to extend to wage discrimination by worker ability types. The most likely reason for this is the employer's unwillingness to create invidious distinctions among his workers which may lead to problems of morale and tension among them. Distinctions by group characteristics (like sex or caste) are more easily accepted, but employer-made distinctions in wage payment on the basis of unobserved individual-specific characteristics like ability are likely to be more controversial. The employer usually compensates the better worker by giving him priority in work in the slack season; when labor demand is low, the inferior workers get rationed out first.

Finally a word about the domain of the wage determination process. We have seen in this chapter that the agricultural wage rate is quite sensitive to demand and supply factors, and in many villages there is a fairly vigorous market for daily agricultural labor, particularly for operations like plowing, sowing, transplantation, and harvesting. But sometimes the operation of this market does not extend very strongly beyond the confines of the village or beyond some local neighborhoods. Employers in one village do not think they possess enough information about the work ability and particularly the dependability characteristics of laborers in other villages, and in hiring "outsiders" they cannot draw upon the considerable reservoir of village loyalty and goodwill they utilize in maintaining their social control over the entire labor process. The laborers on their part look up to their local employers as providers of sustained job opportunities, regular credit, and emergency help over the years. On both sides there are thus serious incentives working toward territorial affinities. Of course, in spite of all this there is considerable out-and in-migration of labor, particularly seasonal, in the village and the local labor market is never completely insulated from the influences of agricultural prosperity, commercialization, or public works programs in the surrounding regions.[14] Much obviously also depends on the state of development of agricultural technology in the village. After a certain stage in the development of the forces of production, local employers are likely to find it much more profitable to break the territorial barriers and enlarge the network of operations of the labor market.

[14] In the Bardhan–Rudra 1979 survey, more than one-third of backward villages report out-migration in 10 months of the year (including some in the peak seasons), whereas more than one-third of advanced villages report out-migration in 5 months of the year (mostly the lean months). More than 20 percent of the advanced villages report in-migration of labor in 4 peak agricultural months.

CHAPTER 5

Labor-Tying in Agriculture

In the model of section V of the preceding chapter the employer, in order to save on his recruitment cost in the peak season (i.e., the cost of ensuring ready availability of labor during peak operations), enters into explicit or implicit labor-tying contracts in the lean season. Here I would like to introduce an alternative, and slightly more complicated, rationale of labor-tying contracts in terms of wage uncertainty for peak operations. In the beginning of the year the employer contracts with some tied laborers, feeding them at a steady rate across the seasons (i.e., giving them consumption credit to survive the lean season) in exchange for their delivering committed labor supply in the peak season; if the peak labor demand is higher than that supplied by tied laborers, the employer then enters the spot or casual market, hiring the additional labor at the uncertain wage rate of that time.

So we have two stylized periods, the "lean" and the "peak", with no work in the lean period, followed by a peak period in which the employer requires a random amount of labor. The labor requirement (say, for harvesting) per unit of output in the peak peiod is given by a fixed coefficient, β. Mean output level is given by x, while the actual yield is Ax, where A is a random variable (representing weather and other production uncertainties) with an expected value of unity. If the total labor requirement in the peak period, βAx, exceeds the amount of tied labor, L_t, hired in the lean period, the employer needs to hire some casual labor, which will be paid at the (random) rate W in the peak period.

The employer's profits, π, are thus given:
if

$$\beta Ax \leqq L_t, \quad \pi = \pi_1 = Ax - (2+\rho)cL_t \qquad 5.1$$

and if

$$\beta Ax > L_t, \quad \pi = \pi_2 = Ax - (2+\rho)cL_t - (\beta Ax - L_t)W, \qquad 5.2$$

where c denotes the minimum consumption level in each period which will induce workers to accept the labor-tying contract and ρ is the unit interest cost to the employer for paying out the consumption amount c to each tied laborer in the lean period. Note that c is the same in both periods. If the workers are risk-averse, but the employer (has sufficient wealth and portfolio-diversification opportunities to) be assumed risk-neutral, and if, for simplification for the time being, we assume that the workers discount utility at the same rate ρ as the employer discounts profits,[1] the optimal risk-sharing considerations will imply labor-tying contracts which smooth worker consumption over the two periods.

Let us now look more closely into the labor supply side. Take the case of a worker who does not enter into labor-tying contracts. Suppose that such a worker obtains a consumption of y_0 in the lean period, and $y \geq y_0$ in the peak period, say, through production on own plot of land or other activities. Assume that y_0 is identical for all such workers, but they differ with respect to y. Let $G(.)$ be a cumulative distribution function which describes the distribution of worker types. Thus $G(\bar{y})$ is the proportion of workers such that $y \leq \bar{y}$.

Of course, if the spot wage in the peak period is W, then a type y worker will enter the spot market if $W > y$. Normalizing the utility function so that $U(y_0) = 0$, the expected utility of a casual worker is $EU[\max(y, W)]$. A worker will choose to work on a labor-tying contract if

$$(2 + \rho)U(c) > EU[\max(y, W)].\qquad\qquad 5.3$$

It is easy to see that if a worker of type y accepts the labor-tying contract, then the contract will be accpeted by any worker of type $y' < y$. Thus it is clear that a contract involving a consumption level of c will attract all workers of a type below some critical value $y(c)$.

Suppose $H(W)$ is a cumulative distribution function of the spot wage W, and assume point expectation, i.e., that there is a unique W for each state A, so that the spot wage is a function $W^e(A)$ in workers' expectation. The supply of contract workers is $G[y(c, W^e(A))]N$, and the supply to the spot market, given any wage W, is $N\max[0, G(W) - G[y(c, w^e(A))]]$. where $y(c, w^e(A))$ is given by

$$(2 + \rho)U(c) = U(y)H(y) + \int_y^\infty U(W)\,dH(W),\qquad\qquad 5.4$$

assuming that workers cannot work part of the time for spot wages and the remaining part in their own farms.

The demand for tied labor is given by the landlord's maximization of the expected value of his profits, $E\pi$, or by

$$\underset{L_t}{Max\,L_t}\; x - (2 + \rho)cL_t - \int^m (\beta Ax - L_t)W^\epsilon(A)\,dF(A),$$

where $z \equiv L_t/\beta x$, m is the maximum value taken by A, $W^\epsilon(A)$ is the spot wage function in the landlord's expectations and $F(A)$ is the cumulative distribution of A. We shall assume that A is never high enough to lead to excess demand or nonharvesting of some part of the field. A sufficient condition for this is $m < G(1/\beta)/b$, where $b \equiv \beta x/N$.

---

[1] The more realistic case of a difference in the discount rates can be introduced with a slight increase in cumbersomeness of the subsequent equations.

Tied labor demand $L_t\{c, W^{\epsilon}(A)\}$ is given by the first-order condition of landlord's maximization:

$$(2+\rho)c = \int_z^m W^{\epsilon}(A)\,dF(A) \qquad\qquad 5.5$$

In the equilibrium, demand for tied labor equals supply, so that

$$L_t\{c, W^{\epsilon}(A)\} = NG[y\{c, W^{e}(A)\}], \qquad\qquad 5.6$$

and the actual distribution of W is

$$W\{A, W^{e}(A), W^{\epsilon}(A)\} = \begin{cases} y\{c, W^{e}(A)\}, & \beta Ax \le L_t\{c, W^{\epsilon}(A)\} \\ G^{-1}(Ab) & \beta Ax > L_t\{c, W^{\epsilon}(A)\} \end{cases}$$

In rational expectations equilibrium $W^{e}(A) = W^{\epsilon}(A) = W(A)$. For $A > z$, the distribution function of W is given by

$$H(W) = Pr\{G^{-1}(Ab) \le W\} = Pr\{A \le G(W)/b\} = F\{G(W)/b\}.$$

Thus we can·write in equilibrium,

$$H(W) = \begin{cases} 0, & W < y(c, W) \\ F\{G(W)/b\} & W \ge y(c, W) \end{cases}$$

From equations 5.4, 5.7, and 5.8 the worker's equilibrium condition reduces to

$$(2+\rho)U(c) = U(y)F\{G(y)/b\} + \int_z^m U\{G^{-1}(Ab)\}\,dF(A). \qquad\qquad 5.9$$

The three equations 5.5, 5.6, and 5.9 may be solved to get the equilibrium values of $y(b)$, $z(b)$, and $c(b)$.

Differentiating totally with respect to b and combining terms,

$$\frac{dz}{db} = \frac{\int_z^m [U'(c) - U'\{G^{-1}(Ab)\}]\dfrac{Af(A)\,dA}{G'\{G^{-1}(Ab)\}} - [U'(y)F(z)z]/G'(y)}{U'(c)f(z)y + [U'(y)F(z)b]/G'(v)} \qquad 5.10$$

The second terms in the numerator and the denominator in equation 5.10 measure the effect of changing b on y. As y is the initial minimum wage rate at which the spot market just opens, we can unambiguously sign dz/db if we assume that the effect of b on this minimum wage is small (a sufficient condition for which is that the cumulative distribution function $G(y)$ is sloped in the relevant range in such a way that $G'(y)$ is very large). Under this sufficient condition all we have to prove for dz/db positive is

$$\int_z^m [U'(c)-U'\{G^{-1}(Ab)\}]\frac{A}{G'\{G^{-1}(Ab)\}}f(A)\,dA>0. \qquad 5.11$$

If we define $G^{-1}(A\,b)=c$, it is easy to see that

$$A[G^{-1}(Ab)-c]\gtreqless\bar{A}[G^{-1}(Ab)-c]\quad\text{for } A\gtreqless\bar{A}.$$

Using this and equations 5.5 and 5.7,

$$\int_z^m A[G^{-1}(Ab)-c]f(A)\,dA>0. \qquad 5.12$$

By similar logic, $\{U'(c)-U'[G^{-1}(Ab)]\}/\{G^{-1}(Ab)-c\}$ is nonnegative for $G^{-1}(Ab)\gtreqless c$. Multiplying the integrand in 5.12 with this, 5.11 is proved. This means that dz/db is positive. The intuitive reasoning is that, as b rises, the effect on marginal rates of substitution between contract and spot work is such that the supply price of risk-averse workers rises more slowly for assured contract jobs than for spot labor, favoring employment of contract workers; but at the same time employment of more contract workers raises equilibrium y, the opportunity cost of the marginal contract worker, and hence makes hiring of contract workers more expensive. Our sufficient condition on $G'(y)$ makes sure that this latter effect on changing the *type* of worker at the margin of contract jobs is not strong enough to upset the more familiar effect through marginal rates of substitution.

If $G'(y)$ is not very large, an alternative set of sufficient conditions for dz/db positive is that y is uniformly distributed and that the utility function is logarithmic. If y is distributed uniformly on, say, $[0,k]$, $G(y)=y/k$ and $G'(y)=1/k$. If the utility function is logarithmic, the numerator in 5.10 then reduces to $(1+\rho)/b$, which is positive. In terms of the intuitive reasoning in the preceding paragraph, the effect through marginal rates of substitution dominates when the workers' risk aversion is strong enough for the utility function to be logarithmic.

The variable z indicates the importance of tied labor as a proportion of total labor employed. From the definition of b, it is increasing in x and β and decreasing in N. So we can now interpret our result of dz/db positive as:

(a) Yield-increasing improvements (raising x) increase the importance of tied-labor as a proportion of total labor employed.

(b) Labor-saving technical progress, like some kinds of agricultural mechanization (lowering β), reduces the importance of tied-labor as a proportion of total labor employed.

(c) The larger the total number of workers (N), the smaller is the importance of tied-labor as a proportion of total labor employed.

In general, the more the demand pressure in the labor market relative to supply (indicated by b), the larger the proportional importance of tied-labor. We have not explicitly introduced unemployment in the model, but if a high rate of unemployment is associated with low demand pressure in the labor market relative to supply, it will lead to a smaller proportional importance of tied-labor. (Note that this result is similar to the positive association of tied-labor with tightness of the labor market derived in the model of peak-season recruitment costs in section V of the preceding chapter).

II

In analyzing the peak-season recruitment cost rationale (in section V of chapter 4) as well as that based on peak-season wage uncertainty (in section I of this chapter) for labor-tying, we have assumed lean and peak periods of given duration. But improved agricultural technology (particularly that using HYV seeds, chemical fertilizers, and more privately controlled irrigation) may change the duration and periodicity of the agricultural crop cycle itself, apart from increasing the importance of timeliness of each operation and the requirement of labor at short notice (raising recruitment costs and sharpening wage peaks in the busy season). With a larger number of shorter-duration crops raised in the year, the seasonality of the labor demand profile may be more evened out, with a corresponding effect on the composition of hired labor. With the consequent decline in the seasonal underutilization of tied-labor and hence in the costliness of "labor hoarding" from the point of view of the employer, his optimal labor mix is likely to shift in favor of tied-labor.[2]

Two additional reasons not captured in our theoretical model may reinforce the result about the increase in the relative importance of tied labor with agricultural development. One is that the employer often finds it riskier to entrust animals to casual workers over whom he has less continued control. The other reason has to do with the general problems of labor supervision and control that the employer faces. With agricultural development, as the hired labor force grows in size, the landlord finds it useful to mobilize the services of his attached laborer in overseeing the work of casual laborers and reporting on cases of delinquency or rebelliousness. In general, the two-tiered labor system on a farm is an important check on the development of class solidarity of farm workers. This divide-and-rule policy is particularly effective for the employer when labor-tying is carefully interlocked with personalized credit transactions and provision of homestead or cultivable land allotment by the employer. In the Bardhan–Rudra 1979 survey in West Bengal, we found that in villages where some form of group bargaining or labor agitation for agricultural wage increase took place, most of our tied-labor respondents reported nonparticipation in the movements, and the majority of them

[2] For an application of the literature on the choice of base and peak load capacities for an electric utility to the choice of the optimal labor mix for an employer, see Kotwal (1981).

cited their ties with the landlord as the primary reason for their nonparticipation.

Let us now turn to some empirical information on the incidence of labor-tying and its relationship with agricultural development and tightness of the labor market. In the Bardhan-Rudra 1979 sample villages in West Bengal, the proportion of tied-labor families to total farm labor families was almost twice as large in agriculturally more advanced villages as in backward villages. Bhalla (1976) shows in her study of the prime Green Revolution area of the state of Haryana that, compared with other less developed regions of the same state or with the same region earlier, a much larger proportion of agricultural laborers are employed on rather long-term contracts.

Bent Hansen has drawn my attention to the fact that even in Danish agriculture, for more than a century after the emancipation of serfs, "permanent laborers" were the major part of the agricultural work force, and their importance declined only after large-scale introduction of mechanization in recent decades.[3] For Sweden, Eriksson and Rogers (1978) report how during the late eighteenth and early nineteenth centuries commercialization of the agricultural sector and the attendant reorganization of the large landed estates in central and southern Sweden resulted in a replacement of corvée labor by the growth of a new proletarian group, the *statare*, year-round workers. This system rapidly expanded over the nineteenth century in Sweden. Richards (1979), in his comparative study of estate labor systems in East Elbian Germany (1750–1860), the Egyptian delta (1850–1940), and central Chile (pre-1930), has noted that, in all these three cases, periods of intensification of agriculture and introduction of new crops and new crop rotations have been associated with an increase in the relative importance of year-round workers—the *Instleute* in Prussia, the *tamaliyya* in Egypt, and the *inquilinos* in Chile.

We now provide some econometric evidence from a variety of cross-sectional data in rural India on the correlates of labor-tying. First, let us take the data from the 1956–57 Agricultural Labor Enquiry Survey in India. In this survey, data were collected from agricultural labor households in nearly 3,700 sample villages in the whole of rural India, divided in 38 zones. The proportion (ATTP) of attached,[4] usually annual-

---

[3] In India, mechanization is still relatively unimportant, and its observed effects on tied labor are somewhat mixed. Parthasarathy and Prasad (1974) note a decline in the demand for permanent labor with the introduction of tractors in a village in Andhra Pradesh. Rudra (1971), however, notes in a survey of large farms in Punjab that, while pumps and tubewells have replaced the labor of permanent workers, tractors have increased their demand.

[4] In this survey attached laborers have been defined as those who are "more or less in continuous employment". For a critique of the concepts and definitions used in the Agricultural Labor Enquiry and a reference to the possibility of their varying interpretations by field investigators in different areas of the country, see Thorner and Thorner (1962: ch 13). We should also note that a household whose major source of *income* is attached labor has been described as an attached labor household, even though some members of the household may have other occupations.

TABLE 5.1

Linear regression analysis of variations in the percentage of attached agricultural labor households across 36 zones, rural India, 1956–57

Dependent Variable:	ATTP (percentage of attached agricultural labor households to total number of agricultural labor households)		
Mean:	31.23 percent		
Standard Deviation:	19.35 percent		

Explanatory Variables	Regression Coefficient	Standard Error	Significant at Percent Level
AGLABP (percentage of agricultural labor households to all rural households)	−0.4634	0.2373	6.0
UNEMD (average number of days unemployed in year for adult male agricultural laborers)	−0.1680	0.0995	10.2
MAXMINW (maximum to minimum agricultural wage ratio across seasonal operations)†	8.7088	4.9922	9.1
PRINDEX (index of land productivity)††	0.2205	0.1512	15.5
DEBTEMP (percentage of total debt of an indebted labor household borrowed from employers)	61.8663	17.7262	0.2
Constant term	10.4227	20.2874	61.1

$R^2 = 0.5163$; $F = 6.4$; no. of observations $= 36$

SOURCE: The data for AGLABP, UNEMD, MAXMINW, and DEBTEMP for thirty-six Agricultural Labor Enquiry (ALE) zones are all from the NSS *Report* relating to the Enquiry.

† Ratio of the daily wage rate for casual adult male laborers in the agricultural operation for which this rate is the highest in a zone to that in the operation for which this rate is the lowest.

†† Estimated by Sharma (1973) for each district, is a weighted average of gross irrigated area as a proportion of gross sown area in 1959–61, average annual rainfall in 1959–61, net sown area as percentage of geographical area in 1959–61, intensity of cropping in 1959–61, gross sown area per head of the total rural population in 1961, and the soil index rating. Our zonal estimates of PRINDEX are simple averages of the estimates of Sharma for the districts each zone consists of (with the all-India average taken as 100). Since we did not have data for PRINDEX for one zone in Assam and one in Bombay, we had to exclude these two zones from the total of 38 (ALE) zones.

contract, agricultural labor households to the total number of agricultural labor households in the sample data set from this source has a mean value of 31.23 percent with a standard deviation of 19.35 percent. Table 5.1 presents the results of a regression equation explaining the variations in ATTP.

The importance of attached labor in a zone seems to be negatively associated with the quantitative importance of total labor households in a zone (a labor supply indicator) and the extent of average unemployment.[5]

[5] Given the numerical preponderance of casual laborers in most areas, it is unlikely that the cross-section variations in the extent of unemployment are themselves significantly affected by variation in the incidence of attached labor.

Attached labor is also more important in areas where the maximum-to-minimum wage ratio across seasonal operations is higher (i.e., where the wage rate shoots up particularly sharply in the peak season relative to that in the lean season, indicating especially tight labor markets in the peak season). All this shows, consistently with our theoretical models, that tighter labor markets lead to more tied-labor contracts, contrary to the common presupposition that it is the need for unemployment insurance for workers in areas of larger unemployment which primarily determines the incidence of tied-labor contracts. In slack labor markets with high unemployment, the employer often does not bother to have long-term contracts with labor since he is surer of his labor supply for peak operations.

The importance of attached labor is positively (though weakly) associated with the land productivity factor (as is consistent with our theoretical model). The positive coefficient of DEBTEMP implies that attached labor contracts are frequently associated with credit provided by the employer. The employer has a special incentive to lend to his attached laborers, not only because recovery of loans is easier but also because it helps cement the labor-tying arrangements or makes it easier to enforce implicit contracts. (In the Bardhan–Rudra 1979 survey of West Bengal villages, the overwhelming majority of labor respondents indicated that they would find it easier to get consumption credit as a tied-laborer than as a casual laborer.)

Our next set of econometric evidence is from the NSS 1972–73 Employment and Unemployment Survey data and the Reserve Bank of India 1971–72 Debt and Investment Survey data across 60 agroclimatic regions in rural India. Let ATTMP denote our estimate for each region what the NSS called regular[6] (as opposed to casual) farm laborers as a percentage of total farm laborers (male, 15–59 age group). In our sample, ATTMP has a mean value of 33.54 percent with a standard deviation of 19.27 percent. Table 5.2 presents the results of a regression equation explaining variations in ATTMP. Consistently with our previous discussion, the proportional importance of tied-labor is again negatively associated with the indicator (as we interpret the variable ASTPOOR to be) of plentiful labor supply in a zone and with the rate of unemployment. It is positively associated with an indicator of inequality in the distribution of land cultivation, possibly indicating that, in areas where land is concentrated in fewer hands, more people can afford to hire year-round or long-term laborers than where land is more equally distributed and the average size of farm is smaller. Larger farms also need more attached workers to oversee and supervise the work of casual laborers.

---

[6] In the survey schedules no rigorous definition of "regular" as opposed to "casual" laborers has been given. In practice the term "regular" has been applied mostly to cover annual-contract attached workers.

TABLE 5.2

Linear regression analysis of variations in the percentage of attached male farm laborers across 60 regions, rural India, 1972–73

Dependent Variable:	ATTMP (regular, as opposed to casual, male farm laborers in 15–59 age group as a proportion of total farm male laborers in that age group)	
Mean:	33.54 percent	
Standard Deviation:	19.27 percent	

Explanatory Variables	Regression Coefficient	Standard Error	Significant at Percent Level
ASTPOOR (proportion of rural households that are asset–poor)†	−0.9004	0.2169	0.0
URR (average rural unemployment rate in the region)†	−0.0058	0.0043	18.1
CVLC (coefficient of variation of cultivated land across size classes of land holdings)	19.5034	9.6822	4.9
Constant term	31.1527	12.0666	1.2
$R^2 = 0.3831$; $F = 11.6$; no. of observations $= 60$			

SOURCE: Data for ATTMP are from NSS, 27th Round, 1972-73. For ASTPOOR: Reserve Bank of India, All-India Debt and Investment Survey, 1971–72. For URR: NSS, 27th Round, 1972-73. For CVLC: Reserve Bank of India, All-India Debt and Investment Survey, 1971-72.

†Also see table 4.6.

Our third set of econometric evidence is from the detailed household-level NSS 1977–78 Employment and Unemployment Survey data for rural West Bengal. Table 5.3 presents the results of a LOGIT analysis of the probability that an agricultural labor household has some male member (in the 15–60 age group) who is a "regular" farm laborer by usual status. It seems this probability is significantly higher if the household is located in a village with better irrigation or in a district where the normal rainfall is higher (indicating association of labor-tying with areas of higher agricultural productivity). It is also not unexpected that this probability is positively associated with households belonging to low castes or with unowned homestead or indebtedness to employers. (As mentioned before, labor-tying agreements are often cemented by provision of credit or homestead by the employer.)

III

In the last two sections we have provided theoretical reasoning and historical and econometric evidence to show how the importance of labor-tying contracts may increase with yield-increasing improvements and with a tightening of the labor market. We should note here that this is somewhat

TABLE 5.3

LOGIT analysis of the probability of any male member (in the 15–60 age group) of an agricultural labor household being a "regular" farm laborer by usual status, rural West Bengal, 1977–78

Explanatory Variables	Estimated Coefficient	Standard Error
RAIN (normal annual rainfall in district in meters)*	0.2417	0.1123
VILIRR (village irrigation level)†*	0.4130	0.0825
SCHCASTE (dummy for scheduled caste)*	0.9551	0.2014
HMUNOWN (dummy for unowned homestead)*	0.4775	0.2672
EMDEBT (dummy for indebtedness to employer)	0.3969	0.2830
Likelihood ratio index=0.6735; no of observations=2,195		

SOURCE: Data for RAIN are from *Statistical Abstract of West Bengal*. Data for VILIRR, SCHCASTE, HMUNOWN, and EMDEBT are from NSS, 32d Round, 1977–78, for rural West Bengal.

†Represents four levels of irrigation in the village.

*Denotes a variable significant at 5 percent level.

contrary to the presumption in the literature on economic development and economic history, in which tied-labor is sometimes automatically equated with "feudal" or "semifeudal" relations and characterized as a symptom of economic stagnation.

Historically, agrarian labor-tying brings to mind the blatant cases of obligatory service by the tenant-serf to the lord of the manor (as in the classic instances of European feudalism) or those of debt-peonage to moneylender-cum-landlord as obtained in many parts of the world. These are clearly cases in which tying involves a continuing lack of freedom on the part of the laborer and the sanctions underlying the employer's authority are based primarily on social or legal compulsion, or what Marxists often call extraeconomic coercion. This is to be distinguished from the case where the laborer voluntarily enters long-duration contracts with his employer and reserves the right to leave unconditionally at the end of the specified period. In situations of widespread poverty and unemployment, this freedom to choose one's employer may sometimes be perilously close to the freedom to starve, yet conceptually the distinction between extraeconomic coercion and economic exploitation on the basis of unequal but voluntary contracts is important.

Although circumstances obviously vary from country to country, it is probably correct to say that today in most parts of the world labor-tying in the sense of bonded and unfree labor is quantitatively not very important and/or is on the decline. Defining bonded laborers as those who are obliged to work *exclusively* for a single employer over an *indefinite* period until some loan taken in the past is repaid, the Bardhan–Rudra 1975–76 survey in a random sample of more than 300 villages in east India (a region where the problem has been alleged to be acute) found that such debt bondage is currently rather infrequent.[7] On the other hand, the incidence of varying degrees of tying in voluntary labor contracts in agriculture is quite significant. This is particularly true if one includes not only the laborers under annual contracts (usually called attached laborers in India), but also those under other contract durations, like a season or the period of a given agricultural operation or a specified sequence of days. One major focus of the 1979 Bardhan–Rudra survey in West Bengal was on this latter variety of contracts relating to what we have called semi-attached laborers.[8] The difference in this intermediate set of contracts from the day-to-day casual or the annual attached labor contracts is not simply one of duration (being less than a year and more than just a few days) but, more significantly, is in terms of freedom to work for more than one employer for most of the agricultural year (which distinguishes them from the annual-contract attached laborers). The survey distinguished three major types of semi-attached laborers: (a) those who are attached to an employer for part of the year (a month or a few months), but for the major part of the year have the freedom to work for other employers; (b) those who are obliged to work for the employer whenever called, but for a stipulated number of days, and are free to work for any other employer for the rest of the time; and (c) those who are obliged to work for the employer whenever called for an unstipulated number of days—sometimes described as a "beck-and-call" relationship, an expression used by Thorner and Thorner (1962) following some earlier authors.[9]

The Bardhan–Rudra survey notes that in general the actual duration of association between a laborer and his employer is much longer than the

[7] Taking an alternative definition of bonded labor, the 1977–78 NSS Employment and Unemployment Survey found that only 0.28 percent of males in the labor force in rural India were "working with an employer under obligation, but work not specifically compensated by any wage or salary".

[8] In the Bardhan–Rudra sample villages in West Bengal, these semi-attached labor families are found to be as large as about 50 percent of the total number of attached farm labor families. For details of the terms and conditions of these labor contracts, see Bardhan and Rudra (1981).

[9] Thorner and Thorner (1962) have described the beck-and-call relationship as unfree. They suggest that quite often long-term outstanding loans which the laborer is not in a position to repay bind him (or his family members) to the employer in such a relationship. In the Bardhan–Rudra West Bengal sample, *none* of the beck-and-call laborers reported hereditary debt or a long-term debt incurred by the laborer himself as a basis for his attachment to the employer. But the overwhelming majority of them reported periodic consumption loans or wage advances from the employer as the basis of their attachment. It is arguable that a laborer who is at the beck-and-call of his employer for an unspecified length of time is not an entirely free participant in the labor market. His relationship with the employer is more often in the nature of a vague understanding of personalized obligation rather than that of an explicit contract.

duration stipulated in the contract each time it is made or renewed and that the majority of workers prefer their existing contract duration and type. This suggests that under the present circumstances and constraints the existing contracts are convenient to both parties. There are no indications whatsoever in the survey data that the phenomenon of working continuously (or intermittently) for the same employer over a long period implies any *extraeconomic* coercion exercised by the employer over the laborer as in precapitalist relations of obligatory labor service. The fact of the labQrer's *economic* dependence on the employer is a part of the universal phenomenon of the unequal and asymmetric relation between the poor and the rich and does not negate the fact that an employer or employee may find it more convenient to work in an environment of mutual understanding and familiarity over a long time and prefer working with the same opposite party rather than changing parties too often. Earlier in this chapter I have argued how such labor-tying arrangements may even be strengthened by the process of capitalist agricultural development.

We should, however, note that our theoretical model in the first section also suggests that there are certain types of agricultural development which may *reduce* the incidence of labor-tying. Agricultural progress in a particular region may involve mechanization of some operations or may induce seasonal in-migration of labor from poorer areas, both resulting, consistently with our model, in a reduction in the employer's need for tied labor. Apart from these theoretical reasons, there may be data-related problems which may vitiate the relevance of the empirical evidence used in testing the hypotheses on labor-tying enumerated in this chapter. As an illustration, let us refer to two kinds of such data problems. One relates to regions where pockets of bonded labor or semi-serfdom still exist. Here the data on tied-labor will often lump together both free and unfree laborers, and with agricultural progress the former may go up in importance while the latter decline in numbers, canceling or dampening the observed trends in the estimates of tied-labor.[10] The second kind of data problem arises because data collectors, particularly in large-scale surveys, often miss out on a variety of *implicit* contracts of labor tying, or confuse the concepts of duration of contract and frequency of wage payment (a laborer whose duration of contract is the whole crop season may still be paid on a daily basis like casual laborers), or fail to count as tied-laborers the whole class of "semi-attached" laborers emphasized above. We should note here that this omission of important cases of labor-tying has also affected our statistical exercises in tables 5.1, 5.2, and 5.3, which are based on NSS data that do not capture tied-laborers other than annual-contract "attached" or "regular" laborers.

Finally, let us note that all of the preceding analysis in this chapter has

---

[10] The problem is sometimes made worse by the further lumping in the data of disguised tenants, whom the landlords may report as attached laborers merely to avoid land reforms that take the form of protective tenancy legislation.

assumed tied and untied labor to be homogeneous. But in actuality they often involve different kinds of work (sometimes the tied-laborer has to work as a part-time domestic servant or do various errands for his master in addition to farm work) or different work hours (usually longer hours for the tied-laborer). The employer also usually looks for special personal traits like docility and, particularly, "dependability" before entering into a labor-tying contract with a worker.

CHAPTER 6
Credit–Labor Linkage

I

As noted in the preceding chapter, even apart from long-term attached laborers who are usually indebted to their employer, there is a large class of laborers who take loans from the employer during the agricultural lean period, when there is little farm work, in exchange for a commitment to provide labor services during peak periods, when labor demand is high. In the 1979 Bardhan–Rudra survey of labor contracts in rural West Bengal, we found that in 78 percent of our random sample of 110 villages, this system of loans against commitment of future labor exists—a system usually known as *Dadan* in this region. In more than two-thirds of these sample villages where the *Dadan* system exists, the number of labor days in which the loan is repaid by the laborer is calculated at a wage rate which is below the market wage rate prevailing at the time of repayment.

Such voluntary credit–labor linkage (terminable and renewable every crop season) is most simply interpreted as a barter transaction executed over time (even if one ignores the risk-sharing argument of the theoretical model in the preceding chapter). The incentive for this is a double coincidence of wants arising from the irregularities of the agricultural crop cycle. In order to survive the slack season, the laborer looks for a credit transaction in which he can repay the loan in the form of future labor services, but this will not be acceptable to all creditors except the employer-creditor who is in great need of labor in the peak season. Such barter transactions are of obvious importance in a poor agrarian economy in which a credit market and a system of monetary exchange are as yet inadequately formed.

Many such village economies are characterized by a dominant landlord who, because of the size of his assets and urban connections, is able to obtain credit more cheaply than other local agents. Thus the landlord is able to act as a financial intermediary between an outside loan market and his laborers. However, the landlord is also positioned as a monopolist in establishing the terms of trade between current consumption and future labor services. If the landlord can obtain unlimited funds at a fixed interest rate, then monopoly profits are earned by a two-part tariff on consumption credit. Laborers pay a marginal interest rate per unit of consumption credit equal to the landlord's opportunity cost plus a fixed "entry fee" for the privilege of borrowing at this rate The provision of labor services in future periods constitutes repayment of principal and interest, including the entry fee, on a consumption loan. The entry fee represent the monopoly profits on the transaction.

The interpretation of credit–labor linkage as a loan transaction raises a certain indeterminancy in the relationship between the landlord and his tied-laborers. Peasants can be viewed as repaying a consumption loan by providing labor services at a discount below the market wage for spot labor. A loan repayment of a given size can be made equivalently by working more hours at a smaller discount or fewer hours at a larger discount. Thus the wage paid to tied laborers is indeterminate, depending on the numbers of hours worked for the landlord. This may be one explanation of why there are variations in the wage rate paid to different tied laborers.

The next section develops a simple model of an agrarian economy in which both the landlord and the laborers are wage takers in the market for spot labor. The relationship of the landlord and tied-laborers is modeled as an implicit contract which stipulates a quantity of consumption credit, a quantity of contract labor, and a contract wage. The analysis establishes the indeterminancy of the contract wage and leads to the interpretation of the equilibrium contract as a barter loan transaction involving a two-part tariff.

II

Consider a stylized agrarian economy with two periods. In the first, there is no work. In the second, a spot labor market opens. Labor services are traded on the spot market at an exogenously fixed wage of w.

There is a single dominant landlord engaged in agricultural production requiring a homogeneous labor input. The landlord's revenues are a monotonically increasing and strictly concave function, $F(L)$, of the quantity of labor employed, L. Also, the landlord is able to borrow and lend unlimited amounts at an exogeneously fixed interest rate of r.

There is a pool of M peasants who can be tied to the landlord. Each peasant has an identical utility function, $U(C_1, C_2)$, defined over consumptions, C_1 and C_2, in each of the two periods, and satisfying the usual properties:

$$U_1 > 0, \ U_2 > 0, \ U_{11} < 0, \ U_{22} < 0, \ U_{12} > 0,$$

where a subscript i indicates a derivative with respect to the ith variable.[1] Thus marginal utility is positive and decreasing in each consumption, and consumptions in the two periods are complementary. Peasants can borrow from a source other than the landlord (say, the professional moneylender in the village or in the nearby small town) at an exogenous interest rate of $r^0 > r$. Each peasant has a second period labor endowment of 1 unit.

The landlord and peasants can trade labor on the spot market or might undertake agreements which entirely bypass the spot market. Such

---

[1] $U_{12} > 0$ is not really necessary. What we need for our results is that consumption in each period is a "normal" good.

extramarket labor agreements might be linked to the landlord's provision of consumption credit. Linked credit–labor transactions are modeled as an implicit contract specifying three items: (1) a quantity of consumption credit, c, which the landlord extends to peasants during period 1; (2) a commitment of labor services, e, to be provided by each peasant in period 2; and (3) a wage, y, at which the committed labor services are compensated. Implicit contracts are, by assumption, costlessly enforceable.

The implicit contract can be interpreted as the sum of two simple barter transactions. The first is a future transaction in which the landlord provides a consumption credit of c in period 1 in exchange for labor services of

$$e' = e \left(1 - \frac{y}{w}\right)$$

in period 2. The second is a spot transaction in period 2 in which the landlord pays the spot wage w for each of $(e - e')$ units of labor. An immediate implication of this formulation is that the contract wage is below the spot wage.

Consider an implicit contract (c, e, y). Each peasant has committed e units of labor to the landlord at a wage of y and trades the remaining endowment, $(1 - e)$, at the spot wage. Hence, under the contract, first period consumption is

$$C_1 = c,$$

and second period consumption is

$$C_2 = ye + w(1 - e).$$

Substituting these into the utility function gives the utility of the contract to peasants,

$$U = U[c, ye + w(1 - e)]. \qquad\qquad 6.1$$

Profits to the landlord are

$$\Pi = F(L) - w(L - eM) - yeM - (1 + r)cM. \qquad\qquad 6.2$$

Note that costs are of three components. First, the landlord must pay the market wage, w, for each of $(L - eM)$ units of spot labor. Second, the landlord must pay a contract wage, y, for each of eM units of contract labor. Finally, the landlord must pay the cost, including interest, of consumption credits.

The implicit contract can now be reinterpreted as follows. The landlord extends to peasants a loan of c which must be repaid by providing labor services, which are compensated at a discount $(w - y)$, below the market wage. The market value of these labor services is ew, whereas the peasant is only compensated by an amount ey. The difference,

$$t = e(w - y), \qquad\qquad 6.3$$

therefore, constitutes repayment of the loan.

Substitution of expression 6.3 into equations 6.1 and 6.2 gives, with some manipulation, a utility function,

$$U = U(c, w - t),\qquad\qquad 6.4$$

and a profit function,

$$\Pi = F(L) + tM - wL - (1+r)cM.\qquad\qquad 6.5$$

Thus both the landlord and the tied laborers care about contract values of e and y only to the extent that they affect the value of the repayment, t. An implication of this result is that the contract wage, y, must be indeterminate in any equilibrium.

Peasants' compliance with an implicit contract must be strictly voluntary. Suppose that a peasant repudiated an implicit contract, sold his entire labor endowment on the spot market, and financed consumption credit at an interest rate of r^0. The budget constraint of this peasant is

$$w = C_1(1 + r^0) + C_2,$$

and the peasant optimally chooses a consumption plan which maximizes utility subject to this constraint. The solution to this problem determines an indirect utility function,[2] $V(w, r^0)$, of the spot wage and the interest rate. Thus, a peasant will voluntarily comply with an implicit contract only if

$$U(c, w - t) \geq V(w, r^0).\qquad\qquad 6.6$$

Profit maximization implies that the voluntary compliance constraint must hold with strict equality, i.e.,

$$U(c, w - t) = V(w, r^0).\qquad\qquad 6.7$$

Otherwise there would exist an alternative contract which would be more profitable to the landlord and still acceptable to peasants.

Equation 6.7 implicitly determines the loan repayment as a function,

$$t = t(c, w, r^0),\qquad\qquad 6.8$$

of the consumption credit, the spot wage, and the peasants' interest rate. Given exogenous values of w and r^0, the function defines a maximum repayment a peasant is willing to make for a consumption credit of c. A preliminary result which will be useful shortly is

[2] A solution to the problem determines first-period consumption as a function, $C_1 = c(w, r^0)$, satisfying the condition

$$\frac{U_1[C_1, w - (1 + r^0)C_1]}{U_2[C_1, w - (1 + r^0)C_1]} = (1 + r^0).$$

Second-period consumption is determined by the budget constraint: $C_2 = w - (1 + r^0)c(w, r^0)$. Substitution into $U(C_1, C_2)$ gives the indirect utility function,

$$V(w, r^0) = U[c(w, r^0),\ w - (1 + r^0)c(w, r^0)].$$

$$t_c = \frac{U_1}{U_2},$$ 6.9

where t_e denotes the partial derivative of the function with respect to c. Thus a peasant's willingness to pay for a marginal increase in consumption credit is equal to the peasant's intertemporal marginal rate of substitution in consumption.

Upon substitution of equation 6.8 into the profit function, defined by equation 6.5, the landlord can be viewed as choosing values of L and c which maximize the resulting new profit function,

$$\Pi = F(L) + t(c, w, r^0) M - wL - (1+r)cM.$$ 6.10

A solution to this problem is characterized[3] by the conditions that the landlord employs labor up to the point where the marginal revenue product of labor equals the spot wage,

$$F'(L) = w,$$ 6.11

and that the landlord equates the marginal return from the provision of consumption credit to the marginal cost,

$$t_c(c, w, r^0) = 1 + r.$$ 6.12

Together these equations determine equilibrium values, (L^*, c^*), of labor input and consumption credit, while

$$t^* = t(c^*, w, r^0)$$

fixes a loan repayment, and

$$e(w - y) = t^*$$

determines values of contract labor, e, and a contract wage, y, which accomplish the repayment. These values constitute an equilibrium of the model.

Some of the comparative-static results are as follows. A higher spot wage (w) lowers labor input (L), increases consumption credit (c), and raises the loan repayment (t). A higher interest rate faced by the landlord (r) leaves labor input unchanged, lowers consumption credit, and lowers the loan repayment. A higher interest rate faced by peasants (r^0) also leaves labor input unchanged, lowers consumption credit, and raises the loan repayment. Note that if the quantity of contract labor (e) is held constant, then the contract wage (y) will move in the opposite direction of the loan repayment.

Substitution of equation 6.9 into equation 6.12 gives the condition,

$$\frac{U_1(c, w - t)}{U_2(c, w - t)} = 1 + r,$$ 6.13

[3] Under the stated assumptions of the model, the subsequent first-order conditions are both necessary and sufficient for a maximum.

that the peasants' intertemporal marginal rate of substitution in consumption is equal to the opportunity cost of credit to the landlord. This suggests a further interpretation of the equilibrium implicit contract. Suppose that the landlord charges peasants an interest rate on consumption loans of r plus an "entry fee" of f for the privilege of borrowing at this rate. A peasant will optimally choose a consumption credit, c, which satisfies the optimal intertemporal consumption condition,

$$\frac{U_1[c, w - (1+r)c - f]}{U_2[c, w - (1+r)c - f]} = 1 + r.$$

If

$$f = t^* - (1+r)c^*,$$

then the peasant will optimally choose a credit of $c = c^*$. Thus the equilibrium implicit contract effects an outcome equivalent to a two-part tariff on consumption loans by which the landlord establishes a fixed entry fee and a marginal interest rate equal to his own cost of credit. The peasant chooses the size of the loan and then repays principal and interest, including the entry fee, in labor services valued at the spot wage. Any further commitment of labor services can be interpreted as a simple spot transaction.

PART B

LAND LEASE

Part B analyzes the rationale and the consequences of the various observed patterns of land-lease contracts. Chapter 7 summarizes some of the essential arguments of market imperfections, uncertainty, and information asymmetry as rationale of sharecropping contracts, and also shows how in the absence of observability of inputs (like fertilizers) other than labor, the landlord provides incentive for their use by effectively paying the tenant a fixed sum: there is cost-sharing, but not at the margin, contrary to the usual analysis of this problem. Chapter 8 formalizes in a two-period model the conflict between the threat of tenurial insecurity as an incentive to tenant performance and the consequential disincentive to tenant application of labor on durable land improvements. Chapter 9 reports the results of a primary survey of 334 sample villages in North and East India on terms and conditions of sharecropping contracts and the nature of relationship between the landlord-creditor and the tenant-borrower. Chapter 10 uses cross-section data at varying levels of disaggregation to test theoretical hypotheses relating the extent of tenancy and technological, economic, and demographic variables. Chapter 11 carries out a similar hypothesis-testing on the different forms of tenancy (particularly, sharecropping vis-a-vis fixed-renting).

CHAPTER 7

Incentives, Sharecropping, and Cost Sharing

I

Even with full property rights in land, the market for buying and selling cultivable land is often rather inactive. Unless forced by extremely difficult circumstances, a resident villager does not usually sell his land. One possible reason is that land prices do not fully compensate for the very high risks in parting with this secure asset as evaluated by the farmer. In the absence of integrated financial markets, the transaction costs of investing the sales proceeds in alternative ventures is also far too high. Besides, the externalities of landownership in terms of social status and credit collateral for the owner may not be fully reflected in the land prices in the market. Land-lease markets, on the other hand, are quite active, at least until recently, before land reforms legislation abolished tenancy in some areas or drove it underground. The theoretical rationale for land lease, particularly in the age-old form of sharecropping, has been the subject of a fairly large literature in recent years. Since some good surveys of this literature exist,[1] we shall only briefly indicate in this section some of the main points of this rationale and, in the next section, go into the relatively unexplored subject of cost sharing. If there were a complete set of perfect markets, tenancy would have been theoretically uninteresting or insignificant. Its rationale lies more in the imperfections and inadequacies of the various input markets in agriculture.

Take, for example, the problem of enforceability of contractual provision of inputs and the particular "moral hazard" problem it raises. Since there is a natural tendency to shirk work, wage contracts with time rates of payment need costly monitoring and supervision. Sharecropping clearly offers more incentive to deliver effort unmonitored. But as the tenant gets only a fraction of his contribution to output, there is still a disincentive problem, which is eliminated in the case of fixed-rent tenancy. Thus in a simple model of a landless tenant facing the landlord, where there is no uncertainty, where production is characterized by constant returns to scale, and if we consider only linear contracts in output, only fixed-rent

---

[1] See, for example, Newbery and Stiglitz (1979), Bliss and Stern (1981) and Bell and Zusman (1979).

tenancy contracts will be observed in equilibrium.[2]

Some authors base their explanation of sharecropping on differential monitoring costs.[3] It is not, however, clear why monitoring *costs* will differ for different contracts. These costs depend on monitoring technology, which is independent of the nature of the contract used. What is true is that the *benefits* of monitoring depend on the type of contract: for example, a landlord who rents out land at a fixed rental rate could monitor the tenant's labor but would receive no benefit from it (as long as the quality of land is unchanged). If in a sharecropping contract the landowner specifies the labor input required and bears the monitoring cost to enforce it, this latter cost is the same between this contract and a wage contract.

The rationale for sharecropping lies, therefore, in market imperfections other than just monitoring costs. This brings us to the case of uncertainty and asymmetric information. In order to emphasize the differential risk-bearing capacities and portfolio-diversification opportunities of landlords and tenants, we shall assume, for simplification, the former to be risk-neutral and the latter to be risk-averse. Under the circumstances, the landlord may decide to monitor application of labor, in which case the contract need not depend on output for the provision of incentives and can provide perfect risk sharing. If the landlord decides not to monitor,[4] the trade-off between risk sharing and incentives will point toward sharecropping.[5] Pure fixed-rent contracts will be ruled out, as the tenant has to bear the full brunt of risks. Production uncertainty makes inferring the supply of unobserved inputs from the observation of output particularly difficult and increases the importance of sharecropping (like the commission system for traveling salesmen) as a compromise between wage and fixed-rent contracts.

Newbery (1977) has shown that, if risk is not confined to production but also affects the labor market with risky wages, share tenancy may be a way of increasing output in every state of nature. Thus, if the labor market is unable to provide needed insurance, sharecropping emerges as a partial solution in response. Reid (1973) has pointed out that sharecropping has a special advantage as much of uncertainty in agriculture is sequential, with one's view of likely prospects changing over the crop cycle, making renegotiation of contract terms desirable for both parties. With wage or

---

[2] This differs from the result in Lucas (1979) because he assumes that the landlord chooses the crop share given the tenant's response function for pure sharecropping contracts but takes the rental rate as given for pure fixed-rent contracts. This behavior is consistent neither with the landlord choosing the best linear contract given the tenant's response function nor with his taking the contract terms as parametric.

[3] See, for example, Datta and Nugent (1981).

[4] Whether the landlord in this case will be better off with monitoring or without will depend on how risk-averse the tenant is, how sharply his dislike for additional effort supply goes up, and how rapidly monitoring costs rise.

[5] For a thorough analysis of this problem, see Stiglitz (1974).

fixed-rent contracts, one party has no incentive to renegotiate.

We have assumed so far that the landlord has full information about the abilities of workers. If there is information asymmetry and the landlord requires more information, the worker's choice of contract will itself reveal something of his abilities. The most productive workers will self-select themselves by choosing fixed-rent contracts; those who are least productive will work for wages; and, those of intermediate ability will opt for share tenancy. But this role of sharecropping as a screening device, emphasized by Hallagan (1978) and Newbery and Stiglitz (1979), is relatively unimportant in the small closed world of a traditional village where the landlord has a fairly good idea of the ability characteristics of the different members of the village work force.

An inadequately developed credit market may also contribute to the rationale of sharecropping. If the fixed-rent contract involves advance payment of rent, a capital-poor or credit-rationed tenant is likely to prefer share tenancy where the rental share is collected at the time of harvest. Besides, the risk-averse tenant will prefer the risk sharing involved in an equity loan from the landlord paid as a share in the harvest to fixed-charge loans under other rental contracts. The landlord, under share tenancy, has also a special incentive to give a production loan, since he shares in the outcome of its use.[6]

An additional factor explaining the advantage of sharecropping as opposed to wage contracts is the indivisibility and imperfect marketability of some factors of production. As Bell (1976) and Bliss and Stern (1981) have emphasized, in the absence of an active market for hiring services of draft animals, leasing of land under sharecropping is a way of ensuring a fuller utilization of the household endowment of such animal power. A similar argument applies with respect to endowment of underutilized but indivisible managerial and husbandry skills of cultivators and to underemployed family laborers (particularly women and children), for whom there are various social and economic constraints for participating in the wage labor market. The ownership of such nontraded factors may impose barriers to entry for new tenants, and both landlords and existing tenants stand to gain from cooperation through bilateral lease contracts. The division of these gains will depend on their respective bargaining strength. Bell and Zusman (1976) have analyzed the set of equilibrium contracts in this context, which will be the outcome of a system of Nash cooperative games.

The alternative solution concept that has been used in most of the "principal–agent" literature on sharecropping is that of Nash non-cooperative games based on free entry of tenants and utility equivalent contracts (with parametrically given "reservation utility" levels available to

---

[6] This incentive effect will, however, depend on the degree of complementarity between the production loan and the tenant's supply of effort as well as on the income effect on effort.

them elsewhere in the economy). If contractual enforcement is costly, the landlords in these models press the tenants down to the reservation utility levels by controlling the rental share and the plot size. The tenant is assumed unable to split his time between sharecropping and wage labor: he has to choose one or the other contract exclusively.

If the tenant's reservation utility level depends on his initial wealth position (the reservation level being higher for better-off tenants), then equilibrium will be characterized by a heterogeneity of contracts, differing wealth levels of tenants implying differing local risk-aversion properties and differing possibilities for rationing in the use of capital inputs. In general one would then expect landowners to prefer wealthier tenants, other things remaining the same. The latter, with usually better risk-bearing capacities and access to entrepreneurial and financial resources, will be better able to repay necessary production loans (or require smaller loans) from the landlord. In cases in which the landlord is not well informed about the tenant's ability, he may also take the more easily observed wealth of the tenant (particularly as this wealth takes the form of land, livestock, or residential property) as an indicator of his ability. In either case, whether the landlord has information about the tenant's ability or not, a "tenancy ladder" is likely to emerge, with the wealthiest and least risk-averse tenant getting fixed-rent tenancy, the poorest settling for wage labor, and the sharecroppers inbetween.

II

Most analyses of sharecropping in terms of a principal agent relationship assume only one decision variable for the tenant (namely, his effort supply). But quite often the tenant controls more than one decision variable (particularly when there are several inputs), and the terms of the sharecropping contract reflect this. Take, for example, the decision about the use of an input like fertilizers. If the tenant has to pay for it himself, there will in general be underapplication of this input. The presumption in the literature has been that, if the landlord shares in the cost of fertilizers in the same proportion as in the output, efficient application of this input will follow.[7] Recently, Braverman and Stiglitz (1981 b) have shown that this "equal share" rule breaks down when one introduces uncertainty and information asymmetry. In this section we shall first present an exposition of their model and then argue why we find their particular specification for the choice of inputs like fertilizers implausible in the context of a principal-agent problem. We then provide an alternative specification and compare the predictions of the two approaches.

It is assumed that tenants are identical. They lease from the landlord a plot of land whose size is exogeneously fixed. A tenant chooses his labor

---

[7] See, for example, Adams and Rask (1968).

input (effort) and the level of one other input, say, fertilizer, given the terms of the contract. The landlord chooses the contract terms given the tenant's behavioral functions. The tenants' actual behavior is not observable and hence cannot be directly controlled. The production function is concave in effort and fertilizer. In addition, output is subject to exogeneous uncertainty, modeled as a multiplicative random variable. All choices are made before the outcome of this random variable is observable. (In fact, the landlord never observes it, only the level of output; that is what creates the "moral hazard".) Finally, the landlord is assumed to be risk-neutral and the tenant risk-averse.

The notations, which here are kept the same as in Braverman and Stiglitz (1981 b) are:

e: labor effort
x: fertilizer input
α: tenant's output share
β: tenant's cost share
g: a random variable, $E(g)=1$
f: expected output
P: fertilizer price
Y: tenant's income, $\alpha g f(e,x) - \beta px$
Π: landlord's expected profit, $(1-\alpha)f(e,x)-(1-\beta)Px$
$U(y,e)$: tenant's utility, $U_1>0$, $U_2<0$, $U_{11}<0$, $U_{22}<0$.

Subscripts denote partial derivatives. The choice of contract and inputs may now be formally expressed as a sequence of optimization problems:
The tenant maximizes his expected utility of income and effort, i.e.,

$$V(\alpha,\beta) \equiv \max EU[Y(e,x),e] \qquad 7.1$$

The first-order conditions are

$$\alpha f_x EU_1 g - \beta PEU_1 = 0 \qquad 7.2$$

$$\alpha f_e EU_1 g + EU_2 = 0 \qquad 7.3$$

These imply the fertilizer and effort supply functions $x(\alpha,\beta)$, $e(\alpha,\beta)$. The landlord chooses the terms of the tenancy contract subject to equations 7.2 and 7.3. Furthermore, he is constrained to provide the tenant with the latter's reservation level of expected utility, $\bar{V}$. The landlord's optimization is therefore

$$\max_{\{\alpha,\beta\}} \Pi = (1-\alpha)f[e(\alpha,\beta),x(\alpha,\beta)] - (1-\beta)Px(\alpha,\beta) \qquad 7.4$$

subject to $V(\alpha,\beta) \geq \bar{V}$.

Under plausible conditions on the utility function, the constraint will be binding. Hence we may rewrite the maximization as (suppressing the argument $\bar{V}$),

$$\max_{\beta} \Pi(\beta) = \{1 - \alpha(\beta)\}\, f\{e(\beta), x(\beta)\} - (1 - \beta)\, P x(\beta) \qquad\qquad 7.5$$

Note that we ignore sufficient conditions and possible nonuniqueness of optimal choices (as do Braverman and Stiglitz), as they are not the issue here.

We may now summarize the Braverman - Stiglitz results for the four cases they consider.

Case 1: $e = \bar{e}$ (i.e., no incentive effects) and no uncertainty. The equilibrium involves $\alpha = \beta$. This clearly leads to an optimal allocation of fertilizer.

Case 2: $e = \bar{e}$, with uncertainty present. Here a sufficient, but not necessary, condition for $\beta < \alpha$ is $x_\beta \big|_{\bar{v}} < 0$. The last inequality says that, not only the landlord can reduce the tenant's risk, he can also increase his input of fertilizer by reducing β. Clearly it pays to subsidize fertilizer input (in the sense that $P\beta/\alpha < P$). Braverman and Stiglitz also consider special cases where $x_\beta \big|_{\bar{v}} < 0$ is valid.

Case 3: No uncertainty but incentive effects on effort. In this case, $\beta \lesseqgtr \alpha$ as $e_\beta \big|_{\bar{v}} \lesseqgtr 0$. A low elasticity of substitution between inputs will tend to make $e_\beta \big|_{\bar{v}} < 0$.

Case 4: Both uncertainty and incentive effects. Here $\beta < \alpha$ only if (1) $e_\beta \big|_{\bar{v}} < 0$, or (2) the positive incentive effects are dominated by the negative risk-sharing effects.

Next let us examine the specification of observability and control of inputs in the above model more closely.

The Braverman–Stiglitz model assumes that the landlord cannot control x. However his income depends on x, and he pays a predetermined share of the cost Px. The question therefore arises: if he knows x, why can he not specify to the tenant what its level should be?[8]

What is a more reasonable specification of the problem facing the landlord who cannot observe a tenant's fertilizer input but wishes nevertheless to provide incentives for its use? We postulate that the landlord chooses the amount of fertilizer to be bought. He also chooses what fraction of this cost will be paid by the tenant. The tenant, however, may not use all the fertilizer supplied, but secretly may sell some on the open market or, equivalently, use it on his own land (if he has any). The

---

[8] One answer to this question may be that one should distinguish between monitoring and enforcement costs: the input of fertilizer can be monitored at no cost but enforced only at a prohibitively high cost. We do not find this argument realistic. If x can be monitored, its level can be enforced by an appropriate payment scheme depending on x, probably in a discontinuous way. This takes us outside the class of linear reward functions, but not in any complex manner, and restricting our analysis to that class is justified only if it is a reasonable approximation to the best that the landlord can do. What I am arguing, therefore, is that the ability to monitor implies the ability to enforce at no extra cost.

landlord, of course, realizes this possibility is available to the tenant. Let N be the amount of fertilizer purchased. Then we have

$$Y = \alpha g f(e, x) - \beta PN + P(N - x)$$

and

$$\Pi = (1 - \alpha)f(e, x) - (1 - \beta)PN.$$

The tenant chooses e and x given β, α, N. Knowing this behavior, the landlord decides on α, β, and N. Let us now examine the alternative implications of this, in my view more plausible, characterization of the cost-sharing issue.

In order to examine our alternative, I will recast it slightly. The tenant's income, Y, may be rewritten as

$$\alpha g f(e, x) - Px + (1 - \beta)PN.$$

Clearly, the tenant's marginal cost of fertilizer is always P, rather than βP in the standard model. Furthermore, define $c \equiv (1 - \beta)PN$. Then we have

$$Y = \alpha g f(e, x) - Px + c$$

and

$$\Pi = (1 - \alpha)f(e, x) - c.$$

Since the landlord does not manipulate the tenant's marginal cost of fertilizer, he effectively pays the tenant a fixed sum, and the latter decides how much fertilizer to use. There is cost sharing, but not at the margin: β and N are not separately determined. Whereas in the standard model β had to partly do the work of sharing risk as well as sharing costs, here c plays that dual rule.

By way of comparison, we may write down the tenant's first-order conditions for this model:

$$\alpha f_x EU_1 g - PEU_1 = 0 \qquad\qquad 7.6$$

$$\alpha f_e EU_1 g + EU_2 = 0. \qquad\qquad 7.7$$

Consider first the case $e = \bar{e}$, with no uncertainty. The solution obviously involves $\alpha = 1$, with $c < 0$ (the fixed-rent case). Just as in the Braverman—Stiglitz case 1, the full optimum is attained: the different specification is irrelevant.

Next consider the case in which there is certainty but effort is determined by the tenant. This corresponds to case 3. Here equation 7.6 reduces to $\alpha f_x - P = 0$, just as in the case $e = \bar{e}$. However, here we must also reckon with cross-effects, since x and e are determined jointly by 7.6 and 7.7. Under plausible conditions, however, the solution involves $\alpha = 1, c < 0$, as in the no-incentives-effect case (see appendix to this chapter). As long as there is no uncertainty, the landlord can achieve the first-best: he does not have to worry about risk sharing. The case 3 is inferior to the first-best because Braverman and Stiglitz do not permit the landlord to charge a fixed fee. Equilibrium in their model must involve $\alpha < 1$ and $\beta \neq \alpha$ in general.

The analog of case 2 yields a more interesting comparison. With $e = \bar{e}$, but with uncertainty, we have

$$\Pi(\beta) = \{1 - \alpha(\beta)\} f(x(\beta), \bar{e}) - (1 - \beta) P x(\beta)$$

and

$$\Pi(c) = \{1 - \alpha(c)\} f(x(c), \bar{e}] - c,$$

where once again $\bar{V}$ is suppressed in the arguments of α, x.

Now we have $\alpha_\beta = Px/\rho f$, and $\alpha_c = -1/\rho f$, where $\rho \equiv EU_1 g / EU_1$ and $0 < \rho < 1$ by risk aversion. More complicated expressions are x_β and x_c. Let $k \equiv (1 - \beta) Px(\beta)$.

Then

$$\beta_k = \frac{1}{(1 - \beta) P x_\beta - Px} .$$

Hence

$$\alpha_k = -\frac{1}{\rho f} \cdot \frac{1}{1 - (1 - \beta) x_\beta / x} .$$

Therefore, if $x_\beta < 0$, we have $0 > \alpha_k > \alpha_c$. Furthermore, if $x_\beta < 0, x_k = x_\beta \cdot \beta_k > 0$.

Now

$$\Pi_k = -\alpha_k f + \alpha f_x x_k - 1$$

and

$$\Pi_c = -\alpha_c f + \alpha f_x x_c - 1.$$

Using the expressions for α_k and α_c and the first-order conditions, we have

$$\Pi_k = \frac{1}{\rho} \left(\frac{1 - \alpha}{\alpha} \cdot \beta x_\beta - x \right) \cdot \frac{1}{(1 - \beta) x_\beta - x} - 1$$

and

$$\Pi_c = \frac{1}{\rho} \left(\frac{1 - \alpha}{\alpha} \cdot P x_c + 1 \right) - 1.$$

Now, if β is fixed at 1, and c at 0, the equilibrium in the two models must be the same. Hence we have that $\Pi(\beta^*) > \Pi(c^*)$ if and only if $\Pi_k > \Pi_c$ at $k = c$. From the above, we have $\Pi_k > \Pi_c$ if and only if

$$\frac{1 - \alpha}{\alpha} \cdot P x_c [(1 - \beta) x_\beta - x] > (\frac{\beta}{\alpha} - 1) x_\beta.$$

Since $x_\beta < 0$ by assumption, $\beta / \alpha < 1$, and the right-hand side is positive. Therefore a necessary condition for the above inequality is $x_c < 0$. The intuition behind this is that, while decreasing β provides risk sharing as well as subsidizing the tenant's fertilizer input, increasing c involves some conflict between risk sharing and incentives when $x_c < 0$. When is $x_c < 0$? It turns out that two of the sufficient conditions for $x_\beta < 0$ derived by Braverman and Stiglitz are also sufficient for $x_c < 0$, i.e., constant absolute risk aversion or small enough risk (see appendix to this chapter). If both uncertainty and elastic labor supply are features of the problem, the comparison becomes harder. All we can say is that the landlord will be better off charging a fixed amount if the incentive effects dominate the risk-sharing effects.

The main purpose of this section has been to provide a more plausible alternative to the standard model of cost sharing under sharecropping, when other inputs cannot be perfectly controlled by the landlord, and also to explore some of the predictions of our model and compare them with the Braverman–Stiglitz formulation. We found that the welfare comparisons of the two formulations were ambiguous. However, the nature of cost sharing is very different in the two models. In the Braverman–Stiglitz model, βP is the tenant's marginal cost of fertilizer: the landlord can subsidize fertilizer at the margin. In our specification, we might define an effective cost share $\beta = 1 - c/px$. However, this does not reflect any cost sharing at the margin. We may add that this applies to the case where the landlord can control x (in our model, $x \equiv N$). In that situation, the landlord is better off than in either model considered here, but his choice of β does not serve to subsidize the input at the margin. We hope this sheds some light on the degree of effective control exercised by an imperfectly informed person in situations where parties to a contract are constrained by one side's lack of information

Appendix

I. *The Certainty Case.*

The tenant's first-order conditions are

$$\alpha f_x - P = 0$$

$$\alpha f_e U_1 + U_2 = 0$$

Taking the total differential, and using $\alpha_c = -\dfrac{1}{f}$,

$$\begin{bmatrix} \alpha f_{xx} & \alpha f_e x \\ \\ \alpha f_{ex} U_1 & \alpha (f_{ee} U_1 + \alpha f_e^2 U_{11} + 2f_e U_{12}) + U_{22} \end{bmatrix} \begin{bmatrix} dx \\ \\ de \end{bmatrix} = \begin{bmatrix} \dfrac{f_x}{f} \\ \\ \dfrac{f_e U_1}{f} \end{bmatrix} dc$$

The second-order conditions are

$$\alpha f_{xx} < 0, \ \alpha(f_{ee}U_1 + \alpha f_e^2 U_{11} + 2\ f_e U_{12}) + U_{22} < 0 \ \text{and} \ \Delta > 0,$$

where Δ is the determinant of the left-hand matrix.

Hence, we get

$$\frac{de}{dc} = \frac{\alpha U_1}{\Delta f}(f_{xx}f_e - f_{ex}f_x)$$

and

$$\frac{dx}{dc} = \frac{1}{\Delta f}\{f_x[\alpha(f_{ee}U_1 + \alpha f_e^2 U_{11} + 2U_{12}f_e) + U_{22}] - \alpha f_{ex}f_e U_1\}.$$

Now if $f_{ex} \geq 0$ or, if negative, is not large in magnitude, we have $de/dc < 0$, $dx/dc < 0$. For example, with constant returns to scale, $f_{ex} > 0$. Now $\Pi_c = (1 - \alpha)(f_x x_c + f_e e_c)$.

Therefore Π has a stationary point at $\alpha = 1$, and if $de/dc < 0$, $dx/dc < 0$, this is a maximum (if $\alpha < 1$, x_c, $e_c < 0$ imply $\Pi_c < 0$, i.e. the landlord can do better by reducing c and increasing α).

II. *The Fixed-Effort Case.*

In this case, we have from the first-order condition,

$$\alpha f_x E U_1 g - P E U_1 = 0,$$

$$x_\alpha \big|_c = -\frac{1}{\gamma}[f_x E U_1 g + \alpha f_x f E U_{11} g^2 - P f E U_{11} g]$$

$$x_c \big|_\alpha = -\frac{1}{\gamma}[\alpha f_x E U_{11} g - P E U_{11}]$$

where

$$\gamma = \alpha f_{xx} E U_1 g + \alpha^2 (f_x)^2 E U_{11} g^2 - \alpha p f_x E U_{11} g < 0$$

therefore

$$x_c \big|_{\bar{v}} = x_c \big|_\alpha + x_\alpha \big|_c \cdot \alpha_c \big|_{\bar{v}} = x_c \big|_\alpha - \frac{1}{f\varrho} \cdot x_\alpha \big|_c.$$

With no uncertainty,

$$x_c \big|_\alpha = 0, \ x_\alpha \big|_c = -\frac{f_x}{\alpha f_{xx}} > 0.$$

Hence $x_c \big|_{\bar{v}} < 0$, and by continuity, this will hold if there is not much uncertainty.

With constant absolute risk aversion, $U_{11} = -A U_1$, where A is the index of absolute risk aversion. Hence we see that $x_c \big|_\alpha = 0$. Then $x_c \big|_{\bar{v}} < 0$ requires $x_\alpha \big|_c > 0$. Without going into details, we may argue that this must be true at the optimum, else α would be too high (since $x_c \big|_\alpha = 0$). Hence the required result holds.

CHAPTER 8

Tenurial Insecurity and Land Improvements

I

Most of the theoretical analysis of sharecropping is in terms of a static framework and relates to a single period. When contracts are recognized as renewable for a second period or beyond, one may take note of two general ideas somewhat loosely floating in the literature:[1] that the threat of eviction prods the sharecropping tenant to avoid any underapplication of inputs; and that such a threat seriously discourages long-term improvements on the land that a tenant would otherwise have carried out. The purpose of this chapter is to formalize the conflicting effects of this threat in terms of a two-period principal–agent model of sharecropping, with landlord as the principal and tenant as the agent. In spite of a number of simplifications adopted, the model soon gets rather complicated, and we shall confine ourselves to pointing out only the broad, intuitive results, bypassing details as well as analytical rigor.

In the basic principal–agent model, output is determined by the agent's effort (unobservable by the employer) and the outcome of a random variable. The agent chooses a level of effort given the terms of the contract (like the sharing rule) but before observing the true state of the world. The principal knows how the agent will behave and takes this into account in drawing up the contract which maximizes his own welfare. In addition to the essential incentive constraint, the principal is constrained to provide the agent with at least some minimum level of expected utility (the latter's opportunity cost). Finally, the contract is constrained by the resources available to both parties. Inefficiency arises when the principal is less risk-averse than the agent and must therefore end up sharing risks as well as providing proper effort incentives. If the outcome of the one-shot game is inefficient compared with the full-information game, can the parties involved do better in a repeated game? Radner (1981) has examined this question in detail. Roughly his results are as follows. While a finitely repeated game does not differ from the one-period case (working backward from the last period) if each player is fully rational, with "bounded

---

[1] Classical economists have emphasized the adverse effects of tenurial insecurity on investment by the tenant; J. S. Mill, in particular, regarded this as the major defect of *metayage* in France. In the more recent literature on sharecropping, Johnson (1950) was the first to emphasize the importance of the short-term lease for the landlord to enforce a given intensity of cultivation.

rationality" there exists, for sufficiently many repetitions of the game, an epsilon-equilibrium of the "supergame" that is arbitrarily close, in terms of expected utility, to the full-information outcome. If the game is repeated infinitely often, the full-information outcome can be attained.

This chapter considers a repeated principal–agent relationship in a spirit rather different from that of the Radner model. Instead of examining how prolonging a contractual relationship can increase efficiency as the length of the relationship approaches infinity, we see how the threat of termination can provide an increased incentive for effort on the part of the agent and how at the same time this threat adversely affects the incentive for improvements that enhance productivity in future periods. In order to do this we must first focus more closely on the agent's opportunity cost. Consider the two-period case. Can the threat of dismissal after the first period, for unsatisfactory performance, provide the agent with a greater incentive to work in the first period? For an affirmative answer, the threat must be both *real* and *credible*: a threat is real if the agent is made worse off by being dismissed, i.e., he would be strictly better off working for the principal in period 2 than in his next best occupation; a threat is credible if the principal is made no worse off by dismissing the agent. Credibility of the threat is ensured if the principal has access to a pool of homogeneous agents; the first-period agent is then easily replaced at no cost. However, in the usual model, the principal always forces the agent down to his opportunity cost (or reservation utility level) in each period. Hence the latter is indifferent between working for the principal and his best alternative, so that the threat of dismissal is not real. In order to ensure that the threat is real, we will construct a case under a proportional sharing rule where the agent's one-period benefit from working for the principal *exceeds* his opportunity cost. In section II we shall show why the principal may be interested in allowing this. For the time being let us anticipate the argument and take the dismissal threat to be real as well as credible.

Suppose output x is determined jointly by the agent's effort, e, and the outcome g of a random variable $\tilde{g}$, with range $(0, \infty)$. Let $F(x; e)$ be the distribution function for x given e, induced by the distribution of $\tilde{g}$ and the production function. Let the agent's utility function in terms of income and effort be separable, i.e., of the form $U(\alpha x) - H(e)$, where α is the tenants's crop share, and $U' > 0$, $H' > 0$, $U'' < 0$, $H'' > 0$. While the agent is thus risk-averse, the principal is assumed risk-neutral, and the agent's opportunity cost is $\bar{V}$, the reservation level of utility.

In the second period of a situation where each person lives for just two periods, the principal's problem is precisely the standard one:

$$\underset{\alpha, e}{\text{Max}} \; E\left[(1-\alpha)x\right]$$

subject to

$$e \; \epsilon \; \text{argmax}\{E[U(\alpha x)] - H(e)\}$$

and

$$E[U(\alpha x)] - H(e) \geq \bar{V}.$$

Let us assume that a solution to the above maximization problem exists and in equilibrium, the level of the agent's expected utility, say Φ^A, exceeds $\bar{V}$. Next consider the situation in the first period. Let us suppose the principal uses a simple rule for determining whether to dismiss the agent or not: the agent is dismissed if his performance, as measured by output, falls below some level, say $\underline{x}$. If the agent is dismissed, the principal hires someone from a pool of readily available and identical agents. Normalizing for $\bar{V}$, the agent's expected utility is therefore given by

$$\int_0^\infty U(\alpha x) f(x;e) \mathrm{d}x - H(e) + \rho \Phi^A [1 - F(\underline{x};e)], \qquad 8.1$$

where ρ is the agent's discount factor and f is the density of x induced by the production function $x = q(e, g)$ parametrized by e. The agent's first-order maximization condition is given by

$$\int_0^\infty U(\alpha x) f_e(x;e) \mathrm{d}x - H'(e) - \rho F_e(\underline{x};e)\Phi^A = 0, \qquad 8.2$$

where subscripts denote partial derivatives. Since we would expect F_e negative (i.e., increased effort reduces the probability of output falling below a given level), and Φ^A is positive, the sum of the first two terms on the left-hand side of equation 8.2 is negative. Thus the dismissal threat in period 2 increases the agent's effort, for any first-period contract (given α).

At this stage let us indicate the difference made by the possibility that some effort carried out in period 1 increases productivity in period 2 (for example, through simple land improvements). If this land improvement effort (which may be carried out in the slack parts of period 1), called l, is in addition to the direct production effort, e, in the same period, then the total effort in period 1 is $(e+l)$, and in period 2 the density of output is $f(x;e,l)$. It is reasonable to assume $F_l < 0$ and $F_{el} > 0$. The agent's first-order conditions of maximization are:

$$\int_0^\infty U(\alpha x) f_e \mathrm{d}x - H'(e+l) - \rho F_e(\underline{x};e)\Phi^A(l) = 0 \qquad 8.3$$

and

$$-H'(e+l) + \rho \Phi^{A\prime}(l)[1 - F(\underline{x};e)] = 0. \qquad 8.4$$

Condition 8.4 requires $\Phi^{A\prime}(l)$ positive, otherwise l would obviously be set equal to zero. I shall discuss the conditions of $\Phi^{A\prime}(l)$ positive in the next section.

II

The preceding section assumes that the dismissal threat is real. Let us now see how this may come about. Given the share α, in a one-period problem the agent's labor choice is given by:

$$\int_0^\infty U(\alpha x) f_e\ (x;e) - H'(e) = 0. \tag{8.5}$$

From 8.5,

$$\frac{de}{d\alpha} = -\int_0^\infty U'(\alpha x) x f_e(x;e) dx / [\ \alpha \int_0^\infty U(\alpha x) f_{ee}(x;e)\ dx - H''(e)\ ]. \tag{8.6}$$

By the second-order condition of maximization and if relative risk aversion is less than unity, $de/d\alpha$ is positive. If $f_{ee}(x;e)$ and $H''(e)$ are both small, i.e., the second-order effects on expected utility and on disutility of changes in e are small, then $de/d\alpha$ is large, so that changes in α have a large impact on labor supply. Now for a given level of expected utility, $\bar{V}$, for the tenant, the landlord's expected utility is:

$$\Phi^P(\bar{V}) \equiv [1 - \alpha(\bar{V})] \int_0^\infty x f[x;e(\bar{V})] dx, \tag{8.7}$$

with

$$\Phi^{P'}(\bar{V}) > 0,$$

if

$$-\int_0^\infty x f[x;e(\bar{V})] dx + [1 - \alpha(\bar{V})] \int_0^\infty x f_e[x;e(\bar{V})] dx \cdot \frac{de}{d\alpha} > 0 \tag{8.8}$$

If $de/d\alpha$ is large, then for $\alpha(\bar{V})$ small enough, i.e., $\bar{V}$ small enough, 8.8 will be valid. This means it is not worth reducing α beyond a point because of the adverse impact on the tenant's labor supply. The utility possibility frontier may thus look like the curve in figure 8.1. For $\bar{V} < \bar{V}^*$, the principal will pay the agent more than his opportunity cost.[2]

Let us now go back to the case where the second-period output is favorably affected by off-time first-period land-improving labor, l. The second-period equilibrium is described by equations 8.9, the tenant's first-order condition, and equations 8.10 and 8.11, the landlord's first-order conditions of maximization:

$$\int_0^\infty U(\alpha x) f_e dx - H' = 0 \tag{8.9}$$

$$-\int_0^\infty x f dx + \mu \int_0^\infty U' x f_e dx = 0 \tag{8.10}$$

---

[2] An alternative reason for the tenant to get more than his opportunity cost may be when the tenant can observe something about production possibilities or his alternative opportunities before choosing his level of effort, with the possibility of his effectively, if secretly, reneging on the contract (or "moonlighting") after this observation.

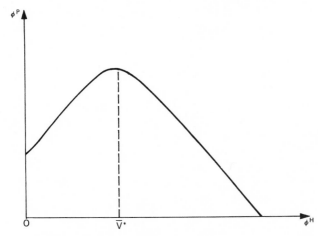

Figure 8.1 Expected Utility Frontier of the Principal and the Agent

$$(1-\alpha)\int_0^\infty x f_e \, dx + \mu[\int_0^\infty U f_{ee} - H''] = 0, \qquad\qquad 8.11$$

where μ is the Lagrange multiplier associated with the incentive constraint facing the landlord. To see how α varies with l, we have to differentiate totally in these three equations with respect to l. This leads to three very cumbersome equations. If, however, we assume the second- and third-order effects to be negligible,[3] we get

$$\frac{d\alpha}{dl}\int_0^\infty -f_e \, dx + (1-\alpha)\int_0^\infty x f_{el} \, dx \approx 0. \qquad\qquad 8.12$$

Equation 8.12 implies that, if the expected marginal product of labor in period 2 increases with land improvement in period 1, $d\alpha/dl$ is positive. Let us next note that

$$\frac{d\Phi^A}{dl} = \frac{d\alpha}{dl}\int_0^\infty U'xf \, dx + \int_0^\infty U f_l \, dx. \qquad\qquad 8.13$$

The first integral on the right-hand side of equation 8.13 indicates the impact on the tenant's expected utility of a change in the equilibrium crop share; the second integral shows the direct impact as the distribution of output is more favorable. Thus as long as increased l affects α favorably, or not too unfavorably, the tenant's expected utility in period 2 goes up if he puts in land-improving labor in period 1.

In period 1, the tenant's total effort is $(e+l)$. The tenant's optimal choices of e and l in period 1 are given by first-order conditions of maximum as given in equations 8.3 and 8.4. The second-order conditions of the tenant's maximum require $M<0$, $N<0$ and $MN-P^2>0$, where

[3] Apart from ignoring third derivatives of f, we have assumed $\int_0^\infty xf_{ee} \, dx \approx 0$ (i.e., the expected marginal product of labor does not fall rapidly).

$$M \equiv \int_0^\infty U f_{ee} - H'' - \rho f_{ee} \Phi^A,$$

$$N \equiv \rho \Phi^{A''}(1-F) - H'',$$

and

$$P \equiv -[H'' + \rho F_e \phi^{A'}],$$

M and N are the second-order effects on the tenant's expected utility over periods 1 and 2 of changes in e and l, respectively. P represents the cross-effects of a change in l on the marginal benefit of changing e. Now,

$$\frac{dl}{dx} = \rho[M\Phi^A f - P\Phi^A f_e]/[MN - P^2] \qquad 8.14$$

Similarly,

$$\frac{de}{dx} = \rho[\Phi^{A'} f P + \Phi^A f_e N]/[MN - P^2] \qquad 8.15$$

The appendix to this chapter shows that 8.14 is negative if the production function is concave and there is multiplicative uncertainty and that 8.15 is positive if the second-order terms (like the change in marginal disutility of effort) are small. It is implied by dl/dx negative and de/dx positive that a higher performance standard (i.e., a larger threat of dismissal) encourages application of labor for current output but discourages land-improving labor, l, as the tenant is less likely to be around to enjoy the latter's benefits. The model thus formalizes the conflict between "static" and "dynamic" efficiency involved in sharecropping with tenurial insecurity.

Appendix

In equations 8.14 and 8.15, the denominator is positive from the second-order conditions of maximization. So we have only to sign the numerators. Take 8.14 first. The bracketed expression in the numerator on the right-hand side may be rewritten as:

$$\Phi^{A'} f \int_0^\infty U f_{ee} \, dx + H''[\Phi^A f_e - \Phi^{A'} f] + \rho \Phi^A \Phi^{A'} [f_e F_e - f F_{ee}] \qquad 8.16$$

The first two terms in 8.16 are nonpositive, as f_e evaluated at x is negative, and Φ_A' is positive from 8.13. A sufficient condition for 8.16 to be negative is, therefore,

$$f_e F_e - f F_{ee} < 0.$$

Or,

$$\frac{\partial}{\partial e}\left[\frac{f(x;e)}{F_e(x;e)}\right] < 0. \qquad 8.17$$

We can show 8.17 to be valid with a concave production function and multiplicative uncertainty. Suppose $x = q(e)g$, and $s(g)$ is the density of the random variable g. In that case,

$$\frac{f}{F_e} = - q(e)/x\, q'(e),$$

and 8.17 is equal to $[\, q\, q'' - (q')^2]/x(q')^2 < 0$, since $q'' < 0$. Now take equation 8.15. The bracketed expression of the numerator on the right-hand side may be rewritten as:

$$- H''[\Phi^A f_e + \Phi^{A'} f] + \rho \Phi^{A'}[\Phi^A f_e(1 - F)\Phi^{A''} - f F_e \Phi^{A'}]$$

8.18

If all second- and third-order terms are ignored, as in 8.12, this amounts to $[-\rho(\Phi^{A'})^2 f F_e]$, which is positive.

CHAPTER 9

Terms and Conditions of Sharecropping Contracts: An Analysis of Village Survey Data in India

I

Compared with the sizable theoretical literature on sharecropping tenancy in agriculture, the literature on the actual nature of sharecropping contracts empirically observed in peasant agriculture is rather small. In India neither the large-scale Land Holdings Surveys carried out by the National Sample Survey Organization nor the small-scale village surveys carried out by the Agro-Economic Research Centers in different parts of India collect data on the contractual details in the land-lease markets. Some field surveys by individual economists[1] or social anthropologists in a handful of purposively chosen villages have sometimes been quite intensive and useful in terms of their coverage of tenancy contracts, but their microscopic nature and purposive sample inhibit statistically valid generalization. This chapter is based on what may have been the first intensive and yet fairly large-scale survey of contractual relationships in rural India. We shall be reporting here data collected in 1975–76 from 334 randomly chosen villages in four states in northern and eastern India: West Bengal, Bihar, Uttar Pradesh, and Orissa.

In these states, villages were randomly selected;[2] in each such village four types of questionnaires were canvassed: one to be answered by two (purposively chosen and, if possible, different types of) tenants separately, one by two casual laborers separately, one by two permanent farm servants separately, and one general village questionnaire to be filled in on the basis of information obtained from all these six respondents and cross-checked

---

[1] See, for example, Bharadwaj and Das (1975), Bell (1977), Bliss and Stern (1982), and Jodha (1981).

[2] It was decided to take about 100 villages in each of the three states other than Orissa. The villages were allocated to the districts in proportion to the agricultural population of the districts; and within each district villages were selected randomly with probability proportional to the village agricultural population. The numbers allocated to West Bengal, Bihar, and Uttar Pradesh were 110, 101, and 100, respectively. The 23 villages of Orissa were not selected by following this procedure or any other strictly defined procedure. On account of the largeness of the state of Uttar Pradesh, we covered by our sample only the western and eastern districts. So, although in our subsequent discussion we refer to Uttar Pradesh without any qualification, it should be understood that our analysis refers only to western and eastern Uttar Pradesh.

with other people living in the village. Since this chapter is concerned with the terms and conditions of sharecropping contracts, the main focus will be on the tenancy schedules in each village; for some of the other results of the survey, the reader may refer to Bardhan and Rudra (1978). The tenant (and laborer) respondents were asked questions about the contract they themselves had entered into and those others prevailing in the village and other particulars about themselves; in addition, they were asked about the characteristics of their landlords, employers, or creditors and about general features, institutions, and trends in the village economy as perceived by them. We did not canvas any questionnaire with the village landlords, employers, or moneylenders as such.[3]

The ultimate unit of investigation is the village. Most of the questions relate to the standard type or types of contracts prevailing in the village, and the answers given by one respondent belonging to a particular category (say, tenant) about the prevailing contractual type in the village have been cross-checked with those given by the other respondents in the same category. Although villages were randomly selected, the respondents within a village were purposively chosen in order to gain in the quality of information. The respondent from a given group was selected by the investigator on considerations of the cooperation that was sought and given as well as that of knowledgeability.

Table 9.1 presents the number of sample villages and tenancy patterns in the four states. In the overwhelming majority of the villages surveyed,

TABLE 9.1

Number of sample villages and tenancy patterns

State	Number of Villages Surveyed	Number of Tenancy Patterns Reported	Crop for Which Tenancy Patterns Observed
West Bengal	110	188	Paddy
Bihar	101	106	Paddy
Orissa	22	29	Paddy
Uttar Pradesh	100	90	Wheat

NOTE: By a tenancy pattern we mean a combination of crop-sharing and cost-sharing patterns involving one or more crops and several inputs. Whenever any one element in the combination is different, we have considered that as two different patterns. Thus in the same village we have often encountered more than one pattern. We have counted for each village the number of different patterns prevailing there. However, an identical pattern occurring in different villages has been counted not once but as many times as it has occurred. This gives the total number of patterns observed. All the percentages in tables 9.2–9.6 and 9.11 refer to the number of patterns of a certain kind occurring in the total number of patterns defined as above.

---

[3] We avoided them deliberately, as it is our understanding that they are much more inclined toward falsifying information on tenancy contracts than laborers, poor tenants, etc.

TABLE 9.2

Frequency distribution of crop shares

Crop Shares (Tenant: Owner)

State	3:1 (75%)	2:1 (66.7%)	10:6 (62%)	3:2 (60%)	9:7 (56%)	1:1 (50%)	18:22 (45%)	7:9 (44%)	2:3 (40%)	6:10 (38%)	7:13 (35%)	1:2 (33.3%)	6:17 (26%)	1:3 (25%)
(1)	(2)	(3)	(4)	(5)	(6)	(7)	(8)	(9)	(10)	(11)	(12)	(13)	(14)	(15)
							PADDY							
West Bengal	6.4	4.7	1.2	1.8	0.0	66.9	3.5	0.0	3.8	0.0	0.6	6.4	0.6	4.1
Bihar	0.0	0.5	0.0	1.0	0.0	86.5	0.0	1.6	0.0	2.6	0.0	6.2	0.0	1.6
Orissa	3.4	0.0	6.9	6.9	3.4	79.4	0.0	0.0	0.0	0.0	0.0	0.0	0.0	0.0
							WHEAT							
Uttar Pradesh	0.6	0.0	0.0	0.0	0.0	83.8	0.0	0.0	6.0	0.0	0.0	6.0	0.0	3.6

sharecropping is the predominant form of tenancy. Although there are some signs of increase in the incidence of fixed-rent tenancy in some areas and for some crops, as high as 91 percent of the cases of tenancy reported in West Bengal and Bihar, 100 percent in Orissa, and 93 percent in Uttar Pradesh in our survey take the form of sharecropping. An important feature of the sharecropping arrangements is that the share proportion clusters around certain simple rational fractions, the most important of which is, of course, that of 50:50. Table 9.2 presents frequency distributions of the share of the principal crop in crop-sharing arrangements in the four states. While in all four states more than two-thirds of the cases report 50:50 share, the tenant's share is *less* than 50 percent in 19 percent of cases in West Bengal, 12 percent of cases in Bihar, and 16 percent of cases in Uttar Pradesh. In 21 percent of cases in Orissa and 14 percent of cases in West Bengal, the tenant's share is *more* than 50 percent.

Much of sharecropping theory assumes *either* that the (exogenously or endogenously determined) crop share is uniform for all tenancy contracts in a village, *or* (less frequently) that the crop share varies from one contract to another in the same village depending on the varying bargaining power of individual lessors and lessees or on their differential risk aversion or on farm size used as a screening device. Neither of these neat theoretical alternatives seems to fit our data. Table 9.3 shows that, while the majority of villages have only one prevailing share pattern, in a significant number of villages more than one share proportion coexists in the same crop in the same village; on the other hand, there is no evidence that the share varies from one pair of lessor–lessee to another or that the share is sensitive to the particular characteristics of individual parties.

TABLE 9.3

*Incidence of single and multiple crop shares
in the same village*

	Number of Share Patterns in Same Village				Number of Villages	
State	One†	Two	Three	Four	No crop sharing in paddy/wheat††	Total
(1)	(2)	(3)	(4)	(5)	(6)	(7)
West Bengal	63	35	9	1	2	110
Bihar	78	10	2	0	11	101
Orissa	17	4	1	0	0	22
Uttar Pradesh	65	11	0	0	24	100

†For West Bengal, Bihar, and Orissa, all cases (e.g., 63, 78, and 17) are of 50:50 share. For Uttar Pradesh, out of the 65 cases of mono-share pattern, 62 are cases of 50:50 share.
††For West Bengal, Bihar, and Orissa, the figures refer to sharecropping arrangements in paddy. For Uttar Pradesh, the figures refer to share arrangement in wheat.

Land Lease

In fact, it is not very easy to find a definite pattern in the intravillage or intervillage variations in crop shares. But from table 9.4 it seems that high-yielding varieties (HYV) of grains are more frequently associated with higher tenant share than in the case of ordinary varieties, and in West Bengal and Orissa we encounter a significantly larger incidence of the tenant's share being greater than 50 percent in the case of HYV than for ordinary paddy. In West Bengal it is also observed that the crop-sharing proportion is very much more concentrated on the 50:50 share when fertilizer is *not* used than when it is.

There is also a remarkable association between the crop share and the incidence of cost sharing by the landlord. As table 9.5 shows, when the landlord does not share in the costs, the tenant's crop share is in general higher in all the four states; and, when the landlord shares in the costs, the tenant's crop share is 50 percent or lower. A chi-square test, carried out separately on the data for each state, shows that the association between the landlord's crop share and the existence of cost sharing is significant for all the states except Bihar.

The widespread prevalence of the cost-sharing arrangement as a part of the tenancy contract is a strikingly new phenomenon in Indian agriculture.[4] In West Bengal and Uttar Pradesh two-thirds of the cases report some cost-sharing by the landlords: in Bihar 58 percent of cases and in Orissa 48 percent of cases do so. The phenomenon is, of course, more frequently observed in the "advanced" villages (where tubewells and pumps are used

TABLE 9.4

Difference in crop shares for
ordinary and high-yielding varieties

		Tenants Share of Crops		
State	Crop	Less than 50%	Equal to 50%	More than 50%
(1)	(2)	(3)	(4)	(5)
West Bengal	Paddy (ordinary)	21.4	68.4	10.2
	(HYV)	22.8	61.4	15.8
Bihar	Paddy (ordinary)	12.0	86.4	1.6
	(HYV)	4.2	95.0	0.8
Orissa	Paddy (ordinary)	0.0	88.0	12.0
	(HYV)	0.0	76.0	24.0
Uttar Pradesh	Wheat (ordinary)	17.9	81.4	0.7
	(HYV)	15.5	83.8	0.7

[4] This has been noted by several authors in different parts of India. See, for example, Parthasarathy (1975) for evidence in West Godavari (Andhra Pradesh) and Rao (1975) for evidence in Kota (Rajasthan) and Karnal (Haryana).

TABLE 9.5

Association between cost shares and crop shares

(1)	West Bengal Cost Sharing (%)			Bihar Cost Sharing (%)			Orissa Cost Sharing (%)			Uttar Pradesh Cost Sharing (%)		
	Exists	Does not exist	Total	Exists	Does not exist	Total	Exists	Does not exist	Total	Exists	Does not exist	Total
	(2)	(3)	(4)	(5)	(6)	(7)	(8)	(9)	(10)	(11)	(12)	(13)
Tenant's share less than 50%	98.5	0.5	100.0 (19.0)	65.2	34.8	100.0 (12.0)	0.0	0.0	0.0	96.2	3.8	100.0 (15.6)
Tenant's share and owner's share 50:50	69.4	30.6	100.0 (67.0)	57.8	42.2	100.0 (86.5)	56.5	43.5	100.0 (79.3)	61.4	38.6	100.0 (83.8)
Tenant's share above 50%	10.4	89.6	100.0 (14.0)	33.3	66.7	100.0 (2.5)	16.7	83.3	100.0 (20.7)	0.0	100.0	100.0 (0.6)
Total	66.7	33.3	100.0	58.3	41.7	100.0	48.3	51.7	100.0	66.5	33.5	100.0

NOTE: Figures in parentheses are the percentages of different crop shares.

TABLE 9.6
Frequency distribution of cost shares
Cost Shares (Tenant: Owner)

State	Input	0:1 (0%)	1:3 (25%)	1:2 (33.3%)	8:12 (40%)	18:22 (45%)	1:1 (50%)	2:1 (66.7%)	3:1 (75%)	1:0 (100%)
(1)	(2)	(3)	(4)	(5)	(6)	(7)	(8)	(9)	(10)	(11)
West Bengal	Seed	9.9		1.5	1.2	1.5	36.2			49.17
	Manure	10.2					15.2			74.0
	Fertilizer	9.1					51.7			24.3
Bihar	Seed	6.2					16.7			76.6
	Manure	2.1		0.5			3.6		0.6	93.8
	Fertilizer	2.1					40.1		0.5	31.2
Orissa	Seed									100.0
	Manure									100.0
	Fertilizer						48.3			37.9
Uttar Pradesh	Seed			1.2			36.5			62.3
	Manure	3.6		1.2			6.6			88.6
	Fertilizer	2.4		1.2			44.3	1.2		50.3

NOTE: Row totals do not necessarily add up to 100 because some of the input items, fertilizer in particular, do not get used in all the cases for which sharecropping systems have been reported.

and use of chemical fertilizers and HYV seeds are highly prevalent and/or spreading) in our data set than in other villages.

As for the extent and the pattern of cost sharing, there are many variations. In the traditional arrangements, the tenant is supposed to provide his own labor and his own bullock and plow; the landlord is expected to pay the land taxes as well as irrigation taxes when they exist. With the introduction of new inputs, new crops, and new irrigation devices, however, new cost-sharing arrangements have developed. Table 9.6 shows that while in the overwhelming majority of cases in Bihar, Orissa, and Uttar Pradesh and in half the cases in West Bengal tenants bear all of the costs of seed and manure, 50:50 cost sharing with the landlord is much more common in the case of chemical fertilizers, a new input. There is also evidence that in West Bengal (unlike in Bihar) the use of fertilizer is positively associated with cost sharing not only in fertilizer but also in seed and manure, the incidence of cost sharing of seed and manure being much higher when fertilizer is used than otherwise. In West Bengal some (though not many) cases are observed where the sharing of a paddy byproduct—straw— depends on the sharing of fertilizer costs: if any one of the parties pays for the entire cost of fertilizers, it gets the entire output of straw; if the fertilizer cost is shared, the straw is also shared in the same proportion.

III

Let us now look at some of the contractual terms other than those of crop and cost shares. Thus the tenancy contract is predominantly a short-term contract holding good for a year or less than a year (say, for a crop season). There are indications that the practice of lease for a specific crop and for a specific season is on the increase. Tenancy arrangements which leave all decision making to the tenant, the landlord being interested only in the rent, seem to be far from being typical (except possibly in the case of Bihar), as may be seen from table 9.7. The landlord does not confine himself to supervision of harvesting alone, which, of course, is an activity to which he attaches much importance; quite frequently he participates in making decisions, singly or jointly with the tenant, about such matters as what crops to grow and what inputs to use. This phenomenon is more often observed in the advanced (by our earlier definition) than the backward villages. Harvest sharing and threshing taking place on the landlord's premises (which usually works to the landlord's advantage) is again not always typical: in West Bengal it is observed in slightly less than half of the cases, in Orissa and Uttar Pradesh in considerably less than half of the cases; in Bihar, however, it is observed in about 60 percent of the cases. In the remaining cases harvest sharing and threshing take place either in the field, on the tenant's premises, or in some public place.

The terms and conditions of the tenancy contract are often enmeshed in various social relations between landlords and tenants which are of the

Land Lease

TABLE 9.7

Other particulars of tenancy contracts

Contract Particular	West Bangal %	Bihar %	Orissa %	Uttar Pradesh %
(1)	(2)	(3)	(4)	(5)
Duration of one year	76	53	98	78
Duration less than one year	24	53	20	21
Crop decisions made by owner jointly with tenant or singly	56	29	50	96
Input decisions made by owner jointly with tenant or singly	54	30	46	90
Supervision of harvesting by employer or his representatives	91	89	87	95
Harvest sharing to take place in owner's house	49	58	26	35
Threshing to take place in owner's house	49	61	44	14

nature of dominance and dependence. It is sometimes a common practice in the literature to treat these relations as characteristics of "feudalism" or "semifeudalism". Our survey results, however, suggest that the institution of sharecropping tenancy as it has been evolving in India does not at all conform to the stereotype of the landlord–serf relationship familiar from European or Japanese history. On the contrary, there is a considerable amount of evidence that the institution has been adapting itself more and more to the needs of increasing production and profit by enterprising farmers, both owners and tenants.

First, on the question of freedom of the tenant to enter into tenancy contracts with other landlords. On the basis of the answers of our tenant respondents, it seems it is indeed very rare in any of the four states that the tenant cannot lease in land from more than one landlord. Such instances of the tenant being tied to a particular landlord occur in 4 percent of tenants surveyed in West Bengal, 2 percent in Bihar, 8 percent in Uttar Pradesh and none in Orissa (see table 9.8).

Take again the question of unpaid and obligatory services by the tenant to the landlord, typical of the classical model of feudalism. As seen in table 9.8, 70 percent or more (in Bihar and Uttar Pradesh nearly 80 percent) of the tenants in our survey reported rendering *no* (paid or unpaid) labor services to the landlord. Even among purely landless tenants (who render labor services to the landlord more often than the landed tenants), more than 40 percent (in Uttar Pradesh, about two-thirds) reported rendering no labor service to the landlord. Among those tenants who do work for the landlord, nearly all in the case of Orissa, nearly two-thirds in West Bengal, and nearly half in Bihar reported being "properly" (in the tenant's

TABLE 9.8

Dominance–dependence relations
between landlords and tenants

Relations	West Bengal	Bihar	Orissa	Uttar Pradesh
	Percentages of Respondents			
(1)	(2)	(3)	(4)	(5)
Tenant cannot lease in land from more than one landlord	4	2	0	8
Tenant sells product to landlord	9	3	2	2
Tenant has to render services to landlord against				
Full payment	18	10	28	0
Less than full payment	5	6	2	1
No payment	5	5	0	22
Tenant has to render labor services (fully paid, less than fully paid, or unpaid) for landlords				
Among landed tenants	10	14	19	12
Among landless tenants	52	55	57	34
Among all tenants	28	21	30	23

judgment) paid for the work. In all, a relatively small proportion (10 percent in West Bengal, 11 percent in Bihar, 2 percent in Orissa, and 23 percent in Uttar Pradesh) of all the tenants in our survey reported rendering "unpaid" or "underpaid" services to the landlord.

Another binding constraint of the tenancy contract may be that of the landlord being the principal marketing channel for the tenant's share of the crop. But in our sample this seems to be quite unimportant. In less than 5 percent (in West Bengal, less than 10 percent) of the cases do our tenants report selling their product to their landlords (table 9.8).

IV

A major factor of the tenant's dependence on the landlord works through the former's indebtedness to the latter. The institution of sharecropping tenancy often dovetails in a land-lease contract and a credit contract. This is not unexpected in a situation of inadequately developed credit market: while a poor sharecropper may have few assets acceptable as collateral in the outside credit market, his landlord would accept the tenancy contract itself as collateral. The landlord has the incentive to supply production credit (since he shares in the outcome of its use) and also is in the best position to enforce repayment (of both production and consumption loans) at the time of harvest sharing.

TABLE 9.9

*Incidence of consumption loans to tenants by landlords
with and without interest*

State	Percentage of Tenants Taking Consumption Loans from Landlords		
	With interest	Without interest	Total
(1)	(2)	(3)	(4)
West Bengal	28	23	51
Bihar	48	2	50
Orissa	46	2	48
Uttar Pradesh	48	6	54

In our surveyed villages the landlord is undoubtedly an important, though not the only source of credit to his tenant. Tables 9.9 and 9.10 indicate that about half of all the tenants reported taking consumption loans (as well as general purpose loans for ceremonial expenditures, etc.) from their landlords. In West Bengal nearly half of these consumption loans are interest-free; however, the proportion is much lower in the other states.

Some recent theorists of "semi-feudalism" would have us believe that in the landlord–tenant relationship usury dominates as the mode of exploitation and the landlord's considerations of usurious income from the indebted tenant dampens his incentive to increase production through productive investments.[5] It is obviously difficult to test this hypothesis directly from empirical data: the same phenomenon of adoption or

TABLE 9.10

Incidence of general purpose loans to tenants with and without interest

State	Percentage of Tenants Taking General Loans from Landlords		
	With interest	Without interest	Total
(1)	(2)	(3)	(4)
West Bengal	50	5	55
Bihar	57	1	58
Orissa	35	4	39
Uttar Pradesh	55	3	58

[5] See, for example, Bhaduri (1973).

TABLE 9.11

Association between cost shares and owners giving production loans to tenants

(1)	West Bengal Cost Sharing (%)			Bihar Cost Sharing (%)			Orissa Cost Sharing (%)			Uttar Pradesh Cost Sharing (%)		
	Exists	Does not exist	Total	Exists	Does not exist	Total	Exists	Does not exist	Total	Exists	Does not exist	Total
	(2)	(3)	(4)	(5)	(6)	(7)	(8)	(9)	(10)	(11)	(12)	(13)
Owners giving production loans to tenants	84.4	15.6	100.0 (42.9)	81.8	18.2	100.0 (28.7)	55.9	44.1	100.0 (58.6)	61.0	39.0	100.0 (35.3)
Owners not giving production loans to tenants	53.3	46.7	100.0 (57.1)	48.9	51.1	100.0 (71.3)	37.5	62.5	100.0 (41.4)	69.4	30.6	100.0 (64.7)
Total	66.7	33.3	100.0	58.3	41.7	100.0	48.3	51.7	100.0	66.5	33.5	100.0

NOTE: Parentheses indicate column percentages.

nonadoption of yield-increasing innovations may have various explanations quite different from that implied in the hypothesis. All we can say is that the indirect evidence from our large-scale survey in north India is not at all consistent with this hypothesis.

In our survey, we asked the tenants about the principal occupation (in terms of income source) of their landlords. In our sample of 109 villages reporting tenancy in West Bengal, *not a single* tenant reported money lending as a principal occupation of his landlord. In the overwhelming majority of cases the tenant reported self-cultivation as the principal occupation of his landlord. What is more important to note for our present purpose is that in 43 percent of cases in West Bengal, 59 percent of cases in Orissa, 35 percent of cases in Uttar Pradesh, and 29 percent of cases in Bihar the landlord gives advances to the tenant to meet his production needs of seeds, fertilizers, etc. (see table 9.11). In West Bengal and Orissa, about half of these cases of tenants receiving production loans from landlords were reported to be interest free (see table 9.12). The common practice is for the advance to be paid by the landlord in kind in the form of fertilizers, seeds, etc., and to be repaid by the tenant in terms of grains at the time of harvest. One also observes in table 9.11 a positive association between cost sharing and giving of production loans by the landlord in West Bengal, Bihar, and Orissa. A chi-square test carried out on the data suggests a highly significant association in West Bengal and Bihar. Production loan as well as cost sharing obviously indicate a strong interest on the part of the landlord in productive investment on the tenant farm. On their self-cultivated land, 60 to 70 percent of the landlords of our tenant-respondents are reported as using HYV seeds and chemical fertilizers (see table 9.13). All this is a far cry from usurious landlords uninterested in productive investments.

In the literature on production relations it has become an uncritically

TABLE 9.12

Incidence of production loans to tenants by landlords with and without interest

State	Percentage of Tenants Taking Production Loans from Landlords		
	With interest	Without interest	Total
(1)	(2)	(3)	(4)
West Bengal	21	23	44
Bihar	26	15	41
Orissa	30	27	57
Uttar Pradesh	34	8	42

TABLE 9.13

Landlords of tenants making productive and unproductive investments

	Percentage of Landlords				
State	Using chemical fertilizers	Using HYV seeds	Principal occupation: self-cultivation	Buying grains from tenants	Giving loans to poor peasants other than own tenants
(1)	(2)	(3)	(4)	(5)	(6)
West Bengal	62	59	62	19	38
Bihar	68	63	72	11	25
Orissa	61	61	72	2	33
Uttar Pradesh	73	68	82	2	56

accepted habit of thought to equate tenancy with feudalism and indebtedness by poor peasants to their landlords with debt-bondage. This has been a source of considerable confusion in the recent discussion on modes of production. First of all, in most regions tenancy involves only a relatively small part of agriculture—less than 20 percent of all cultivated area is under tenancy in the four states of north India under our consideration, according to estimates from 1970–71 NSS Land Holdings Survey data. Moreover, a substantial proportion of area under tenancy is leased by enterprising farmers who already are large owners of land (sometimes leasing land from small landowners). But even in villages where the institution of tenancy is important and where many poor tenants enter into land-lease, labor, and credit relationship with their landlords, our survey results indicate that the institution as it operates is far from being anything akin to feudalism by most accepted definitions of the term. It is commonly agreed that one essential feature of feudal relationship is associated with the appropriation of surplus in the form of unpaid labor services and other obligatory payments by primarily rentier landlords through *extraeconomic coercion*, that is, through various social and politico-legal compulsions. In our surveyed villages, unpaid and obligatory service by the tenant for the landlord is quite uncommon; even less common is the phenomenon of a tenant being tied to any particular landlord. The landlord quite often (though certainly not always) gives production loans to the tenant, shares in costs of seeds, fertilizers, etc., participates in decision making about the use of these inputs, and in general takes a lot of interest in productive investments on the tenant farm (as well as on his self-cultivated land), quite contrary to the prevailing image of rentier or usurious landlords. Needless to say, desperate conditions of poverty and underemployment often afflict the small sharecropper and push him into unequal relationships of mutual dependence with the landlord-creditor-employer. But, surely, unequal contracts giving rise to economic dependence–dominance relationships are not distinguishing features of feudalism as opposed to other modes of production.

CHAPTER 10

Cross-Section Variations in the Extent of Tenancy

I

In chapters 7 and 8 we have discussed some factors in the abstract which are likely to affect contractual choice in land cultivation. In chapter 9 we have gone to the other pole of describing the details of terms and conditions of actual tenancy contracts from a primary survey of villages we have carried out in north and east India. This chapter turns to tne large body of cross-section evidence available from some secondary sources in different parts of India on broad magnitudes (like the proportion of cultivated area under tenancy—we shall call this variable LSPROP) but without many details about the terms of the lease contracts and examines whether statistically some patterns can be deciphered in the variations of these magnitudes and whether those patterns are economically meaningful.

This clearly is a hazardous exercise, much more than that involved in our analysis of cross-section variations in agricultural wage rates in chapter 4. Tenancy as an institution has complex historical, sociological, political, and legal dimensions, and variations in a statistical magnitude like the area under tenancy cannot capture the qualitative nuances associated with them. Even in narrow economic terms, the same value of LSPROP may have different economic implications if the terms and conditions of the tenancy contract are different. In addition, there is the inevitable statistical problem of underreporting of tenancy in the data particularly on account of protective tenancy legislation.[1] All this should be borne in mind in evaluating the empirical exercises in this (and the next) chapter. It should also be remembered that the tenancy variable is meant to be nothing more than a very crude proxy in the absence of better information.

Regional variations in LSPROP are indeed substantial. Taking the NSS agroclimatic regions in India, it varies from 1.23 percent in Saurashtra region of Gujarat to 53.86 percent in the Coastal and Ghats region of Karnataka, according to the 1971–72 Land Holdings Survey. It is relatively high in Assam, Punjab, Haryana, West Bengal (except in the western plains region), Himalayan and southern Uttar Pradesh, Bihar (except southern region), coastal Orissa, coastal southern Tamil Nadu, and coastal and

---

[1]All the data on LSPROP in this chapter refer to area reported as leased *in* by the tenant respondent, rather than area leased *out* by the landlord respondent. The extent of underreporting, on account of tenancy legislation, is usually larger for the latter than for the former.

northern inland Karnataka. It is very low in Gujarat (except in the northern plains region), Rajasthan (particularly in southern and western regions), inland western Maharashtra, and Jhelum Valley of Kashmir. The aim in this chapter is to indicate some of the economic, demographic, and technological factors that may partially explain these variations. Since our theoretical analysis of the influence of these factors on tenancy contracts is conducted at the micro level, there are difficulties in transferring the results of that analysis to the macro level of aggregative tenancy in an NSS region or a State. We, therefore, also consider variations in individual household-level data on tenancy (from the Farm Management Survey as well as NSS). But some of the ecological, demographic, and institutional factors are much more divergent across broad regions than across households within a homogeneous region, so a cross-sectional statistical analysis may be able to capture the effects of these factors more clearly at the level where the divergences are sharper. This empirical exercise is thus conducted at both levels of aggregation.

Chapter 7 suggests that tenancy is an economic response to inadequacies and imperfections of various markets linked to agriculture. One major problem that any empirical exercise in this area will face is that it is impossible to get "hard" quantitative evidence on the *extent* of these market failures which could be statistically related to variations in tenancy. We are therefore compelled to confine our attention in this chapter to technological and demographic variables on which there is somewhat more information. Does one expect higher or lower incidence of tenancy in areas of higher rainfall or better irrigation or lower production uncertainty or higher unemployment or more labor-intensive crops and methods of cultivation? We first formulate a simple model designed to show why in cases of all of the latter ecological-technological-demographic conditions the extent of tenancy may be expected to be *higher*, other things remaining the same, and then try to test these hypotheses with the cross-section evidence.

This section describes the main building blocks of the theoretical model in this chapter. There are two seasons in the crop cycle: season 1 for land preparation, sowing, interculture, etc.; and season 2 for harvesting. Land and labor (and, in one variant of the model, fertilizers) produce "seedlings" at the end of season 1; "seedlings" and labor produce crop output at the end of season 2. There is thus complementarity in production in the two seasons. The seasonal distinction is also important from the point of view of the conditions in the various input markets. Take, for example, the labor market. Season 1 also happens to be in part what is known as a "lean" season. In this season the market wage rate does not clear the labor market and there is unemployment. On the other hand, in season 2, which coincides with the "peak" season, there is full employment and the wage rate is competitively determined. (We are abstracting from the effects of labor market imperfections in peak season and of labor-tying that we discussed in earlier chapters.)

The seasonal distinction is also important because of the nature of the credit market. The landless tenant is dependent on the landlord for credit to finance his subsistence consumption in the lean season, and he pays back the loan along with interest at the end of the harvest. Since the interest rates are usually very high, it matters a great deal as to how long one has to wait until income accrues. For example, the landless tenant knows that, as a wage laborer (provided he is lucky to get employment), he can get some wage income immediately in season 1, whereas as a tenant he has to wait until the crop is harvested in season 2. The landlord also notices that if he increases his hiring of labor in season 1, he thereby reduces the credit needs of his borrowers.

In the land-lease market we can assume that there is a conventional (commonly 50:50) crop share[2] and at that rental rate the landlord decides how much land to lease out to sharecroppers. The latter do not participate in this decision. This reflects some monopoly power on the part of the landlord, which is not unrealistic in the general context of acute tenurial insecurity, heavy demographic pressure on land, and a highly skewed distribution in its ownership.

Suppose $Q(BA, L)$ is the number of seedlings produced at the end of season 1 on the landlord's farm. In this production he uses L amount of labor (entirely hired) and A amount of land acreage. B is a land-augmenting improvement factor.[3] The total area owned by the landlord, $\bar{A}$, is given, and out of this he leases out A_t and $A(=\bar{A} - A_t)$ is what remains with him for cultivation. $Q_t(BA_t, L_t)$ is, similarly, the number of seedlings produced at the end of season 1 on the sharecropping tenant's farm, and L_t is the amount of labor the sharecropper uses on his farm in season 1. For simplification we can assume that the seedlings production functions, Q and Q_t, are similar and that both display constant returns to scale with changes in effective acreage and labor (ignoring the tendency toward corner solutions that constant return to scale generate in models of sharecropping.)

Notice that we have used the same land-augmenting factor B in both the production functions. To the extent the land improvement term refers to natural fertility factors, we are assuming that the land on the landlord and

In order to avoid cumbersomeness we assume for the theoretical model that all tenancy takes the form of sharecropping. The model in the next chapter incorporates the other major form of tenancy, renting at a fixed rate per acre. We consider production uncertainty later in this chapter.

[3] In the traditional agriculture of densely populated peasant economies, most important forms of technical progress tend to increase the effective supply of land. See, for example, Ishikawa (1967) and Hayami and Ruttan (1971). At any rate, the Indian data that we have used in our subsequent empirical analysis relate mostly to a period or areas where use of labor-saving machinery in agriculture was not very significant. The chemical-biological breakthrough in production with the use of high-yielding variety of seeds, chemical fertilizers, pesticides, etc.—the so-called green revolution—has been largely land augmenting in nature. In section III there will be comment on the impact of introducing labor-saving changes in this model.

the tenant farms is homogeneous with respect to soil rating, rainfall, evapotranspiration rates, etc. To the extent the land improvement factor is due to public irrigation, assuming the same B implies that both the tenant and the landlord have equal access to such irrigation. To the extent the land-augmenting technical progress is due to adoption of high-yielding varieties of seeds, etc., assuming the same B implies that both the tenant and the landlord have equal access to the seeds and to the requisite knowledge. Later in this chapter I shall comment on the cases in which there are landlord–tenant differences in the land-augmenting improvement factor due to unequal access either to irrigation facilities (the insecure tenant may be uninterested in digging field channels or investing in tubewells) or to new varieties (due to, say, maket imperfections particularly in credit).

With the use of harvesting labor seedlings produce output, say, in fixed proportions. Let us suppose one unit of seedlings ends up in one unit of crop harvest. We can now write the landlord's income at the *end* of the crop cycle as

$$Y = [1 - \beta w_2] Q(BA, L) + rQ_t(BA_t, L_t) + iC - (1 + i)w_1 L \qquad 10.1$$

In equation 10.1, r is the conventional crop share, i the interest rate (per season), w_1 the given wage rate in season 1, and w_2 the competitively determined wage rate in season 2, β the amount of harvesting labor used per unit of seedling, and C the given subsistence consumption of the tenant family that the landlord finances with credit. The landlord thus has three sources of income: rental income from leased-out land; income from self-operated land net of wages paid in season 1 and 2; and interest income. There is only one final commodity in this model, and all rental, wage, and interest payments are in terms of this commodity.

The tenant's income at the end of the crop cycle is given by

$$Y_t = (1 - r) Q_t(BA_t, L_t) + (1 + i)w_1 \mu(1 - L_t) + w_2(1 - \beta Q_t) - iC \qquad 10.2$$

As indicated before, in lean season 1 the wage rate w_1 does not clear the labor market. In that season the tenant is prepared to supply $(1 - L_t)$ amount of wage labor but expects only a fraction, μ, of it to get wage employment on the landlord farm and the rest to be unemployed. In both seasons the total number of potential workers in the tenant family is given at unity. It is assumed for simplification that the tenant does not own any land of his own.[4] The landlord maximizes Y with respect to his decision variables, A_t and L (assuming that he cannot control the tenant's use of labor intensity per acre, a_t) and gets the necessary conditions of interior maximum as follows:

$$r \frac{q_t}{a_t}(a_t) - [1 - \beta w_2] q'(a) = 0 \qquad 10.3$$

---

[4] We shall later comment on the effect of owned land on the extent of area leased in.

$$[1-\beta w_2][q(a)-q'(a)a]-(1+i)w_1=0, \qquad 10.4$$

where q and q_t are the average productivities of labor in season 1 and $a(=BA/L)$ and $a_t(=BA_t/L_t)$ are the effective land–labor ratios in season 1 on the landlord and tenant farms respectively. If marginal productivity of each factor is diminishing, the Jacobian, J, of equations 10.3 and 10.4 is positive and the second-order condition of maximization are satisfied. From 10.3 and 10.4,

$$\frac{\partial A_t}{\partial w_2}=-\frac{\beta}{J}[1-\beta w_2]\,\frac{a}{L}\,\,q(a)q''(a)>0 \qquad 10.5$$

$$\frac{\partial L}{\partial w_2}=[\frac{\beta}{J}]\,\frac{-r(q_t-q_t'a_t)}{a_t\,A_t}\,[q(a)-q'(a)a]+[1-\beta w_2][\frac{a}{A}q(a)q''(a)]<0 \quad 10.6$$

As expected, a higher harvesting wage, other things remaining the same, makes the landlord hire fewer laborers in seedlings production and induces him to lease out more land.

The tenant maximizes his income, Y_t, with respect to his only decision variable, L_t, and gets as a necessary condition of interior maximum:

$$\mu(1+i)w_1-(1-r-\beta w_2)[q_t(a_t)-q_t'(a_t)a_t]=0. \qquad 10.7$$

Note that in the interior $(1-r-\beta w_2)$ has to be positive (which is generally the case with r at 50 percent and βw_2—the share of harvest paid as wages—usually not more than 10 or 12 percent). This implies in equation 10.3 that

$$\frac{q_t}{a_t}(a_t)>q'(a), \qquad 10.8$$

10.8 is consistent with $a_t \gtrless a$, even if production functions Q and Q_t are similar. In this model the standard effects of output sharing tend to raise a_t above a, while the effect of unemployment tends to lower it.

In peak season 2 there is full employment so that

$$\beta Q(BA,L)=1-\beta Q_t(BA_t,L_t), \qquad 10.9$$

where the left-hand side represents the demand[5] for wage labor for harvesting on the landlord's farm and the right-hand side the corresponding supply. Equation 10.9 determines the equilibrium harvesting wage rate, w_2. Using 10.5 and 10.6 in 10.9, we can see that the demand for wage labor for harvesting is a declining function of the harvesting wage, given L_t. Also, L_t is a declining function of w_2 from equation 10.7. But the supply of wage labor for harvesting—the right-hand

[5] We assume that the landlord is a monopolist in the land-lease market but not in the labor market where the harvesting wage is determined. The landlord recognizes himself as only one of the many demanders of labor in the harvesting season. Demand for labor by others has been suppressed from equation 10.9, but if we introduce on the left-hand side of equation 10.9 a term $D(w_2)$ to represent the net demand for labor by others with usual properties, our subsequent results do not change.

side of 10.9—may or may not be an increasing function of the wage rate, w_2 (because a higher w_2, by inducing more leasing out on the part of the landlord, increases tenant output of seedlings and therefore labor required for harvesting them on the tenant farm). For the standard Walrasian stability (and uniqueness) condition to be satisfied, we need

$$K = \frac{\partial[Q+Q_t]}{\partial w_2} = B\frac{\partial A_t}{\partial w_2}(q_t'-q') + (q-q'a)\frac{\partial L}{\partial w_2} + (q_t-q_t'a_t)\frac{\partial L_t}{\partial w_2} < 0$$

10.10

But of the three terms on the right-hand side of equation 10.10, the last two are negative and the first is uncertain. Let us assume this stability condition to be satisfied.

III

Given the basic model in section II, let us now work out some comparative-static propositions. Let us first carry out a parametric variation in the land-augmenting improvement factor, B.

From equations 10.3 and 10.4, after simplification,

$$\frac{\partial A_t}{\partial B} = -\frac{A_t}{B}$$

10.12

$$\frac{\partial L}{\partial B} = \frac{\bar{A}}{a}$$

10.13

Using 10.12 and 10.13 in the equilibrium condition 10.9,

$$\frac{dw_2}{dB} = -\frac{1}{K}\left[\frac{q}{a}\bar{A} + 2\frac{A_t}{a_t}(q_t - q_t'a_t)\right] > 0.$$

10.14

So an increase in the land-augmenting improvement factor increases the equilibrium harvesting wage rate.

Now,

$$\frac{dA_t}{dB} = \frac{\partial A_t}{\partial B} + \frac{\partial A_t}{\partial w_2}\frac{dw_2}{dB}$$

10.15

10.15 indicating the two conflicting influences of land-augmenting agricultural progress on the extent of land leased out by the landlord: $\partial A_t/\partial B$ being negative or self-cultivation being more profitable, the landlord tends to lease out *less* at constant, w_2, the harvesting wage rate; but the harvesting wage rate does not remain constant, it actually goes up, which induces the landlord to self-cultivate less and lease out more. Using 10.5, 10.12, and 10.14, we can see that the latter effect will dominate and dA_t/dB is positive under the *sufficient* conditions that the elasticity of substitution does not exceed unity and that the labor elasticity of output on the sharecropper's farm is small enough,[6] which is not unrealistic to assume for a peasant economy. In that case land-augmenting improvement in our model leads to a higher percentage of area under tenancy.

This is for the case when the land improvement parameter, B, is the same for both landlord and tenant farms. But as we have indicated in the preceding section the landlord and the tenant may have unequal access (or incentive) to land improvement. This will tend to modify our result. Take the extreme case when B appears as before in the landlord's production function $Q(BA, L)$, but disappears altogether from $Q_t(A_t, L_t)$, the tenant's production function. Reworking equations 10.3 through 10.15, it turns out that even in this case dA_t/dB is positive, if the elasticities of substitution are very small.

Suppose, however, that land-augmenting technical progress (say, in the form of high-yielding varieties of seeds) requires the purchase of some current inputs or services (like chemical fertilizers, water from tubewells, or renting the service of a pumpset) *and* the market for the latter is imperfect (may be because the landlord has better connections and access to the government-subsidized distribution of fertilizers or because the landless tenant has fewer channels of cheap credit open to him with which to buy these inputs) so that the landlord has a differential advantage over the tenant. In this case it is easy to prove that the larger the degree of imperfection in the market for these inputs, the lower the percentage of area under tenancy, other things remaining the same (unless the landless takes part in cost sharing, which we ignore in this chapter).

Now let us take up the case in which there is a parametric variation in β, the harvesting labor coefficient. From equations 10.3, 10.4, and 10.7,

$$\frac{\partial A_t}{\partial \beta} = \frac{\partial A_t}{\partial w_2} \frac{w_2}{\beta} > 0. \tag{10.16}$$

$$\frac{\partial L}{\partial \beta} = \frac{\partial L}{\partial w_2} \frac{w_2}{\beta} < 0. \tag{10.17}$$

$$\frac{\partial L_t}{\partial \beta} = \frac{\partial L_t}{\partial w_2} \frac{w_2}{\beta} < 0. \tag{10.18}$$

From the equilibrium condition 10.9,

$$\frac{dw_2}{d\beta} = -\frac{B(q_t'-q')\dfrac{\partial A_t}{\partial \beta} + (q-q'a)\dfrac{\partial L}{\partial \beta} + \dfrac{(Q+Q_t)}{\beta} + (q_t - q_t'a_t)\dfrac{\partial L_t}{\partial \beta}}{K} \tag{10.19}$$

---

[6] For example, if production functions are Cobb–Douglas, rental share is 50 percent, and share of harvest paid as wages does not exceed 25 percent, any value of the labor elasticity of output of "seedlings" less than or equal to 0.75 is sufficient for our result. In the development literature the labor elasticity of output in peasant agriculture (in the lean season) is often put at a much lower value, sometimes even at zero.

Using 10.16, 10.17, 10.18, and 10.19 and that K is negative as a stability condition,

$$\frac{dA_t}{d\beta} = \frac{\partial A_t}{\partial \beta} + \frac{\partial A_t}{\partial w_2} \cdot \frac{dw_2}{d\beta} = -\frac{\partial A_t}{\partial w_2} \frac{(Q+Q_t)}{\beta K} > 0, \qquad 10.20$$

implying that an increase in the harvesting labor coefficient β *increases* the percentage of area under tenancy in equilibrium, other things remaining the same. This suggests that tenancy would be larger in areas where the crop is more labor-intensive. Alternatively, if there is a labor-saving technical change reducing the harvesting labor requirement per unit of output, tenancy will tend to decline.[7]

Similarly, if the parametric variation is in μ—the objective probability of getting wage employment for the tenant in the lean season—it is easy to see from 10.3 and 10.4 that $\partial A_t/\partial \mu = \partial L/\partial \mu = 0$ and $\partial L_t/\partial \mu$ is negative, and that $dA_t/d\mu$ is negative. In other words, the larger the extent of unemployment in the lean season, the higher the incidence of tenancy.

We now briefly introduce production uncertainty (say, due to vagaries of weather) and consider the impact of a parametric variation in the riskiness of output on the extent of tenancy. We shall consider only the simpler multiplicative form of uncertainty so that $G(u)Q(BA, L)$ is the production function on the landlord's farm,[8] with u as the random variable representing some index of weather; similarly $G(u)Q_t(BA_t, L)$ is the production function on the tenant farm. If the landlord maximizes his expected utility function with respect to A_t and L, he gets as necessary conditions for an interior maximum equation 10.3 as before and, instead of equation 10.4,

$$EU'(Y)[(1-\beta w_2)[q(a)-q'(a)a]G(u)-w_1(1+i)]=0, \qquad 10.21$$

where E is an expectation operator and U is the utility function. Similarly, on the tenant side, instead of equation 10.7, we now have

$$EU'(Y_t)[(1-r-\beta w_2)\{q_t(a_t)-q_t'(a_t)a_t\}G(u)-\mu w_1(1+i)]=0. \qquad (10.22)$$

The equilibrium condition determining w_2 is given, as before, by 10.9—with the difference that $G(u)$ is appended to the production functions—and we shall take this equilibrium to be unique and stable.

Let us define an increase in the riskiness of output in the Rothschild-Stiglitz (1971) sense of a "mean-preserving spread" It is then relatively easy to show with the use of equations 10.3, 10.9, 10.21, and 10.22 that an increase in production uncertainty induces the landlord to lease out more at a given wage rate, w_2, under the sufficient condition that the degree of

---

[7] This is consistent with the observation by Day (1967) that large-scale mechanization substituting for handpicking of corn and cotton contributed to a rapid decline in sharecropping in the Mississippi Delta.

[8] We shall assume that the production uncertainty is only for season 1; by the time the harvesting season comes the uncertainty is over (this ignores, for example, the possibility of unseasonal rain or hail damaging the ripe crop).

absolute risk aversion does not increase as income increases; under a similar condition on the tenant's utility function, an increase in production uncertainty induces him to go more for wage labor at the same wage rate, w_2.[9] But the equilibrium wage rate itself changes, and in general it is quite cumbersome to find out which of these conflicting forces prevail. But it is easy to show that in the special case when the landlord is risk-neutral and the tenant is risk-averse, an increase in production uncertainty *reduces* the equilibrium percentage of area under tenancy.

IV

Summarizing the comparative-static propositions of section III, we have shown under the conditions in our model that:

(A) LSPROP, the percentage of area under tenancy, will be higher in areas where the land improvement factor is larger (i.e., soil fertility, rainfall, irrigation, etc., is better);

(B) lower production uncertainty increases LSPROP;

(C) the larger the labor intensity of the crop harvested, the higher the LSPROP (alternatively, if there is a labor-saving technical change reducing the harvesting labor requirement, say, through the introduction of harvesters, tenancy will decline);

(D) the larger the extent of unemployment in wage labor market facing the landless households, the higher the extent of tenancy.

We should note that in the case of irrigation particularly from relatively secure sources (like canals or tubewells) our propositions A and B should go together, since such irrigation improves land as well as protects against weather fluctuations.

Proposition C is strengthened by the consideration, not included in the model above but emphasized in chapter 7, that the more labor-intensive the agricultural operation, the more serious the labor supervision problem under wage contracts, making tenancy a more attractive option for the landlord. Another issue raised in chapter 7 is that the tenancy contract serves the purpose of enabling a fuller utilization of the nonmarketable or not easily marketable resources of the potential tenant family (like family labor, particularly female and child labor, given the various social and economic constraints on their participation in the wage labor market, and draft animal labor, when the market for animal labor renting is not active). This suggests an additional proposition:

(E) LSPROP, the percentage of area under tenancy, is likely to be higher for households with relatively plentiful endowments of family labor or draft animals.

[9] In this model, even though we have not introduced any independent source of wage uncertainty, an increase in output uncertainty itself, by affecting demand for and supply of wage labor, changes the equilibrium wage rate.

The model in the preceding sections of this chapter has assumed, for simplification, that the tenant family is landless. In reality the majority of tenants are landed. According to NSS Land Holdings Survey data, in 1970–71 in all the States in India (except Kerala and, marginally, Karnataka), more than 80 percent of the holdings reporting area under tenancy were cultivated by landed tenants (even though they are often small owners, particularly in the densely populated areas of East and South India). So the question arises as to what relationship one expects between LSPROP for a household and its owned area. The answer is not clear-cut. For reasons mentioned in chapter 7 (such as the larger size of the tenant's owned land, giving him more access to entrepreneurial and capital resources), landlords may prefer wealthier tenants; on the other hand, the smaller peasant may be facing more unemployment and may have a larger supply of underutilized family labor, both tending to raise LSPROP for him, according to propositions D and E above. Besides, socially and politically, the landlord may have less fear (of the tenant acquiring rights on the land) if he leases out to a smaller tenant, over whom he may have more control.

We shall now carry out a statistical analysis of the cross-section evidence to test some of the hypotheses enunciated in the preceding paragraphs in this section. We shall use four alternative sets of cross-section data, the first two at the individual household level, the third at the level of NSS agroclimatic regions, and the fourth at the aggregative level of states. The first set relates to the detailed NSS 1977–78 data for individual cultivator households in rural West Bengal. The mean value of LSPROP for this set is about 14 percent with a standard deviation of 27.9 percent. Table 10.1 presents the regression results. LSPROP is positively and significantly related to IRRCULT, the percentage of cultivated area irrigated for the household,[10] and the district-level indices of normal rainfall (RAIN) and foodgrain productivity (YHA). This suggests that the percentage of area under tenancy is positively linked to what we have called the land improvement factor, consistent with proposition A above. VAR is a district-level index of the variation of agriculture output around the trend line over the preceding 18 years: for our purpose this may serve as a proxy for production uncertainty. The significant negative association between LSPROP and VAR is, therefore, consistent with proposition B. LSPROP is positively associated with the number of economically active family members, male (ACTMALE) and female (ACTFEM), pointing to proposition E. We have noted that the relation between LSPROP and the size of the household's owned area (OWNED) is not clear-cut a priori. In the regression equation OWNED has a significant negative sign, suggesting that small owners have a larger percentage of area under tenancy, but the

---

[10] Since we do not have data on the effectiveness of particular types of irrigation, IRRCULT is at best a crude proxy for land improvement due to irrigation. The same applies for IRRP in tables 10.3 and 10.5.

TABLE 10.1

Linear regression analysis of determinants of percentage of area under tenancy in cultivator households, rural West Bengal, 1977–78

Dependent Variable:	LSPROP (proportion of cultivated area leased)	
Mean:	0.1399	
Standard Deviation:	0.2786	

Explanatory Variables	Regression Coefficients	Standard Error	Significant at Percent Level
RAIN (normal annual rainfall in district in meters)	0.0521	0.0086	0.0
YHA (yield in tons per hectare of foodgrains in the district)†	0.0873	0.0252	0.1
VAR (variation in agricultural output in the district)††	−0.1081	0.0377	0.4
OWNED (area owned by household)	−0.0772	0.0033	0.0
(OWNED)^2	0.0028	0.0002	0.0
IRRCULT (percentage of cultivated area irrigated)	0.0457	0.0167	0.6
ACTMALE (no. of economically active males in household)	0.0496	0.0049	0.0
ACTFEM (no. of economically active females in household)	0.0183	0.0101	7.1
SCHCASTE (dummy for scheduled caste)	0.0219	0.0133	10.0
Constant term	−0.1452	0.0715	4.2

$R^2 = 0.2541$; $F = 69.7$; no. of observations $= 2,264$

SOURCE: Data for RAIN, YHA, and VAR at the district level are from the *Statistical Abstract of West Bengal.* Data for all other variables are from NSS, 32nd Round, Employment and Unemployment Survey.

†Since the yield data for all agricultural output for 1977–78 were not available, YHA relates only to foodgrains.

††Computed by taking the district agricultural output figures for eighteen years between 1960–61 and 1977–78, fitting a regression line to estimate the rate of growth of output, and then looking at the residual sum of squares of that regression to derive an index of the variation of output around the trend for each district.

quadratic term has a positive coefficient, indicating that the relationship gets reversed after a point. The positive relationship between LSPROP and scheduled caste status probably indicates the sociological fact that upper-caste households tend to lease out rather than directly cultivate their land.

The next data set relates to Farm Management Survey data for 150 individual farms in Hooghly (West Bengal) in 1970–71. The mean value of LSPROP is 28 percent with a standard deviation of 35.47 percent. Table 10.2 presents the regression results. Again, LSPROP is positively and significantly associated with an irrigation variable (the percentage of leased-in area irrigated from secure sources like canals and tubewells) and

TABLE 10.2

Linear regression analysis of determinants of percentage of area under tenancy on sample farms, Hooghly, 1970–71

Dependent Variable:	LSPROP[†]
Mean:	0.2801
Standard Deviation:	0.3547

Explanatory Variables[†]	Regression Coefficients	Standard Error	Significant at Percent Level
OWNED	−0.1331	0.0240	0.0
(OWNED)^2	0.0091	0.0022	0.0
ADCULT (number of adult cultivators in family)[††]	0.0431	0.0180	1.8
CTIRLS (percentage of leased-in area irrigated from canals and tubewells)	0.5544	0.0918	0.0
OBKPA (owned bullock labor days used per acre of cultivated area under paddy)	0.0067	0.0025	0.7
Constant term	0.2856	0.0436	0.0
$R^2 = 0.4250$; F = 21.3; no. of observations = 149			

SOURCE: Farm Management Survey for Hooghly in 1970–71.
[†] LSPROP refers to *net* leased-in area. Also see table 10.1 or Glossary of Variables.
[††] Earners in family with cultivation as main occupation.

the number of active family members (adults with cultivation as main occupation), consistent with propositions A, B, and E. Again, OWNED has a significant negative sign, but the quadratic term has a positive coefficient, indicating a reversal in the direction of the initial relationship between OWNED and LSPROP. Finally, LSPROP has a positive and significant relationship with OBKPA, the number of owned bullock labor days used by the farm per acre of cultivated area under paddy (the main crop). This indicates that farms with more bullock labor per acre get more tenancy, consistent with proposition E.

The third set of data relates to 53 NSS agroclimatic regions and is, therefore, at a much more aggregative level than that of the household or the farm. Table 10.3 presents the regression results. Again, consistent with proposition A, LSPPROP is positively and significantly associated with land improvement factors, like normal annual rainfall, percentage of area irrigated, and index of soil rating. In general, the high-rainfall areas are also associated with the preponderance of highly labor-intensive crops, like rice or jute. This indirectly suggests consistency with proposition C.

Finally, the inter State cross-section data for India in the early 1950s is presented in table 10.4 and the regression results in table 10.5. Again, LSPROP is positively and significantly associated with the percentage of cropped area irrigated (consistent with proposition A, and with RICEP, the proportion of cropped area under rice, *ragi*, jute, and barley (the most

TABLE 10.3

Linear regression analysis of determinants of percentage of area under tenancy across 53 regions, rural India, 1970–71

	Dependent Variable:	LSPROP†	
	Mean:	12.71 percent	
	Standard Deviation:	9.12 percent	

Explanatory Variables	Regression Coefficient	Standard Error	Significant at Percent Level
NRAIN (normal annual rainfall in region in meters)	0.0062	0.0015	0.0
SOIL (index of soil rating of land in region)	0.2430	0.1438	9.8
IRRP (percentage of area irrigated in region)	0.2770	0.0895	0.3
Constant term	−14.3349	8.3755	9.3
$R^2 = 0.3872$; $F = 10.3$; no. of observations $= 53$			

SOURCE: Data for LSPROP: NSS, Land Holdings Survey, 26th Round. Region-level estimates for NRAIN have been worked out after taking simple averages of district-level data given in the *Season and Crop Reports*. SOIL has been similarly computed after taking averages of the district-level indices prepared by K. B. Shome and S. P. Raychaudhuri and reported in *Reserve Bank of India Bulletin*, October 1969. IRRP for each region is taken as the area of owned irrigated land as percentage of total owned land as of June 30, 1971, as reported in Reserve Bank of India, All-India Debt and Investment Survey.

NOTE: Some regions had to be left out for lack of data on at least one variable.
†See table 10.1.

labor-intensive crops in the Indian cropping pattern),[11] thus indicating consistency with proposition C. LSPROP is positively associated with UNEMD, the average number of days in the year that males in agricultural labor households remain unemployed. Although our focus is on the tenant households, it is very likely that in areas where UNEMD is high (or low), the prospect of unemployment on wage work for our tenant households is also correspondingly high (or low). This indicates indirect consistency with proposition D. Table 10.5 also shows a negative relationship between LSPROP and EJECTP, the proportion of total leased-in area in which the tenant, under the existing contract (usually oral), could be evicted at will by the landlord. One possible interpretation is that high tenurial insecurity, by adversely affecting the tenant's incentives for long-term improvements on land, has a negative relationship with tenancy.

Let us now add a general comment on the significant positive relation

[11] National Sample Survey Report no. 170 gives data on human labor days utilized per acre for a number of crops. Except for sugarcane (which being a "perennial" crop is on a different footing altogether), rice, *ragi*, barley, and jute are by far the most labor-intensive crops; human labor days used per acre on these crops are substantially larger than (sometimes more than twice) those for other crops like wheat, cotton, jowar, bajra, pulses, and oilseeds.

Land Lease

TABLE 10.4

Interstate tenancy and other data for rural India in the early 1950s

State	LSPROP	IRRP	RICEP	EJECTP	UNEMD
Uttar Pradesh	11.38	25.91	28.90	63.34	59
Bihar	12.39	17.66	55.72	66.32	107
Orissa	12.58	12.89	64.55	48.89	60
West Bengal	25.43	18.65	78.49	58.47	111
Assam	43.54	20.54	76.02	19.37	82
Andhra	19.07	26.47	29.15	53.54	n.a.
Madras	27.53	24.61	38.15	40.64	145
Mysore and Coorg	16.37	13.01	33.13	47.01	98
Travancore and Cochin	23.63	27.80	30.24	30.00	108
Bombay	26.81	5.46	9.18	23.01	190
Saurashtra and Kutch	6.22	3.22	0.93	26.20	126
Madhya Pradesh	18.61	5.36	27.06	16.08	90
Madhya Bharat	19.54	4.62	2.34	46.32	123
Hyderabad	18.04	5.16	7.18	40.77	110
Vindhya Pradesh	21.33	4.52	28.08	41.49	n.a.
Rajasthan and Ajmer	20.92	11.23	5.14	39.05	119
Punjab (including Delhi and Himachal Pradesh)	40.42	34.82	9.09	48.09	226
Pepsu	37.71	41.03	3.92	28.37	171
Jammu and Kashmir	22.17	39.03	29.37	33.29	175

SOURCE: Data for LSPROP from NSS, 8th Round, 1953–54; for IRRP and RICEP from Ministry of Food and Agriculture data, 1952–53; for EJECTP from NSS, 8th Round; 1953–54; for UNEMD from First Agricultural Labor Enquiry Report, 1950–51.

NOTE: LSPROP=percentage of cultivated area under tenancy in 1953–54.
IRRP=percentage of gross sown area irrigated in 1952–53.
RICEP= Proportion of total cropped area under rice, *ragi*, barley, and jute.
EJECTP=percentage of leased-in area under contracts where tenant may be evicted at will.
UNEMD=number of days unemployed in 1950–51 for male workers in agricultural labor households.

between the land improvement factor and tenancy, which seems to be corroborated in one way or another by all the four sets of cross-section evidence considered in this section: areas with larger rainfall, or better irrigation, or a higher index of soil fertility seem in general to be areas with a larger incidence of tenancy. Yet this cross-section evidence conflicts with the intertemporal evidence in recent years, that over the last two or three decades (a period in which any index of irrigation or of land improvement shows a significant rise) the percentage of cultivated area under tenancy declined considerably. One primary reason has to do with the impact of protective tenancy legislation in most States in India or even outright

TABLE 10.5

Linear regression analysis of determinants of percentage of area under tenancy in Indian states, 1953–54

Dependent Variable:	LSPROP†	
Mean:	22.30 percent	
Standard Deviation:	9.82 percent	

Explanatory Variables	Regression Coefficient	Standard Error	Significant at Percent Level
IRRP (in the region)	0.4200	0.1652	2.9
RICEP	0.1996	0.0859	4.2
EJECTP	−0.3405	0.1239	2.1
UNEMD (in the year)	0.1473	0.0551	2.3
Constant term	3.1638	10.0615	76.0
$R^2 = 0.7596$; $F = 6.3$; no. of observations = 19			

SOURCE: See table 10.4.
†See table 10.4.

abolition of tenancy in some states. It has led to large-scale eviction of tenants by landlords. In other cases the absentee landlords finally gave up on their already tenuous links with the land, which now passed on to the peasant proprietors who were tenants before. These are institutional factors obviously not incorporated in the model in the preceding sections.

In this model the land improvement factor tends to increase the extent of tenancy mainly by raising the wage rate and thereby canceling the enhanced profitability of self-cultivation. It is possible that in areas of recent agricultural progress in India significant in-migration of labor (particularly in the peak season) from poorer areas (and nonagricultural occupations) along with the flooding of the labor market by the newly evicted tenants may have dampened the rise in wage rates and hence induced less leasing out by landlords. The introduction of labor-saving devices in some areas may have also contributed to the decline in tenancy, which is consistent with the proposition C derived from the model. Bell (1976) has noted another tenancy-reducing effect of tractorization. If a partial rationale of tenancy was to use the underutilized and imperfectly marketed bullock power in the possession of tenants, the introduction of tractors, by activating an alternative specialized market for draft power, may reduce the operation of that rationale. On top of all this, as noted before, the new agricultural technology makes heavier demands on entrepreneurial decision-making factors as well as on capacity to raise finance and investable capital, which the small sharecroppers of yesteryear are ill equipped to provide.

CHAPTER 11

Cross-Section Variations in Forms of Tenancy

I

In India the major forms of tenancy are sharecropping, fixed rental (in kind) per acre, and fixed rental (in cash) per acre. Sharecropping is the predominant form of tenancy in the eastern and the northwestern parts of India, whereas fixed-rent tenancy is the predominant form in the southern states. Much of this difference is undoubtedly due to complex historical, political, and sociological factors peculiar to different regions. But an economist persists in believing that at least some of the variations may be explained by economic structural factors. The object of this chapter is to identify some of these relevant economic, technological, ecological, and demographic factors in terms of a simple theoretical framework and then check for their actual significance in an empirical analysis of interregional cross-sectional data relating to Indian agriculture.

We shall confine our model to the case of a single homogeneous crop and, ignoring the problem posed by price fluctuations, regard both fixed-rental tenancy types described above as equivalent and focus our attention on the simple alternative tenancy contracts of sharecropping and fixed renting. We shall particularly concern ourselves with the case when factor markets are highly imperfect and asset endowment characteristics of different types of tenants differ. There are two types of tenants in this model: the landless sharecropper, and the landed farmer who enhances the size of his farm by leasing in land under a fixed-rental contract.[1] The landless sharecropper takes whatever amount of land he gets at the conventionally fixed (usually 50:50) rental share of output; the landlord who enjoys some monopoly power vis-a-vis the sharecropper decides how much land to lease out to sharecropping, and the latter does not participate in this decision. The landed tenant, on the other hand, has more bargaining power and decides how much land he would like to lease in. In the labor market, the landed tenant hires labor, whereas the landless sharecropper family is a net supplier of wage-labor.

[1]The presumption is that the risk-bearing capacity of the landless sharecropper is too low to enable him to operate in the fixed-rental market where the full brunt of production uncertainty is on the tenant. Our classification of the two types of tenants is clearly an extreme one, intended only as a simplification for sharpening results. In the real world, various types of tenancy and asset characteristics intermix: there are many cases of landless fixed-rent tenants (particularly where production uncertainty is relatively low as, for example, in Kerala before tenancy abolition) and of landed sharecroppers (as in Punjab).

As in the model of the preceding chapter, there are two seasons in the crop cycle: season 1 for land preparation, sowing, interculture, etc., and season 2 for harvesting. Land and labor produce "seedlings" at the end of season 1; "seedlings" and labor produce crop output at the end of season 2. Season 1 also happens to be in part a lean season, the market wage rate in this season does not clear the labor market, and there is persistent unemployment afflicting the landless sharecropper family. In season 2, the peak season, there is full employment of labor at the going wage rate. The seasonal distinction is also important because of the nature of the credit market. The landless sharecropper, unlike the landed tenant, is dependent on the landlord for credit to finance his subsistence consumption in the lean season, and he pays back the loan along with interest at the end of the harvest. The credit market is imperfect, and the interest rate that faces the landless sharecropper is significantly larger than that for the landed tenant (or the landlord) when they try to get credit from outside sources.

Suppose $Q_f(A_f, L_f)$ is the number of seedlings produced at the end of season 1 on the fixed-rent tenant farm. In this production he uses L_f amount of labor (let us assume it is entirely hired, although none of the results will change if we take into account family labor as well) and A_f amount of land acreage. The tenant owns A_f amount of land and leases in the difference $(A_f - \bar{A}_f)$ at rent R per acre. Hired labor, L_f, is paid at a given wage rate, assumed without loss of generality at the value of unity. In season 2, with the use of harvesting labor, seedlings produce output, say, in fixed proportions. As before, let us suppose one unit of seedlings ends up in one unit of crop harvest. We can now write the fixed-rent tenant's income *at the end of the crop cycle* as

$$Y_f = (1 - bw) Q_f(A_f, L_f) - R(1 + i)(A_f - \bar{A}_f) - (1 + i)L_f, \qquad 11.1$$

where i is the interest rate (per season), w is the wage rate in the harvesting season, and b is the amount of harvesting labor used per unit of seedlings. Since the rent, R, and the lean-season wage is paid before the onset of the harvest season, they are multiplied by the interest factor $(1 + i)$.

Similarly, the landless sharecropper's income at the end of the crop cycle is given by

$$Y_s = (1 - r) Q_s(A_s, L_s) + (1 + \rho) \mu (1 - L_s) + (1 - bQ_s)w - \rho C, \qquad 11.2$$

where r is the conventionally given rental share to be paid to the landlord, Q_s is the output of seedlings and harvest, A_s is the amount the landlord has leased out to the sharecropper, L_s is the amount of labor the sharecropper decides to use on his farm in season 1, and C is the given subsistence consumption of the sharecropper family, the excess of which over its wage earnings in this season the landlord finances with credit. In the lean season the wage rate does not clear the labor market. In that season the sharecropper family is prepared to supply $(1 - L_s)$ amount of wage labor, but expects only a fraction, μ, of it to get wage employment outside and the rest is unemployed. In the peak season, on the other hand, whatever the amount of wage labor this family is prepared to supply (after using bQ_s amount of labor in harvesting on its own farm) is absorbed at the going wage rate, w.[2] In both seasons the total number of potential workers in the sharecropper family is given at unity. As a result of credit market imperfections, the interest rate facing the family, ρ, will be assumed to be larger than i, the interest rate the landed families face.

The noncultivating landlord has three sources of income: crop share from the sharecropper, rental income from land leased out to the fixed-rent tenant, and interest income from loans to the sharecropper family. His income at the end of the crop cycle is, therefore,

$$Y_l = rQ_s(A_s, L_s) + R(1+i)(\bar{A} - A_s) + \rho[C - \mu(1 - L_s)], \qquad 11.3$$

where $\bar{A}$ is the total land owned by the landlord.

For simplification let us consider only the Cobb–Douglas form of the seedlings production function so that

$$Q_i = B_i A_i^{\alpha} L_i^{\beta}, i = f, s, \qquad 11.4$$

where B_i is a constant. Since diseconomies of scale can be important in agriculture, let us assume $\alpha + \beta < 1$.

Now the landlord maximizes Y_l with respect to his decision variable, A_s. He cannot control the sharecropper's use of labor intensity *per acre*, l_s; his decision of A_s, however, affects $L_s(=l_s.A_s)$. So,

$$r(\alpha + \beta)Q_s + \rho\mu\ L_s - R(1+i)A_s = 0. \qquad 11.5$$

The landless sharecropper maximizes Y_s with respect to his decision variable, l_s, and gets as a necessary condition of interior maximum,[3]

$$(1 - r - bw)\frac{Q_s}{L_s}\beta - \mu(1+\rho) = 0. \qquad 11.6$$

The landed fixed-rent tenant maximizes Y_f with respect to his decision variables, A_f and L_f, and gets as necessary conditions of interior maximum,

$$(1 - bw)\alpha\frac{Q_f}{A_f} - R(1+i) = 0 \qquad 11.7$$

$$(1 - bw)\beta\frac{Q_f}{L_f} - (1+i) = 0. \qquad 11.8$$

The equilibrium in the land market is given by:

[2] Since this model is more cumbersome than that in the preceding chapter on account of the introduction of two types of tenants, we give up here on the endogenous determination of the harvesting wage rate, which we now assume to be given.

[3] As we noted in the preceding chapter, in the interior $(1 - r - bw)$ has to be positive, which is generally the case. Also note that my assumption of Cobb–Douglas functions rules out the corner solution with only fixed rent in equation 11.5. Since our subsequent interstate data do not have corner cases, in the model we have confined ourself only to the interior solution.

$$\bar{A} - A_s = A_f - \bar{A}_f. \qquad\qquad 11.9$$

Equation 11.9 implies that the supply (by the landlord) of land under fixed-rent lease is equal to the demand for it by the tenant. Given the parameters in the system, equation 11.9 determines R, the rent per acre. The other prices in the model like the interest rates i and ρ, or the wage rate w, are determined outside the model. Parametric variations in them shall be considered later in this chapter.

From equations 11.5 and 11.6,

$$\frac{\partial A_s}{\partial R} = -\frac{(1-\beta)A_s}{(1-\alpha-\beta)R} < 0. \qquad\qquad 11.10$$

Equation 11.10 implies that the supply of land for fixed-rent lease is an increasing function of the rent per acre.

From equations 11.7 and 11.8,

$$\frac{\partial A_f}{\partial R} = -\frac{(1+i)(1-\beta)A_f^2}{\alpha(1-\alpha-\beta)(1-bw)Q_f} < 0. \qquad\qquad 11.11$$

Equation 11.11 implies that the demand for land on fixed-rent lease is a declining function of the rent per acre.

Equation 11.10 and 11.11 imply that the standard Walrasian stability condition for equilibrium in equation 11.9 holds:

$$K = -[\frac{\partial A_s}{\partial R} + \frac{\partial A_f}{\partial R}] > 0. \qquad\qquad 11.12$$

II

Given the equilibrium described in the previous section, I shall now work out some comparative-static propositions, starting with a parametric variation in the harvesting wage rate, w.

From equations 11.5 and 11.6,

$$\frac{\partial A_s}{\partial w} = -\frac{bA_s[\beta r(\alpha+\beta)Q_s + \rho\mu L_s]}{(1-r-bw)(1-\alpha-\beta)[r(\alpha+\beta)Q_s + \rho\mu L_s]} < 0. \qquad\qquad 11.13$$

Equation 11.13 implies that the landlord tends to lease out less to the sharecropper when the harvesting wage rate is higher for the same rent per acre on fixed-rent tenancy.

From 11.7 and 11.8,

$$\frac{\partial A_f}{\partial w} = -\frac{bA_f}{(1-\alpha-\beta)(1-bw)} < 0. \qquad\qquad 11.14$$

Equation 11.14 implies that the fixed-rent tenant tends to lease in less when the harvesting wage rate is higher for the same rent per acre.

Using equations 11.12, 11.13, and 11.14 in 11.9,

$$\frac{dR}{dw} = \frac{1}{K}[\frac{\partial A_s}{\partial w} + \frac{\partial A_f}{\partial w}] < 0. \qquad\qquad 11.15$$

Equation 11.15 implies that a higher harvesting wage rate reduces the equilibrium rent per acre on fixed-rent tenancy.

Now,

$$\frac{\mathrm{d}A_s}{\mathrm{d}w} = \frac{\partial A_s}{\partial w} + \frac{\partial A_s}{\partial R}\frac{\mathrm{d}R}{\mathrm{d}w}. \qquad\qquad 11.16$$

Substituting equations 11.10, 11.11, 11.13, and 11.14 in 11.16 and using 11.5 and 11.7, it is easy to see that $\mathrm{d}A_s/\mathrm{d}w$ is positive under the alternative sufficient conditions

$$1 - \frac{r}{1-bw} > \beta(1 + \frac{\beta}{\alpha}) \qquad\qquad 11.17$$

or, alternatively,

$$> \beta(1+\rho).$$

We can assume that β, the elasticity of output with respect to labor on seedlings production, is small enough to satisfy 11.17. If the rental share is 50 percent and bw, the share of harvest paid as harvesting wages, is 10 percent (it is usually much lower than that), any β less than 0.3 will satisfy 11.17 if the interest rate ρ *per season* is less than 48 percent or if the land elasticity α is more than 0.62. In the development literature the labor elasticity of output in peasant agriculture (in the lean season) is often put at a very low value, sometimes even at zero.

A positive $\mathrm{d}A_s/\mathrm{d}w$ implies that a higher harvesting wage rate leads to a larger equilibrium percentage of tenanted area under sharecropping. Since in equations 11.5, 11.6, 11.7, and 11.8 w always appears coupled with b, the harvesting labor coefficient, we can now also say that $\mathrm{d}A_s/\mathrm{d}b$ is positive, so that the larger the harvesting labor coefficient, the higher the percentage of tenanted area under sharecropping. This suggests that sharecropping tenancy will be larger in areas where the crop is more labor-intensive. Alternatively, if there is a labor-saving technical change reducing the harvesting labor requirement per unit of output, the relative importance of sharecropping will tend to decline.

I have noted that credit market is imperfect so that ρ, the interest rate facing the landless sharecropper, is higher than i, the interest rate for the landed. Given i, the larger ρ is, the larger we presume is the extent of imperfection in the credit market. In equations 11.5–8, ρ appears only in equations 11.5 and 11.6. It is now easy to check that $\partial A_s/\partial\rho$ is negative, $\mathrm{d}R/\mathrm{d}\rho$ is negative, and

$$\frac{\mathrm{d}A_s}{\mathrm{d}\rho} = \frac{\partial A_s}{\partial\rho} + \frac{\partial A_s}{\partial R}\frac{\mathrm{d}R}{\mathrm{d}\rho} < 0 \qquad\qquad 11.18$$

if α, the land elasticity of output is high enough.

Equation 11.18 implies that, given i, the higher ρ is, or the larger the degree of imperfection in the credit market, the lower the equilibrium percentage of tenanted area under sharecropping.[4]

In equations 11.5–8, μ appears only in equation 11.5 and 11.6 coupled with ρ or $(1+\rho)$, so we can now say that $dA_s / d\mu$ is negative. Since μ is the objective probability of getting wage employment for the landless sharecropper in the lean season, the larger the extent of unemployment in the lean season facing the sharecropper family in the labor market, the larger the equilibrium percentage of tenanted area under sharecropping.

Now suppose there is parametric variation with respect to the technical progress factor B_i in the production functions in equation 11.4. If B_i is the same for both the sharecropper's and the fixed-rent tenant's production functions, it is easy to see from equations 11.5–12 that dR / dB_i is positive, but dA_s / dB_i is zero. Technical progress that is equally accessible to both types of tenants raises the rent per acre but does not change the allocation of tenanted land between the two types of tenancy. The technical progress factors are, however, quite often likely to be different due to unequal access to irrigation facilities (the landless sharecropper with higher insecurity of tenure may be uninterested in digging field channels or investing in tubewells or may not have the resources or credit for such investment). In the extreme case, when there is technical progress only on the fixed-rent tenant's farm (i.e., B_s drops out of the sharecropper's production function altogether), it is easy to see that dA_s / dB_f is negative. Similarly, it is not difficult to show that if the market for fertilizers (and other such current inputs embodying technical progress) is imperfect and the landless sharecropper pays a higher price for buying fertilizers than the landed tenant (possibly because the latter has better "connections" and access to the frequently subsidized distribution of fertilizers, whereas the sharecropper may have to depend more on the black market), then the larger the degree of such market imperfection (i.e., the larger the price differential paid by the sharecropper), the lower the percentage of tenanted area under sharecropping. Much, of course, will, depend on the type of cost-sharing arrangements the sharecropper may work out with the landlord.

III

This section briefly introduces production uncertainty (say, due to vagaries of weather) and considers the impact of a parametric variation in the riskiness of output on the relative importance of sharecropping. I shall consider only the simpler multiplicative form of uncertainty so that $Q_i = G(u) F_i(A_i, L_i)$, $i = s, f$, is the production function with u as the

---

[4] If in equation 11.3 the third term in the landlord's maximand is taken not as his interest income from the sharecropper, $\rho[C - \mu(1 - L_s)]$, but his *differential* interest income, i.e., $(\rho - i)[C - \mu(1 - L_s)]$, it can be checked that our results here do not change.

random variable representing some index of weather. If now the landlord,[5] the sharecropper, and the fixed-rent tenant each maximizes his respective expected utility function with respect to the relevant decision variables, the necessary conditions of maximization given in equations 11.5–8 will now change as follows:

$$EU'(Y_l)[r(\alpha+\beta)\frac{Q_s}{A_s} - R(1+i)]=0 \qquad\qquad 11.19$$

$$EU'(Y_s)[(1-r-bw)\beta\frac{Q_s}{L_s} - \mu(1+\rho)]=0 \qquad\qquad 11.20$$

$$EU'(Y_f)[(1-bw)\alpha\frac{Q_f}{A_f} - R(1+i)]=0 \qquad\qquad 11.21$$

$$EU'(Y_f)[(1-bw)\beta\frac{Q_f}{L_f}-(1+i)]=0, \qquad\qquad 11.22$$

where E is the expectation operator, U is utility function, and Y_l, Y_s and Y_f are the incomes of landlord, sharecropper, and fixed-rent tenant, respectively. It can be checked that the second-order conditions of maximization are satisfied under the sufficient conditions on risk aversion familiar from Arrow's (1971) portfolio model: the degree of absolute risk aversion does not increase as income increases; and the degree of relative risk aversion does not decrease with increase in income.

From equations 11.19 and 11.20 it can be checked that $\partial A_s/\partial R$ is negative under the sufficient condition that relative risk aversion for the landlord does not exceed unity. From 11.21 and 11.22, $\partial A_f/\partial R$. is negative. So, as in the first section, the Walrasian stability of the equilibrium described by equation 11.9 is ensured, and condition 11.12 holds.

In characterizing the increase in weather uncertainty we take the approach of Sandmo (1970) in a slightly different context (the alternative Rothschild–Stiglitz (1971) approach should give similar results) and examine two kinds of shift in the probability distribution of $G(u)$. One is an additive shift which is equivalent to an increase in the mean with all other moments constant; the other is a multiplicative shift by which the distribution is stretched around zero. A pure increase in dispersion can be defined as a stretching of the distribution around a constant mean. This is equivalent to a combination of additive and multiplicative parameter changes.

Let us write,

$$G=\lambda u+\sigma, \qquad\qquad 11.23$$

---

[5] For simplification we shall ignore, for the time being, the role of the landlord as a moneylender to the sharecropper.

where λ is the multiplicative shift parameter and σ the additive one. Taking the differential in EG and putting it to zero,

$$\frac{\mathrm{d}\,G}{\mathrm{d}\,\lambda} = \frac{(G-EG)}{\lambda}.$$ 11.24

From equations 11.19–22 it is tedious, but not difficult, to check that under the sufficient conditions that the Arrovian conditions on risk aversion mentioned above hold and that the landlord's relative risk aversion does not exceed unity, both $\partial A_s / \partial\lambda$ and $\partial A_f / \partial\lambda$ are negative. This implies that $\mathrm{d}R / \mathrm{d}\lambda$ is negative: an increase in production uncertainty reduces the equilibrium rent per acre. Now,

$$\frac{\mathrm{d}A_s}{\mathrm{d}\lambda} = \frac{\partial A_s}{\partial\lambda} + \frac{\partial A_s}{\partial R}\frac{\mathrm{d}R}{\mathrm{d}\lambda}$$ 11.25

On the right-hand side of equation 11.25, the first term is negative but the second term is positive, i.e., an increase in production uncertainty at the same R induces the landlord to lease out less to sharecropping and more to fixed-rent tenancy, but there is an opposite influence from the fact that R goes down. It is difficult in general to be sure which of the two conflicting effects dominate. It is very easy to show that, in the special case when the landlord and the landed fixed-rent tenant are both risk-neutral but the landless sharecropper is risk-averse, an increase in production uncertainty reduces the percentage of tenanted area under sharecropping. The same result holds if the landed fixed-rent tenant is risk-neutral but both the landlord and the landless sharecropper are risk-averse. In the case when both the fixed-rent tenant and the sharecropper are risk-averse, we have not found any clear-cut result: the only result we can report in this case is that, if the landlord is risk-neutral *and* if we allow the sharecropper's production function to be separable so that the marginal product of land is not affected by labor used (thus departing from our Cobb–Douglas assumption), an increase in production uncertainty will tend to *increase* the percentage of tenanted area under sharecropping.[6]

Let us now consider, instead of an increase in production uncertainty, a parametric variation in the asset characteristics of the tenants. Suppose $\bar{A}_f$, the amount of land owned by the landed tenant is larger. From equation 11.21 and 11.22, $\partial A_f / \partial\bar{A}_f$ is positive if we assume a slightly stronger version of Arrow's risk-aversion postulate described above (i.e., if we assume that the degree of absolute risk aversion for the landed tenant decreases as income increases). Since $\bar{A}_f$ does not affect equations 11.19 and 11.20, $\partial A_s / \partial\bar{A}_f$ is zero and hence $\mathrm{d}R / \mathrm{d}\bar{A}_f$ is positive: the wealthier the fixed-rent tenant, the higher the rent per acre. This also means that

---

[6] This is essentially because in this model the landlord himself decides about the extent of land to be put under sharecropping, and if the landlord is risk-neutral, the risk-averse sharecropper's reaction to an increase in uncertainty in terms of his labor use decision does not affect the extent of land leased out by the landlord if the production function is separable.

dA_s/dA_f is negative: the wealtheir the landed fixed-rent tenant, the lower the equilibrium percentage of tenanted area under sharecropping. The result is essentially due to the wealthier tenant taking more risks (under the assumption that risky investment is not an "inferior" good).

IV

Summarizing the comparative-static propositions of sections II and III, we

TABLE 11.1

Interstate data on sharecropping and other variables for rural India in the early 1950s

State	SHPROP	HARVW	NRAIN	MCI	CRLOP	CBOR
Uttar Pradesh	54.17	25.3	39.04	1.21	0.6128	61
Bihar	68.47	28.8	51.23	1.30	0.6577	63
Orissa	60.28	13.6	57.70	1.06	0.6488	54
West Bengal	89.57	28.0	66.74	1.16	0.6466	81
Assam	22.64	30.4	98.16	1.16	0.5671	56
Andhra	43.05	n.a.	32.35	1.14	0.7769	n.a.
Madras	21.54	14.4	74.14	1.16	0.7195	60
Mysore and Coorg	24.72	14.7	36.37	1.03	0.6223	65
Travancore and Cochin	9.70	25.6	100.21	1.17	0.7136	61
Bombay	48.95.	17.6	59.26	1.00	0.6881	45
Saurashtra and Kutch	18.13	28.8	18.19	1.04	0.6291	84
Madhya Pradesh	64.03	14.4	49.54	1.11	0.7027	37
Madhya Bharat	37.06	18.6	35.89	1.04	0.5956	57
Hyderabad	40.11	14.4	33.06	1.01	0.7363	57
Vindhya Pradesh	17.91	n.a.	45.08	1.14	0.6573	68
Rajasthan and Ajmer	23.21	20.0	19.31	1.06	0.6344	57
Punjab (including Delhi and Himachal Pradesh)	76.89	39.8	41.46	1.19	0.7019	59
PEPSU	56.25	58.2	41.46	1.16	0.6761	66
Jammu and Kashmir	67.31	25.6	38.37	1.10	0.4849	n.a.

SOURCE: Data for SHPROP from NSS, 8th Round, Land Holding Survey; For HARVW from First Agricultural Labor Enquiry Report; for NRAIN and MCI from the *Statistical Abstract of India*; for CRLOP from NSS, 8th Round, Land Holding Survey; for CBOR from the *All-India Rural Credit Survey Report*.

NOTE: SHROP=area under sharecropping as percentage of area under sharecropping plus fixed-rent tenancy in 1953-54; HARVW=harvesting wage rate per day (in annas) for males in agricultural labor households in 1950-51; NRAIN=normal annual rainfall (the rainfall data are given for Punjab and PEPSU together, so the same figure has been used for both): MCI =multiple cropping index for 1952-53; CRLOP=concentration ratio of operational holdings: CBOR=percentage of total annual borrowing by small cultivator households for meeting household expenses.

have derived under the assumptions in the model the following propositions:

A. The percentage of tenanted area under sharecropping will be higher in the case of more labor-intensive crops (assuming that harvest labor-intensive crops are also labor-intensive overall).

B. It will be higher in areas where the harvesting wage rate is higher.

C. It will be higher in areas with larger unemployment facing the landless families.

D. It will be lower the larger the extent of imperfection in the credit market (i.e., the higher the differential interest rate that the landless sharecropper has to pay over that paid by the landed).

E. It will be lower the larger the extent of imperfection in the market for inputs like fertilizers.

F. It will be lower if there is less technical progress in the sharecropper's farm than in the fixed-rent tenant's farm due to, say, insecurity of tenure on the former or unequal acess to irrigation facilities.

G. It is not clear in general if an increase in production uncertainty will increase or decrease the percentage of tenanted area under sharecropping. The latter will fall if the landed tenant is risk-neutral but the sharecropper is risk-averse; it will rise with larger production uncertainty if both types of tenants are risk-averse, the landlord is risk-neutral, and the sharecropper's production function is separable.

H. The wealthier the fixed-rent tenant, the smaller sharecropping is.

Table 11.1 brings together some interstate cross-section data for India in the early 1950s (in addition to those already presented in table 10.4), which we are going to use in testing *some* of the propositions above. The dependent variable, SHPROP, the area under sharecropping as a percentage of total area under sharecropping and fixed-rent tenancy varies from 9.7 percent in the (old) state of Travancore and Cochin to 89.57 percent in West Bengal in 1953–54. In general, sharecropping seems to be the predominant form of tenancy in east (except Assam), north, and northwest India, and fixed-rent tenancy predominates south and west India.[7] Table 11.2 presents the results of the regression analysis explaining the variations in SHPROP. Since unlike in the statistical analysis of the preceding chapter the harvesting wage rate is now taken as an independent variable, it can be expected that this itself is influenced strongly by other independent variables (like rainfall, irrigation). So we have a two-stage regression analysis, with the first stage yielding a predicted harvesting wage

---

[7] This pattern is by and large true even in the estimates for 1970–71 from the NSS 26th Round Land Holdings Survey. SHPROP now varies from 12–13 percent in Kerala to 96.44 percent in West Bengal. One major difference between the earlier pattern and that in 1970–71 is that in some of the areas (like Assam, Gujarat, Madras, Mysore, and Rajasthan) where sharecropping was relatively unimportant in 1953–54, it now involves quite a substantial part of the area under tenancy.

TABLE 11.2

Linear regression analysis of determinants of proportional importance of sharecropping as a form of tenancy from interstate data, rural India, 1953–54

Explanatory Variables	Regression Coefficient	Standard Error	Significant at Percent Level
PHARVW (predicted harvesting wage rate)	1.1804	0.5419	6.1
RICEP (proportion of cropped area under rice and other labor-intensive crops)	0.1777	0.0667	2.9
EJECTP (percentage of leased-in area under contracts in which tenant may be evicted at will)	−0.2812	0.1170	4.3
UNEMD (average number of days unemployed in the year for male workers in agricultural labor households)	0.1372	0.0472	2.0
CBOR (percentage of total annual borrowing by small cultivator households taken to meet household expenses)	−0.2740	0.1437	9.3
Constant term	94.6610	37.0378	3.4
$R^2 = 0.8612$; $F = 7.1$; no. of observations $= 16$			

NOTE: This table reports the results of the second-stage regression analysis, of which the first-stage equation relates HARVW to IRRP, NRAIN, CRLOP, and MCI (see table 11.1). In this table the variable PHARVW represents the predicted harvesting wage rate on the basis of the first-stage equation. IRRP and NRAIN were used as independent variables in the second stage as well, but they turned out to be highly insignificant.

rate, PHARVW, which we then use as an independent variable in the second-stage equation reported in table 11.2. SHPROP is positively and significantly associated with this predicted harvesting wage rate, in conformity with proposition B above. SHPROP is also positively and significantly associated with RICEP, the proportion of cropped area under rice, *ragi*, jute, and barley (as noted in the preceding chapter, these are by far the most labor-intensive crops in the Indian cropping pattern) and with UNEMD, which, as in the preceding chapter, is an index of the prospect of unemployment on wage work, thus indicating consistency with propositions A and C, respectively. There is a negative relationship between SHPROP and EJECTP, the proportion of total leased-in area in which the tenant under the existing contract (usually oral) could be evicted at will by the landlord, indicating consistency with proposition F above, dealing with the effect of insecurity of tenure on land improvements. Testing proposition D requires data on interest rates and credit rationing, which, needless to say, are extremely scarce. As all field investigators know, credit is one of the most sensitive issues, and related data are very difficult to get, particularly in large-scale surveys; besides, even the most cooperative and accounting-minded peasant borrower may not have a good idea of the effective interest rate he pays, since interest is charged, as shown in the preceding chapters, in so many different ways in the inextricably interlinked transactions between the moneylender-landlord-employer-trader and the borrower-tenant-employee-seller. To measure the extent of imperfection in the credit market facing the landless sharecropper we have thus used, for whatever it is worth, a very crude proxy, CBOR, which indicates the extent of dependence of small cultivators on borrowing for household consumption. The presumption is that, the larger this dependence, the lower the bargaining power of the borrower and the higher the differential interest rate he will have to pay. If this is the case, proposition D suggests that we should expect a negative relationship between SHPROP and CBOR, which is confirmed by the regression results.

Unlike in the statistical analysis of the preceding chapter, we do not have data at different levels of aggregation for testing the hypotheses on variations in forms of tenancy. The State is too aggregative a level to capture some of the complexities of the relationship between forms of tenancy and economic, technological, and demographic factors. Besides, at that level of aggregation the widely divergent legal and political histories of land tenure and property rights in the different States may cast shadows deep enough to block out some of the simple economic relationships based on household behavior that these crude theoretical models focus on.

PART C

PRODUCTION RELATIONS AND POVERTY

Two chapters (14 and 15) of Part C discuss the possibly ambiguous relationship between agricultural growth and poverty of agricultural laborers and the complexities in the relationship of poverty and child mortality. In the other three chapters I comment on the institutional environment of persistent poverty and how the nature of production relations makes it difficult for piecemeal policy solutions or isolated remedial efforts to work. In particular, chapter 12 shows how the absence of credit or insurance markets leads to contractual interlinking in land, labor and credit relations, and piecemeal reformist measures tinkering with one part of these transactions without taking care of the interconnections, may even worsen the lot of the poor tenant-laborer-borrower. The same absence of credit or insurance markets leads to labor market segmentation and fractures the process of class formation and class action on the part of the exploited, as noted in chapter 13. This underlines the importance of channeling organizational resources toward the building of viable local community institutions providing alternative sources of credit and social insurance. The need for similar community organizations for water management, which can rise above or supercede the private property interests of landlords and "waterlords" and thus relieve one of the major constraints on broad-based agricultural growth, is emphasized in chapter 16.

CHAPTER 12

Interlocking Factor Markets

I

In chapters 5, 6, 7, and 9 we have referred to cases of interlinkage of credit contracts with labor or tenancy contracts. In this chapter we provide some reflections on the general phenomenon of factor-market interlinkage, its rationale, its socioeconomic context, and its consequences.

Anthropologists have often emphasized the multi-stranded nature of relationships in small face-to-face communities. Gluckman in his studies of tribal Africa has called such societies "multiplex", with each individual playing not one but a variety of roles in interacting with fellow members of his community. Generalizing from his experience with the hill peasants of Orissa, Bailey (1971) notes, "The watershed between traditional and modern society is exactly this distinction between single-interest and multiplex relationships". He goes on to comment that in the cognitive map of the peasant, single-interest functionally specialized relationships are to be made—with due caution—only with outsiders, those who are outside his moral community. Multiplex relationships between the same economic agents in a poor agrarian community that the economists emphasize are often described as interlinked contracts encompassing several markets, particularly those of land, labor, and credit. One should be cautious about this description, since the terms "market" and "contract" need to be interpreted somewhat loosely in this context. When we talk of interlinked factor markets we do not necessarily refer to formal or organized or monetized markets. Any transaction in the services of these factors based primarily on economic principles (as opposed to extraeconomic coercion or obligation) is deemed as a "market" relationship for my present purpose even though the transactors do not always bid their prices or offer their services in the impersonal atmosphere of an open marketplace. Similarly a "contract" does not necessarily refer to explicit contracts with legal sanctions, but more often to implicit agreements enforced by nothing more than the prevailing custom, social interaction, and goodwill in a small closed community and the enlightened self-interest of the individual in a situation of limited alternative opportunities.

Of course, this loose interpretation of a market or contractual relationship still presumes a social formation in which individual gain-oriented exchange is an essential part of the economic organization. Anthropologists like Karl Polanyi have rightly questioned the economist's parochial (and often ahistorical) assumption that the market form of organization is ubiquitous. But in a given historical and institutional context, whether or not the transactional modes through which resource allocation, work organization, and product disposition are arranged resemble those of the market is clearly a matter of empirical judgment. The transactional mode of nonmarket economies is primarily one of obligatory payments and some commitment to sharing[1]—what Polanyi calls the principle of reciprocity and redistribution. Examples abound in the anthropological literature, from the case of constant gift and counter gift giving of tribal life in Malinowski's Trobriand Islands to the patron–client relationship of the Indian *Jajmani* system. But a whole generation of social anthropologists and empirical economists has shown us how over the years the traditional system of obligatory payments, custom-determined rewards, and communal sharing and insurance has been eroded by the steady penetration of market forces. This erosion process is slower in some societies than in others, but even in those former cases the evolving transitional patterns show a remarkable degree of sensitivity to market stimuli, and transactions can hardly be described as mere expressions of social obligations. Under the circumstances, simple economic propositions regarding transactions in such societies made on the basis of a market principle may make sense,[2] even though different historical categories of markets still coexist, interact, and evolve under the same social rubric.

But even when the market principle is active, its domain of operation is quite often rather narrow. As noted at the end of chapter 4, whereas market forces may be reasonably vigorous in the village wage determination process, territorial affinities (both for demanders and for suppliers of labor) interfere with the working of a supravillage labor market. The moral boundaries of the village community tend to have a strong, though not overriding, influence on the economic boundaries of a market. The resultant fragmentation is particularly acute in the rural credit market. Since agriculture is a business with slow turnover of capital and since extreme poverty leaves little scope for "internal financing" by peasants, credit plays a crucial role in a poor agrarian economy, and market fragmentation here inexorably leads to a splintering of all the other markets involved in such an economy. In each of these isolated submarkets, however, different participants enjoy differential access to markets outside their village, and this is clearly reflected in the highly unequal bargaining power of agents in a given submarket. Thus in the localized credit submarket of the village the lender often has the advantage

[1] Even in a nonmarket traditional peasant community, the emphasis on a sharing ethic and communal subsistence guarantees underlined by the so-called moral economists like Wolf (1969) and Scott (1976) has been questioned by Popkin (1979), who shows how the peasants are predominantly motivated by personal gain and how they rely on the family or groups smaller than the village community for their insurance against subsistence crises.

[2] The expression "market principle", as distinct from an organized and explicit market mechanism, has been used by Bohannan and Dalton (1962) in their anthropological studies of primitive markets in Africa.

of exclusive access to organized financial markets outside as well as the power in undervaluing any collateral assets provided by the borrower who has no such access.[3] The outcome of transactions in such isolated credit submarkets, particularly in formation of usurious interest rates, can in principle be analyzed in a standard way by assuming monopolistic power on the part of the lender, both in setting interest rates and in valuing collaterals. But it is important to keep in mind a qualitative distinction between *inadequately formed* markets and the *imperfect* markets of the economics textbooks. In an incomplete market it may sometimes be possible to conceptually construct price analogs, but they are often too far-fetched to be meaningful. In many loan transactions in the village, particularly when they are intertwined with transactions in labor or land lease, it may be very difficult to get an idea of the implicit interest rate charged, taking all the transactions together; the parties involved are themselves unaware or vague about it, not to speak of the question of equality of this implicit rate as between different loan transactions in the same village.

Interlinked transactions, particularly those involving credit, are thus highly *personalized*. Such personal ties between the transacting agents are often automatically described in the literature as fuedal. This kind of careless labeling is worse than inaccurate: it actually blocks our understanding of such ties. While there is no commonly accepted definition of feudalism among historians, the descriptions of its fundamental features as given by most serious analysts, from Karl Marx to Marc Bloch to Perry Anderson, do not contain personalized transactions per se as an essential element.[4] Nor does the persistence of such transactions necessarily signify any other precapitalist mode of production. In a capitalist economy the financial transactions and credit mobilization operations of even big business houses (not infrequently controlled by family networks) and interlocking directorates of companies often display a crucial dependence on personal ties. In a world of costly information, credit systems based on personal trust and interlocking obligations in different transactions between the same parties are a way to insure against either party ending up with too many of Akerlof's (1970) "lemons" and to economize on some of the excessive costs of acquiring information. Arms-length trading with personal anonymity of economic agents may thus be too expensive. In this sense the Parsonian dichotomy of personalism/universalism is much too artificial. Enduring relationships in all economies tend to be somewhat

---

[3] This, as Bhaduri (1977) notes, can considerably reduce the so-called lender's risk, since in case of default the value of transferred collaterals often exceeds the value of defaulted loans.

[4] There are many historians who regard feudalism as a nonuniversal socioeconomic organization specific to the experience of Europe (and, at most, Japan) in a particular period of history. For India, historians like Irfan Habib (1969) and Harbans Mukhia (1981) have seriously questioned the validity of the concept of feudalism for *any* period in Indian history.

personalistic, and this is particularly so in the insecure world of peasant market systems. Among anthropologists Mintz has been most explicit on this point:

> Behind the operation of supply and demand there is a network of person-to-person dealings which persist over time and outlast any single transaction...there are important parallels even in highly industrialized countries. But in the internal marketing systems of peasant societies, these small distinctions based on personal relationships loom more importantly. (1959: 24–25)[5]

Or as Geertz comments on the "bazaar economy" of Sefrou in Morocco:

> Clientelization is the tendency, marked in Sefrou, for repetitive purchasers of particular goods and services to establish continuing relationships with particular purveyors of them, rather than search widely through the market at each occasion of need. The apparent Brownian motion of randomly colliding bazaaris conceals a resilient pattern of informal personal connections. (1978:30)

Even in the buying and selling of labor, the underlying principles behind what we have called the moral boundaries of the village labor market have some basic similarities with those behind what is known as the "internal labor market" of the corporate firm. The microeconomics of "idiosyncratic" relations or "customer markets" that Williamson et al (1975) and Okun (1975) have, respectively, emphasized for an industrially advanced country apply with similar importance, albeit with appropriate contextual differences, to the case of personalized relationships of a poor agrarian economy.

Interlinking of transactions is a way of partially circumventing the problem of incomplete or nonexistent markets (particularly of credit and insurance) and the general problems of moral hazards and inappropriable externalities. An interlinked system of personalized transactions may also reduce some of the market costs of work monitoring, contract enforcement, and search by making the possible discovery of dishonesty or shirking by an agent in one transaction too costly for him in terms of its spillover effects threatening other transactions (and the general loss of goodwill in the small closed world of a traditional village). Apart from economizing on these transaction costs, interlinked personalized transactions may also serve a special role in an inadequately monetized rural economy. Barter economies do not in general possess what Ostroy and Starr (1974) have called the informational efficiency of monetary

---

[5] Mintz (1961) extensively analyzes the distributive trade in the Haitian economy where each market woman seeks to protect her stake within the area of exchange through the institutionalized personal economic relationship referred to in Haiti as *pratik* (from French *pratique*: "good customer"). For examples of continual personalized interdependence creating a sanction system enforcing fulfillment of obligations in debt transactions of traders and peasants in Java, see Dewey (1962).

exchange. The absence of a universally acceptable medium of exchange like money introduces uncertainties about the acceptability of the means of exchange used. A laborer may be looking for a credit transaction in which he can make his interest payments (or hypothecate) in the form of commitment to provide labor services, but this may not be acceptable to all creditors. An interlinked credit and wage contract between the employer-creditor and the employee-borrower is thus a way, as we have analyzed in chapter 6, of ensuring the "double coincidence of wants" without which nonmonetized economies tend to be unfeasible or inefficient.[6]

II

One of the major forms in which land and labor market relations are intermixed is, of course, through the institution of sharecropping tenancy. As is by now well known[7] and as already noted in chapter 7, sharecropping is a compromise between the incentives problems under wage contracts and the risk-bearing problems under fixed-rent contracts. Costs of labor supervision and monitoring induce landowners to look for land-lease contracts instead of self-cultivating with hired labor (monitoring being particularly important when production uncertainty on account of weather or other reasons makes it difficult to infer input from output); on the other hand, the fixed-rent contract imposes too heavy a risk burden on the poor, usually highly risk-averse, tenant. If risks are not confined to production but are also important in the factor markets, sharecropping may again be a partial solution: uncertainty of sustained employment at a given wage or uncertainty of the wage rate (particularly the *real* wage rate) may drive the laborer to sharecropping for needed insurance that the labor market cannot provide him.

As noted in chapter 7, sharecropping also serves the purpose of enabling a fuller utilization of the nonmarketable or not easily marketable resources (like family labor, female and child labor, given the various social and economic constraints on their market participation, and, like draft animal labor, given the fact that the market for animal labor renting is often rather inactive[8]) possessed by the tenant family. The absence of a market in which

---

[6] Bhalla (1976) cites from her study of Haryana villages in India cases of a slightly more complicated, three-cornered interlinked exchange. The worker gets supplies of essential consumer goods on credit from the village shopkeeper or grain dealer, which are repaid with his labor services to the culivator-employer (in the form of underpaid wages), who then in turn repays the original creditor by adjusting his account with the latter for grain deliveries or purchases.

[7] The reader may again be referred to Newbery and Stiglitz (1979) for a survey of the analytic issues involved here.

[8] A complete explanation of why the rental market for draft animal labor is inactive (while the market for buying and selling "stocks" of animals is quite active) is not easy to give, but two partial reasons may be suggested: (1) there is a "moral hazard" problem involved in possible misuse and damage of the rented animals that may not be immediately traceable by the owner and attributable to any particular user; (2) there may be inflexibility in the timing of

he can sell the services of his bullocks or his own farm managerial skills in his spare time leads the person who owns such indivisible factors to lease in land and reap the scale economies arising out of such indivisibilities. Apart from the matter of indivisibility of the farmer's managerial or entrepreneurial abilities, sometimes the landlord may not be fully informed about these abilities of different workers, and under the circumstances their contractual choice may act as a screening mechanism. Workers with better entrepreneurial ability may provide self-selection by going for sharecropping tenancy rather than wage contracts.

Thus sharecropping tenancy in the land-lease market may best be regarded as a partial response to inadequacies or imperfections in other markets. Risky labor markets (uncertain employment or wages), employer's costs of monitoring intensity of labor application by the employees, imperfect marketability of family labor (manual as well as managerial) and of draft animal labor service, asymmetry of information on the abilities of workers—all of these factors contribute to the existence and indeed the historical persistence of the institution of sharecropping. To these may be added the contributing factor of an inadequately developed credit market: although a poor sharecropper may have few assets acceptable as collateral in the outside credit market, his landlord would accept the tenancy contract itself as collateral; the latter has the incentive to supply production credit (since he shares in the outcome of its use) and also is in the best position to enforce repayment (of both production and consumption loans) at the time of harvest sharing. Similarly, imperfections in the (production) credit market or in the market for specific inputs like fertilizers facing the small farmer are partially overcome by the rapidly growing system of cost sharing along with crop sharing.

Several authors have also looked upon the tenancy-cum-credit contract as a way of internalizing the effects of borrowing by a tenant on his effort supply (or risk taking) in the sharecropped farm.[9] The landlord, by altering the terms and amount of the loan that he makes available to the tenant, can induce him to work harder or to undertake projects which are more to the liking of the landlord (for example, projects with yields of higher mean as well as larger variance). If thus there is a positive externality of borrowing, there will be an incentive for the landlord to subsidize loans and to encourage the tenant to become indebted to him. In general when the landlord can force the tenant to a "reservation" utility level (at which there is a perfectly elastic supply of tenants), it is in the interest of the landlord to ensure that the tenant gets his credit from the cheapest source; a linked

---

plowing operations so that both the owner and the possible renter may need the animals at the same time, while at other times they are idle. Neither reason is sufficient to explain why the institution of a specialized team of plowmen (along with animals) available for hire is not fully developed everywhere, although there exist many cases where this is precisely the way the animal labor problem is handled.

[9] See Braverman and Srinivasan (1981), Braverman and Stiglitz (1981c).

tenancy-cum-credit contract is one way of ensurisng this if the landlord's opportunity cost of raising finance is lower than the interest rate charged by the village moneylenders. All this is consistent with the empirical finding noted in chapter 9 that in the Bardhan–Rudra sample villages many landlords offer tenants loans at interest rates below the market rate, and sometimes even at a zero interest rate.

Apart from tenancy-cum-credit contracts, one of the most important aspects of production relations in a poor agrarian economy is the frequently observed link between credit contracts and formal or informal labor-tying arrangements, discussed in detail in chapters 5 and 6. Sometimes such labor-tying does not directly involve a loan transaction, for example, when it is associated with land leased out to the laborer for cultivation or homestead (tenancy-cum-labor contract) or when labor is preferentially hired in the lean season in exchange for a commitment of ready availability in the peak season (intertemporal linking of labor markets discussed in section V of chapter 4). But more often than not credit is the all-important ingredient cementing labor-tying contracts. Labor-cum-credit contracts can be viewed as a risk-sharing device against the uncertainties of wage rates in the peak season (as in section I of chapter 5), or as an intertemporal barter transaction in the case of a double coincidence of wants between employer-creditors and laborer-borrowers arising out of the irregularities of the agricultural crop cycle (as in chapter 6), or as an attempt by the landlord to segment the labor market (for example, the landlord may "bundle"[10] credit and labor transactions in order to discriminate between different types of labor, say, between workers with differential credit needs).

III

There has been some recent literature on the question of the effect of interlinked factor markets on incentives to innovate in agriculture. A widely noted theoretical paper here is that by Bhaduri (1973). He shows that a landlord who is also a provider of consumption loans to his tenant (leasing in land at an exogenously given crop share, borrowing regularly for consumption at the beginning of each crop period, and repaying at harvest time along with interest at an exogenously given rate) may have no incentive to adopt yield-increasing innovations if the landlord's interest income from his loans to the tenant goes down (because the tenant will borrow less as he shares the increase in yield) sufficiently to offset his share of the increased yield. If this is correct, it provides a simple example of interlinked land-lease and credit contracts working as a constraining influence on technical progress.

In criticism it has been suggested by Ghose and Saith (1976), Griffin

---

[10] See Adams and Yellen (1976) for the essential arguments of commodity bundling and its ambiguous welfare effects.

(1974), Newbery (1975), and others that this is a rather weak constraint on adoption of technical progress, particularly in the socioeconomic context of poor villages: if the landlord has sufficient power to exploit his tenant-borrower and to withhold the innovation, then he ought to have sufficient power to extract the extra gain from the innovation by suitably manipulating the rental share, the interest rate, and/or other terms and conditions of the tenancy and credit contracts. In terms of Bhaduri's model these authors are questioning the appropriateness of assuming exogenously given rental shares or interest rates (even when there are legally stipulated maximum rates, there are various easy ways of getting around them) if the power relationships in the village are what Bhaduri portrays them to be.[11] This also means that Bhaduri's further consideration of a conflict facing the landlord between economic gain (in case the innovation is profitable) and loss of social and political control over indebted tenants is largely irrelevant if the landlord uses his instruments of economic control appropriately.

A necessary condition of Bhaduri's result is that the tenant *reduce* his borrowing when his income increases as a result of the yield-increasing innovation. But Srinivasan (1979b) shows that, if the tenant is a maximizer of a standard intertemporal welfare function of a discounted stream of utility from consumption, then at an unchanging pure rate of discount and interest, borrowing cannot be an inferior good for the tenant. If the rate of discount exceeds the interest rate, the tenant's borrowing will actually increase with his increased yield. In a related paper Srinivasan (1979a) shows that, even when one takes into account unanticipated production setbacks (say, due to weather) driving the sharecropper to the unpleasant means of underpaid labor service for meeting his debt repayment obligations to his landlord, the former does not lower his consumption borrowing when his mean income goes up, and thus the landlord's incentive to innovate is not blunted. This result, however, partly depends on the assumption that first-period consumption is entirely out of borrowing, so that the income effect on borrowing is by definition positive. Braverman and Stiglitz (1981a) show that, when an innovation changes the variance of yield as well as the mean, tenant borrowing may decline under some conditions.

It is obviously difficult to test Bhaduri's hypothesis directly from empirical data: the same phenomenon of adoption or nonadoption of yield-increasing innovations may have explanations quite different from that provided by Bhaduri. Most of the available indirect evidence,

---

[11] Ghose and Saith (1976) develop a model of accumulating debt and reach a conclusion opposite to that of Bhaduri: the stronger the domination of the landlord, the more readily he accepts technological improvement. In particular, the possibility of extracting the whole of the increase in the tenants' legal share (on the adoption of the new technology) in the form of usury income makes the returns of the new technology to the landlord the same as those for any owner-cultivator who does not have to share the gains of the increase in productivity.

however, suggests that even in areas (like east India) where Bhaduri considers his hypothesis as particularly relevant usury is not the dominant mode of exploitation by the landlord today, whatever may have been true in the past. As noted in chapter 9 from the findings of the 1975–76 Bardhan–Rudra survey in 334 randomly chosen villages in north and east India, even though the landlord is an important source of credit to his tenant, there are very few cases in which the tenant reported moneylending as the principal occupation of his landlord. The landlord quite often gives production loans to the tenant, shares in costs of seeds, fertilizers, etc., participates in decisiontaking about the use of these inputs, and in general takes a lot of interest in productive investment on the tenant farm, quite contrary to the implications of the Bhaduri hypothesis.

IV

Earlier in this chapter we traced the roots of personalized transactions in a poor agrarian economy to considerations qualitatively similar to those behind the operation of "customer" (as opposed to "auction") markets in more developed countries. But in the former case the isolated village economic community and its dense social network often dictate "captive" interlinking of transactions among the same small number of economic agents, with virtually all-or-nothing choices for the weaker partners. The very nature of the rationale that I have discussed for pesonalized interlinking may at the same time act as a formidable barrier to entry for third parties and is thus a source of additional monopoly power for the dominant partner in such transactions (just as in industrial organizations vertical integration rationalized on the basis of internalizing externalities of information and economies of transaction costs may, by the same token, lead to larger industrial concentration). An interlinked tenancy and credit contract, while having the potential of benefiting both the landlord and the tenant, may thus imply that the landlord can now brandish the stronger stick of withholding both land and credit rather than land alone, whereas the professional moneylender can do no more than deny the tenant the credit he seeks. Similarly, as noted in chapter 5, personalized interlocking of labor commitments and credit transactions often divide the workers and effectively emasculate their collective bargaining strength vis-a-vis employers.

Interlinking of transactions in different markets is also a very effective way for the dominant party to avoid social or legal controls on (and traditional sanctions against) charging high prices in some markets and to select criteria for rationing scarce resources (like credit or land) when prices are inflexible or sluggish in adjustment. The monopolistic landlord or the moneylender who faces conventional or legally stipulated norms of maximum rental share or maximum permissible interest rates (the extreme case being that of Islamic sanctions against usury) may be able to extract additional rent or interest in the form of underpaid labor services from the tenant or the borrower,[12] and in cases of less than full adjustment may even get away with much more than what would have otherwise accrued to him if equilibrium were unconstrained. Well-meaning political attempts to lower the ruling rental or interest rates may, under these circumstances, end up in lowering the agricultural wage rate.

Braverman and Srinivasan (1981) have shown that as long as the landlord can vary the size of the plot given to a tenant and there are enough potential tenants, the tenant will be pressed down to the "reservation" utility level and the landlord can reduce many tenancy or credit reforms to insignificance from the point of view of the tenant's welfare. A legislated reduction in the tenant's crop share will leave the welfare of each potential tenant unaltered; if the government offers the tenant subsidized credit at a cost lower than the landlord's opportunity cost of finance, the resultant surplus will accrue only to the landlord. Nothing short of land reforms conferring landownership to the cultivating tenant will affect the tenant's welfare.

Even if one moves away from utility equivalent contracts (say, by assuming that the worker can split his time between two contracts), piecemeal reforms may not be welfare-improving for the tenant, for reasons similar to those suggested by the theory of second-best. If contractual interlinking is a partial response to a whole host of incomplete and imperfect markets, piecemeal policy changes, without a comprehensive understanding of the underlying institutional features and their interconnections, may even worsen the lot of the poor tenant-laborer-borrower. History is littered with well-intentioned but ill-conceived projects crashing down on their intended beneficiaries.

[12] This increase in the exploitative powers of the stronger sections in the village through interpenetration of markets has been pointed out by Thorner and Thorner (1962) and Bharadwaj (1974), among others, in Indian agriculture, by Wharton (1962) for the marketing-moneylending-merchandising combine in Malayan agriculture, and by Ransom and Sutch (1977) for the territorial monopoly of rural merchants-cum-moneylenders-cum-landlords over sharecroppers in the U.S. South.

CHAPTER 13

Agrarian Class Formation

I

Marx did not define the term "class". But from the way he has used it, it seems that classes are best defined by conflicts of interests arising from the way they are related to ownership (or effective control) of means of production. The concept was first formulated and shaped in the context of industrial, capitalist societies. There are many who believe that it withers or misleads in analyzing social divisions in agrarian or primitive societies. There are others who have not been deterred by the particular associations of its original context and who have followed the lead of Lenin and Mao in harnessing it in their analysis of agrarian relations. This chapter begins with an application of the Marxian concept in the context of Indian agriculture and then dwells upon some extensions and modifications that seem to be called for if it is to retain its analytical sharpness in this alien context. A comment made by the Marxist anthropologist Terray in the course of his application of class analysis to the Abron Kingdom of Gyaman in West Africa is equally relevant in our present context:

> By using the idea of classes to understand precapitalist social formations, we inevitably reduce the distance separating them from the capitalist formation. But Marxist analysis cannot be reduced to the locating of similarities. Equally and above all it will prove itself when it is able to restore these particularities, these specific differences, which give each social formation under consideration a singular essence. (1975:133)

At the level of abstract Marxist economic theory, the neatest demonstration of how classes emerge *endogenously* from unequal endowments of means of production in exchange economies is in the recent work of Roemer (1982). He shows rigorously how with the objective of minimizing labor time spent to produce given subsistence requirements, individuals with differential endowments of means of production will sort themselves out in equilibrium into five classes characterized by:

(1) $SE=0$; $HI>0$; $HO=0$
(2) $SE>0$; $HI>0$; $HO=0$
(3) $SE>0$; $HI=0$; $HO=0$
(4) $SE>0$; $HI=0$; $HO>0$
(5) $SE=0$; $HI=0$; $HO>0$,

where *SE* represents self-employment, *HI* hiring in others' labor power, and *HO* hiring oneself out. How he relates to the buying and selling of labor power defines an individual's class position. In an agrarian economy class 1 above may be described as that of a capitalist landlord, class 2 that of a rich farmer, class 3 that of a family farmer, class 4 that of a poor peasant, and class 5 that of a landless laborer. Roemer also proves a one-to-one correspondence between this hierarchy of class positions and wealth distribution of individuals (the richest in class 1 and the poorest in class 5) and exploitation status (labor-hiring classes 1 and 2 as exploiters and labor-selling classes 4 or 5 as exploited, defining an individual as exploited if at the equilibrium he works more time than is socially necessary and as exploiter if he works less). The results are generalizable to an accumulation economy in which producers maximize revenues and one adopts a more general definition of exploitation: an individual is exploited if he works more hours than what is embodied in any commodity bundle he could have bought with his income; similarly, he is an exploiter if any commodity bundle he could have bought embodies more labor than he performs.

This Lenin–Mao–Roemer hierarchy of agrarian classes can now be applied to the set of detailed household-level data that we have for about 500 sample villages in rural West Bengal from the NSS 1972–73 Employment and Unemployment Survey. This is the largest set of data ever used for the purpose of this classification in India.[1] Since our focus is now on agrarian classes, we select from the sample only those households (in fact, the overwhelming majority of all rural households) which have cultivation or agricultural labor (outside of plantations) as the principal occupation. We then look into the details of labor time disposition by all adults and children in the household on farm work and wage work on others' farms in the reference week and also the amount of farm labor hired by the household in the same period. Applying this classification criteria one gets the percentage distribution of agricultural households in agrarian classes, as presented in table 13.1. It seems capitalist landlords constitute 0.2 percent of all agricultural households in rural West Bengal, rich farmers 14.3 percent, family farmers 29.2 percent, poor peasants 8.7 percent, and landless laborers 35.9 percent. Since in the survey self-employment on the farm presumably includes supervisory labor and general control over the labor process and decision making on the farm, it is likely that many of the capitalist landlords have actually been included in the next category of rich farmers. For our empirical purpose we should therefore consider the top two classes together.

There is in table 13.1 a residual category of "others". This primarily

[1] An alternative source of data on time disposition on the farm and on labor hiring is that of the Farm Management Surveys for several districts scattered in different parts of India (with 10 or 15 sample villages in each district). But these surveys deliberately exclude landless households who do not have a farm. On the other hand, labor time use data in these surveys refer to the whole agricultural year, whereas the NSS data relate only to the reference week.

TABLE 13.1

*Class distribution of agricultural households by land size groups,
rural West Bengal, 1972–73*

Agrarian Class	Percentage distribution of Total Agricultural Households in Cultivated Land Size Groups of:				
	Up to 0.1 Acres	0.1–2.5 Acres	2.5–7.5 Acres	Above 7.5 Acres	All Size Groups Together
	(1)	(2)	(3)	(4)	(5)
Capitalist landlords	0.0	0.0	0.1	0.1	0.2
Rich farmers	0.0	3.3	8.6	2.4	14.3
Family farmers	0.2	14.6	13.3	1.1	29.2
Poor peasants	0.5	6.2	1.8	0.1	8.7
Landless laborers	23.7	11.8	0.3	0.0	35.9
Others †	2.7	4.2	3.4	1.3	11.7
All	27.2	40.2	27.6	5.0	100.0

SOURCE: Estimates are from the author's tabulation of household-level data from the NSS, Employment and Unemployment Survey, 27th Round, 1972–73, in about 500 sample villages in West Bengal.

NOTE: Agricultural households are defined as those whose principal occupation (i.e., the singlemost important source of income) is either cultivation or agricultural labor (excluding plantations). Definition of the agrarian classes are in the beginning of the chapter.

† Includes primarily two categories of households: those whose self-employment (SE), hiring in (HI), and hiring out (HO) are all *positive*, and those for whom they are all *zero*. SE, HI, and HO all refer to labor time spent by adults and children in farm work in the reference week. Since SE includes supervisory labor, it is likely that many capitalist landlords have been included in the class of rich farmers.

consists of two types of households: those for whom *SE, HI,* and *HO* are all positive; and those for whom they are all zero. How is it that a farmer household hires out family labor on farm wage work outside and yet in the same reference week hires in farm labor on wage payment? The survey data do not give us any clue in answering this question, but a number of possible explanations suggest themselves: (1) contractual indivisibility (a small peasant enters into a contract with the landlord committing uninterrupted delivery of his services for, say, a fortnight, while the needed one day's work on his tiny plot is carried out by hired labor); (2) specialized work (a peasant may hire himself out on standard wage work and yet may need others on his own farm to do specialized work like transplanting or plowing, the latter often by plowmen who also bring their bullocks, a scarce resource); or (3) distant location of land fragments (it may be more

TABLE 13.2

Class distribution of agricultural households in districts of rural West Bengal, 1972–73

District	Percentage Distribution of Total Agricultural Households in Agrarian Classes			
	Capitalist landlords, rich farmers	Family farmers	Poor peasants, landless laborers	All classes
	(1)	(2)	(3)	(4)
Darjeeling	26.6	38.2	19.9	100
Jalpaiguri	3.6	53.3	33.7	100
Coochbehar	14.3	49.4	32.8	100
West Dinajpur	16.0	42.0	34.8	100
Malda	17.8	35.2	40.6	100
Murshidabad	15.9	33.1	47.3	100
Nadia	11.8	35.7	46.1	100
24-Parganas	12.6	26.0	54.4	100
Howrah	13.1	24.3	48.7	100
Hooghly	23.3	22.2	52.4	100
Bardhaman	24.1	13.7	54.6	100
Birbhum	33.1	25.3	36.8	100
Bankura	19.3	30.3	40.1	100
Medinipur	11.3	35.9	44.5	100
Purulia	17.4	26.6	41.0	100
All of West Bengal	16.4	31.2	44.9	100

SOURCE: see table 13.1
NOTE: The definitions of agrarian classes in this table are somewhat different from those in table 13.1. Not merely have classes 1 and 2 and classes 4 and 5 of table 13.1 been combined, but in taking HI we have now *netted* for any hiring out by the same household in the reference week (and similarly, for HO we have *netted* for any hiring in by the same household). This means column 1 in the present table refers to SE$\geq$0, NHI>0 (where NHI means net hiring in); column 2 to SE >0, NHI=0; and column 3 to SE$\geq$0, NHI<0. Note that the sample size for Darjeeling district is somewhat low, rendering the estimates for that district not very reliable.

convenient for a small peasant to work for wages on a neighbor's farm and hire labor to cultivate a distant land parcel owned by him).[2] One way of getting rid of this awkward category with *SE, HI,* and *HO* all positive is to introduce the idea of *net* hiring in (*NHI,* hiring in minus hiring out). The

[2] If the reference period is longer than a week (as in the Farm Management Survey data), the likelihood of the same household hiring wage labor some time and selling labor some other time increases on account of family emergencies as well as sharp peaks and troughs in short-run seasonal labor requirements.

estimates in table 13.2 incorporate this netting. As far as the quantitative dimension of exploitation (say, in terms of transfer of surplus value) is concerned, netting of exploitation should not pose any problem.

The other type of households included in the residual category is that of *SE*,*HI*, and *HO* being all zero. This is largely a consequence of the short reference period of a week. Given the periodicity of agricultural operations,[3] it is quite possible for some households to have no farm work in the reference week. This category presumably includes many unemployed landless laborers and small peasants (the data suggest that nearly 90 percent of this type of households have cultivated land of 2.5 acres or below).[4] For all practical purposes these unemployed should be included in the class of poor peasants and landless laborers. One may here note that, insofar as unemployment is disguised through "work spreading" on own farm, the family farmer class also contains members who more appropriately belong to the class of poor peasants.

The households in all categories of tables 13.1 and 13.2 include tenant households. Do they need to be separated out in our classification? Much depends on the actual terms and conditions of the tenancy contract. There are some tenants who have security of tenure and enjoy occupancy rights and effective control on the leased-in land, even though they do not legally own it. For all practical purposes they may be classified with owner-farmers in a hierarchy determined only by buying and selling of labor power, even though their income is smaller by the amount of the rental payment. But a majority of the tenants do not have tenurial security; and, as the Bardhan-Rudra survey of sharecropping contracts (described in chapter 9) shows, the landlord, apart from careful supervision of the harvesting operation by the sharecropper, frequently participates in making decisions, singly or jointly with the tenant, about what crops to grow, what inputs to use, etc. In many of these cases, therefore, the

[3] The periodicity of agricultural operations also suggests that a description of the agrarian class structure given in table 13.1 or 13.2, based as it is on a sample staggered over the seasons in a year, gives us an *average* picture across seasons. A class structure based on current household labor hiring in or out will clearly vary from one season to another (and indeed from a good agricultural year to a bad one). In the data set seasonal variance in the class distribution of agricultural households is significant but not very large. Taking the four subrounds in which the NSS divides the agricultural year and using the concept of *net* hiring, we estimate that for rural West Bengal in 1972–73 the percentage of agricultural households in the category of capitalist landlords and rich farmers varies from 12.3 percent in the January–March quarter to 20.2 percent in the October–December quarter, the percentage for family farmers varies from 28.0 percent in the July–September quarter to 36.2 percent in the January–March quarter, and that for poor peasants and landless laborers varies from 41.5 percent in the January–March quarter to 46.5 percent in the October–December quarter. For systematic class analysis one obviously needs panel data on a long-run basis, which we do not have.

[4] We should, however, note that *SE*, *HI*, and *HO* refer to farm work alone. So an agricultural household which does not have any farm work in the reference week may still be employed in nonagricultural work for the period.

sharecropping tenant may not be clearly distinguishable from a harvest-sharing attached laborer.[5] Besides, the landlord often rotates his tenants so that they do not acquire occupancy rights on the land; thus the same worker may shift from tenancy to wage labor and back to tenancy for the same landlord from one year to another. In all such cases the tenant should more naturally be classified with the poor peasants and landless laborers. This means that in table 13.1 some of the agricultural households classified as "family farmers" on the basis of their nonparticipation in the wage labor market contain tenant households who really belong to the classes of poor peasants and landless laborers. This is not, however, likely to make a big change in the estimates presented in table 13.1. Of course, we do not have data on the details of tenancy contracts for the households involved in table 13.1. If as a crude proxy, we take out from the category of family farmer households in the table all households reporting tenant cultivation as their principal occupation and having cultivated land of 7.5 acres or below, even then the percentage of total agricultural households in the family farmer category will decline only by 2.7 percent. This percentage may be larger for other regions.

Roemer's endogenous determination of the class hierarchy assumes, to start with, that each individual has an equal endowment of labor but differential endowments of wealth. If individuals have differential endowments of labor (or they choose to supply different amounts of labor), the hierarchy remains the same but the correspondence between wealth and class position breaks down: in particular, it is now possible for some asset-poor individuals to belong to the exploiting classes. Class positions are now monotonically ranked not with wealth but with the index of the *ratio* of wealth to the amount of labor supplied. This has an important application in the elaborately hierarchical village societies of India. Upper-caste households will not in general participate in manual work on their farm even when they are poor in terms of wealth, and there are special taboos against women doing field work. So they hire labor even on small farms. Note in table 13.1 the entry for rich farmers with 0.1–2.5 acres. Nearly a quarter of our class of "rich farmers" (strictly speaking, labor-hiring farmers) has cultivated land not exceeding 2.5 acres. Many of these households are poor in terms of assets (unless they have nonagricultural sources of income), but they belong to the class exploiting others' labor.

The correlation between class position and the index of the ratio of wealth to labor endowment has also an implication for the size of "family

[5] One major difference between the insecure tenant and the wage laborer is that usually the former brings his own bullocks to work on the landlord's land, while the latter does not. Like the poor peasant who owns a tiny plot, the bullock-owning tenant does not find his means of production productive enough to allow him to earn a living outside subordination to a landlord. This is similar to Cohen's (1978) proletarian example of a cutter in a dress factory who owns his scissors but needs the capitalist's cutting machine.

farmers" as a class. It is generally observed in India that there is an inverse relationship between wealth (particularly land) and the partitioning of the household:[6] asset-poor households tend to be more often nuclear, whereas the incidence of joint families is larger among wealthier farmers.[7] This means that taking the ratio of wealth to labor endowment for a household, there is some neutralizing adjustment in the denominator in response to a change in the numerator.[8] This process of family formation adjusting to the wealth position contributes to the size of the family farmer class: it contains relatively big farmers with large families (and labor endowment) as well as small farmers with small families.

II

In the preceding section we have adopted a somewhat austere economic-statistical categorization of classes. But in any real agrarian economy the economic structure in relation to which the class positions have been defined is itself embedded[9] in a social matrix in a way that cannot but affect those positions. Apart from the question of class consciousness (discussed in section IV), the *depth* of class cleavages as well as the *nature* and *domain* of the class formation process are significantly influenced by the social, political, and cultural milieu. The statistical categories do not, for example, tell us about the intensity of class divisions: is the class distance between labor-hiring rich farmers and family farmers the same as that between the latter and the labor-sellers? Do these distances between two classes vary from one social context to another, and if so, how? In rural West Bengal the sharpest dividing line is that between *bhadralok* (gentry) and *chhotolok* (the "lower classes"), based less on ownership of means of production and more on participation or nonparticipation in *manual* labor and the attendant life-style differences. Even though the latter differences are usually correlated with differences in asset ownership, the two are sufficiently distinguishable. A labor-hiring upper-caste family may be poorer in assets than, say, a family farmer or even a small peasant, but nonparticipation in manual labor clearly marks the former a "class apart" The manual laborer transfers to his hirer much more than the quantity of surplus value; there is an additional qualitative ("ritual") transfer, as it were: it creates what Terray (1975) calls the "material symbols of domi-

[6] For a discussion of some of the evidence see Krıshnaji (1980).

[7] Some of the reasons have to do with diseconomies of subdivision and fragmentation of land in agricultural production, a larger land base allowing a diversification of economic (both agricultural and nonagricultural) activities, leading to a more than proportionate increase in the capacity to support an extended family, and so on.

[8] In Chayanov's (1966) life-cycle theory, however, the numerator responds to a change in the denominator, with the peasant household acquiring more land as the family size increases, a possibility of limited scope for most peasants in India.

[9] This is a word borrowed from Polanyi (1944) but not to be interpreted in the all-devouring sense of his so-called substantivist followers.

nation."[10] This qualitative dimension[11] of labor-hiring and supervision is associated with a degree of social and symbolic control over people that widens the gulf between the class of labor-hiring farmers and the rest. The extent of the gulf varies with regional variations in ecological and demographic factors. In monsoon paddy areas like West Bengal (or coastal south India) the manual work of agriculture is dirtier than in, say, the dry wheat areas of northwest India,[12] and this is reflected in the differential cultural attitudes to manual work in these areas. Added to this is the fact that the secure agriculture of wet areas has encouraged a greater population density, depressing wages, which makes it relatively cheap to hire someone to do the dirty work and to use nonparticipation in manual work as a social differentiation device. Such nonparticipation by rich farmers as well as the gap between them and the family farmers is observed to be less acute in northwest India. Thus while there are possible materialistic interpretations of the cultural attitudes to manual work, there is no doubt that the attitudes themselves sharpen the class distances in a way that is not captured in the arithmetic of surplus value transfer.

Apart from cultural factors, political factors also influence the determinants of class positions.[13] We have already noted in the preceding section that the class position of the tenant depends on tenurial security. Political processes play an important role in the acquisition and preservation of the rights to tenurial security (particularly when most tenancy contracts are oral), and two regions with differential impact of these processes may lead to a different class positioning of asset-wise similar tenants. A landless tenant in Kerala (even before the recent abolition of tenancy there) could have belonged to the class of "family farmers", but were he located in Bihar would probably be indistinguishable from a landless wage laborer. The local political process is also important in the distribution of water from public irrigation facilities. The same physical amount of land will have substantially different productivity (and hence different implications for labor buying and selling) depending on the politically determined access to irrigation water. In recent years the state apparatus has been increasingly important in the delivery of subsidized production credit and key inputs (like fertilizers), and different farmers'

[10] As Djurfeldt and Lindberg (1975) report from a Tamil village, and as is commonly observed all over India, the payment of wages itself is symptomatic: "When a Harijan (lowest-caste) agricultural laborer is to receive his wage at the end of the working day, a ritual is enacted at the gate of his employer's house. In receiving the money, the Harijan bows, forms his hands into a cup, or beggar-bowl, which he holds in front of him; his employer then drops the money into his cupped hands, and is careful not to touch them."

[11] The recognition of this qualitative dimension of labor hiring in Marxian analysis of stratified agrarian societies will bring it a step closer to the Weberian emphasis on class and status as linked tendencies of group formation.

[12] Beteille (1974) puts some emphasis on this.

[13] I thus disagree with Cohen (1978) when he excludes culture and politics from his "structural definition" of class positions.

access to them depends, to a significant extent, on their political connections and mobilization. Of course, the dominant property owners in the village usually have more political clout in appropriating the flow of publicly distributed resources, but the political process is not a mechanical echo of the property relations, and by banishing it to the realm of "superstructure" we miss some of the integral aspects of production relations and class structure.

When Marxists explain exploitation and class positions in terms of a labor market, they do not usually specify the boundaries of operation of that market. In an agrarian economy these boundaries are often rather narrowly delimited and heavily dependent on social and territorial affinities. Since, as Marx noted, "the peculiar nature of labor power as a commodity is that its use value does not, on the conclusion of the contract between the buyer and the seller, immediately pass into the hands of the owner", the latter has to incur some cost in harnessing labor into the process of production. He therefore puts a premium on what he perceives to be the "dependability" characteristics of a worker to be hired. Costs of information on these characteristics rise rather sharply as one goes outside the normal community of one's village. This means that the employer often limits his recruitment, particularly on sustained employment contracts, to the immediate neighborhood, even when wages are somewhat lower outside, as Rudra (1981) has emphasized (with evidence from Birbhum district in West Bengal) and as noted here at the end of chapter 4. By providing local workers with regular credit (again, information costs and loan default risks are higher for outside borrowers) and emergency help, the employer nurtures their loyalty and consolidates his social control over the labor process. All this implies that the moral boundaries of a village community may significantly circumscribe the process of transfer of surplus value, and thus class formation gets territorilly segmented. (Such segmentation blocks supra-village class solidarity in the same way as national segmentation of labor markets in a capitalist world blocks proletarian internationalism.) Much, of course, depends on the stage of development of the forces of production. With the progress of agricultural technology the capitalist landlord is likely to find it much more profitable to break the territorial barriers of the local labor market and import labor from poorer areas to keep wages down.

Segmentation and clientelization in the rural labor market are crucially linked to the inadequately formed credit and insurance markets. The position of the peasant is often "like that of a man standing permanently up to his neck in water so that even a ripple might drown him" (to use Tawney's telling description of the Chinese peasant). He is therefore desperately in need of subsistence insurance and consumption credit for regular as well as emergency needs. Besides, the particularly slow turnover of capital in agriculture necessitates production credit. In the absence of organized credit or insurance markets, the poor peasant or the landless laborer enters, as noted in the preceding chapters, into various kinds of interlocking tenancy-cum-credit or labor-cum-credit contracts with his landlord-employer-creditor. This complicates the application of the concept of exploitation.

Take, for example, Roemer's (1982) property relations definition of exploitation (which seems to be a more general and in some cases more satisfactory definition than the orthodox surplus-value definition). A group is defined to be *feudally exploited* (since historically the term "feudalism" has other particularistic connotations, I would prefer the term "bondage-exploitation") if it can improve its lot by withdrawing from a present social set-up with its *own* endowments (examples of such a group: tenant-serfs, corvée laborers). As noted in chapters 5 and 9, except possibly in localized pockets, the incidence of obligatory labor service on the part of the tenant or debt bondage is quantitatively insignificant in rural India today. In general it is extremely unlikely that if the poor peasants or landless laborers withdrew with only their own assets and labor power they would have been any better off; in this sense they are not "feudally exploited".

Roemer calls a group *capitalistically exploited* if[14] it can improve its lot by withdrawing from society with its *per capita* share in society's alienable property and with its own labor (example: the proletariat). Applying this counterfactual test to a village economy, one can say it is quite likely that the poor peasants and landless laborers will be better off with an egalitarian redistribution of all alienable property in the village. Whether they will be able to sustain this improvement will, of course, depend on how they reorganize the incentive structure, inheritance practices, and the framework of production and investment decisions. But our present specific purpose is to focus on the credit and insurance needs. These needs will be now somewhat less for each individual whose asset position will improve, although, under the circumstances, the value of per capita assets will still be very small (and may get smaller with each generation under existing practices of subdivision through inheritance). Will there be a viable alternative for provision of credit, subsistence insurance, and protection in general? That this is uppermost in the mind of any peasant even remotely contemplating social change and redistribution is clear. Let us quote an example from the fieldwork account of Joshi in Uttar Pradesh:

> A group of tenants of a big landlord in Almora district vehemently protested against my suggestion that no landowner should be allowed to keep more land than he could cultivate with his family labor. They remarked, "In this village we are all small people and if that landlord is reduced to our level, whom shall we approach in times of need and who would protect us against outsiders?" I attributed the villagers' reply to their fear of the landlord and to their

[14] I am suppressing the other two conditions: that the group concerned improves its lot only at the expense of the group that is its complement in society; and that the latter depends on the former under the present arrangement.

backwardness. But as my understanding of village life became deeper I found their answer realistic, because no alternative source of help was yet available for the villagers. (1981:472)

Of course, the post-redistribution peasants can pool their resources to provide cooperative credit and social insurance to one another. Successful examples like those of Chinese communes providing social insurance will no doubt be cited in this context. But *ex ante* it is quite possible that some peasant groups contemplating Roemer's egalitarian counterfactual may be daunted by the enormity of the organizational task involved, particularly with the organizational diseconomies of small scale in coordinating numerous small asset holders replacing the unified decision taking of the big landlord in provision of vital insurance services. Apart from these diseconomies, there is the additional problem that the peasants after redistributing all alienable assets in the village may lose the landlord's connections and conduits to the outside world to raise finance and other resources. The seriousness of the problem will, of course, depend on the geographical domain and the political level of aggregation at which such redistribution is envisaged. These problems are being mentioned not to suggest that they are insuperable but only to point out that any definition of the exploitation and presumably class status of a group on the basis of an egalitarian counterfactual depends on formidable political and social organizational preconditions.

We should also note here that, while the property rights definition of exploitation may be more general and more satisfactory than the orthodox surplus-value definition at the level of abstract economic theory, it focuses primary attention on the statistical *mean* of the property distribution, and away from an analysis of the *depth* of class cleavages, which may depend not merely on the *variance* of the distribution below and above the mean but more importantly on the associated social and political dimensions of control of the labor process. As noted at the beginning of this section, class distances in an agrarian society are heavily influenced by the qualitative aspects of who works with his own hands and for whom, aspects which, while dependent on the property distribution, clearly go beyond it. By dissociating itself from the labor market the property relations approach takes us further away from this kind of class analysis than the surplus-value approach.

III

The surplus-value definition of exploitation leaves the class of "family farmers" (the local name for it in West Bengal is *grihastha chashi*) in somewhat of a limbo: operating outside the wage labor nexus, it is neither an exploiting nor an exploited class (or in some cases may contain both exploiters and exploited). Besides, it may, of course, be exploited, through the credit market, by moneylending rich farmers, or it may itself exploit by lending to poor peasants. In which direction do the alliance predilections of this "awkward class" point? Like any other petit bourgeois class it is extremely attached to its private property in land, and it feels easily threatened by redistributive movements. In rural West Bengal the egalitarian counterfactual will split this class roughly in the middle. Taking the data behind table 13.1 and assuming for the time being land as the only major alienable asset, the mean value for all agricultural households in West Bengal in 1972–73 comes to about 2 acres per household. So roughly half of the family farmer households will gain, and the other half will lose from a hypothetical redistribution.

Apart from the issue of landed property, state policies which affect agriculture and its means of production are likely to make the family farmers take sides. Rich farmers find them willing allies in their battle to lower taxes, betterment levies, and irrigation charges and to increase the flow of subsidized credit and inputs like fertilizers. On the question of securing higher administered prices for agricultural output, the economic interests of the two classes will tally if the family farmers are net sellers of that output in the market, which the rich farmers usually are. On most of these issues of state policies, which in recent years have become increasingly more important with the modernization of agriculture, the family farmers in general support and collaborate with the rich farmers.[15] This kind of collaboration, with the initiative in mobilization usually taken by the rich farmers, is also evident from studies of most of the major past peasant movements in India in this century,[16] contrary to the idea of Wolf (1969) and Alavi (1973) that the "middle peasants", being free from dependence on the landlords, take the initiative in radical peasant movements.

There are disputes in the literature about the size and stability of the family farmer class. There are some, e.g., Gough (1969) and Rudra (1978), who claim that this class is extremely small or nonexistent in India. The NSS estimate for West Bengal 1972–73 reported in table 13.1 suggests that this class is roughly 30 percent of all agricultural households (this estimate probably would have been somewhat lower had the reference period in the survey been longer). We do not have similar NSS estimates for other parts of India. On the basis of the data on hiring of farm labor days reported by the Farm Management Survey in different districts in India, it seems very likely that this class is relatively small in south India but quite substantial in

---

[15] It is, of course, possible to think of situations in which they withdraw such support when they find out that forming their own class organization may be a better way of preventing the rich farmers from appropriating the lion's share of the subsidized credit and inputs.

[16] For an analysis from this point of view of some of the principal peasant movements in India during the period 1917–50, see Pouchepadass (1980).

North and Northwest India.[17] But there is no question that Chayanov's judgment that such farms constituted over 90 percent of all farms in Russian agriculture in the beginning of the century does not apply to India today.

Table 13.2 presents a cross-section breakdown of the proportional importance of the family farmer class for 15 districts of rural West Bengal on the basis of NSS data. It is interesting to note that the proportional importance of the family farmer class is the lowest (and correspondingly, that of poor peasants and landless laborers highest) in Bardhaman, which is agriculturally one of the most developed districts in West Bengal. Another district with agricultural productivity among the highest is Hooghly, where the proportional importance of the family farmer class is among the lowest. In three districts of northern West Bengal, Jalpaiguri, Coochbehar, and West Dinajpur, agricultural productivity is among the lowest in the state, and the importance of the family farmer class is the highest. All this seems to suggest an inverse relation between agricultural progress and the proportional importance of the family farmer class. But the cases of two other districts, Howrah and particularly 24-Parganas, point to another significant factor. These two are among the agriculturally most stagnant districts in West Bengal, and yet the proportional importance of poor peasants and landless laborers is among the highest in the state and that of family farmers relatively low. This may have to do with the proximity of these two districts to the urban agglomeration of Calcutta, which may have accelerated commercialization of labor transactions in agriculture even without any substantial development of the productive forces on the farm.

The relation between agricultural progress and rural proletarianization is much less clear if one takes cross-section variations across agroclimatic regions over the whole of India. Let us take the proportion of farm wage laborers in the total rural work force for males in the 15–59 age group (we shall call this proportion WMPROP) across 55 agroclimatic regions covering most of rural India in 1972–73. It has a mean value of 21.5 percent and a standard deviation of 10.3 percent. Table 13.3 gives the results of a regression equation explaining regional variations in WMPROP. The first thing to note is that agricultural productivity per hectare is highly *insignificant* in explaining these variations. WMPROP has in fact a negative association with the variable GEMHA, or per hectare gross capital expenditure on agricultural implements, machinery, and transport

---

[17] For example, contrast the Farm Management Survey data for Tanjore (1967–68) to those for Muzaffarnagar (1968–69). Take the range of middle-sized farms in the sample distribution in either district (i.e., farms with land size lying between mean and mean plus or minus 75 percent of standard deviation). On about half of these farms in Muzaffarnagar more than three-quarters of the total labor is supplied by family workers; whereas in Tanjore this is the case for *none* of those farms.

TABLE 13.3

Linear regression analysis of determinants of proportional importance of farm wage workers in male labor force across 55 regions, rural India, 1972–73

Dependent Variable:	WMPROP (proportion of farm wage laborers in rural labor force for males in 15–59 age group)
Mean:	21.48 percent
Standard Deviation:	10.32 percent

Explanatory Variables	Regression Coefficient	Standard Error	Significant at Percent Level
OPH (agricultural output per hectare in Rs.)	0.0025	0.0027	35.3
CRLOP (concentration ratio of land operated)	56.3372	13.7871	0.0
GEMHA (gross capital expenditure on agricultural equipment per hectare of cropped area)	−0.1435	0.0525	0.9
SPARSVIL (proportion of sparsely populated villages in region)†	−0.1881	0.0985	6.2
MSTRIBE (proportion of scheduled tribes in total male population in region)	0.1120	0.0907	22.3
Constant term	−10.7081	8.9283	23.6

$R^2 = 0.3832$; $F = 6.1$; no. of observations $= 55$

SOURCE: Data for WMPROP are from NSS, Employment and Unemployment Survey, 27th Round, 1972–73; for OPH, average of years 1970–71 to 1972–73, estimated by Bhalla and Alagh (1979) using cropped acreage data for nineteen major crops; for CRLOP, from NSS, Land Holdings Survey, 26th Round, 1971–72, for area operated by household operational holdings; for GEMHA, same acreage data estimated by Bhalla and Alagh (1979) have been applied to data on gross capital expenditure (in Rs.) on agricultural implements, machinery, and transport equipment, as collected by Reserve Bank of India, Debt and Investment Survey, 1971–72; for SPARSVIL and MSTRIBE, from 1971 Census.

† Proportion of total inhabited villages in each region where the population is less than 200.

equipment; this means that proletarianization is *less* in regions of relatively high investment in agricultural fixed capital. On the other hand, WMPROP is positively, and very significantly, associated with the index of inequality of distribution of cultivated land in the region. Finally, WMPROP is negatively associated with the proportion of sparsely populated villages in a region, and positively (though weakly) with the proportion of tribal population.

How does one interpret these results? Looking at the data across the regions it seems that WMPROP is high in densely populated, fertile-soil regions of West Bengal and coastal south India, but it is low in highly productive areas of northwest India, but also low in low-productivity areas like Rajasthan, northern Madhya Pradesh, and hilly areas of Jammu and Kashmir, again high in low-productivity areas like eastern Maharashtra, northern Bihar, and southern Orissa. One clear pattern is that in high-rainfall, naturally fertile areas population density is high, the proportion of landless or near landless is large, wage labor is cheaper to hire, and the extent of proletarianization is relatively high,[18] even though these areas are not necessarily technologically progressive.[19] These are historically areas of relatively secure wet agriculture where the mounting population is absorbed with an astonishing elasticity (a process described by Geertz as one of "agricultural involution"), with continuous subdivision and multiplication of rights on land leading to elaborate hierarchies, and with the actual manual work of cultivation done only by those who are at the bottom of the heap (such as the lowest of castes and ethnic groups like tribals). The large numbers of landless and the elaborate vertical layering of land rights also imply that in many of these areas inequality in land distribution is high, which, as we have seen in the regression results, is strongly correlated with WMPROP.

On the other hand, in sparsely populated areas with a lot of remote villages not well-connected with centers of commercialization (which tend to commercialize the labor market and provide easier access to modernizing inputs for agriculture), the extent of use of wage labor is rather low.

Capital investment is relatively large (and accelerated in recent decades) in the agriculture of Punjab, Haryana, and western Uttar Pradesh. But in these areas the land–man ratio is relatively high and the proportion of wage labor low. Unlike in the densely populated areas, the land hierarchy here is relatively simple and oriented to direct cultivation of land by owners, and farmers depend to a large extent on the labor of their extended families.

Regional cross-section evidence thus does not clearly indicate larger proletarianization in agriculturally more progressive areas; instead, it points to other ecological, demographic, and institutional features which influence the degree of proletarianization. The evidence over time, however, points to an increase in the use of hired labor in agriculture along with economic growth. On the basis of Farm Management Survey data for all

---

[18] One may object to the term "proletarianization" by pointing out that some of this wage labor may be unfree or "bonded". As we have stated before, the incidence of "bonded labor" is quantitatively insignificant except in localized pockets. Cases of bonded labor are often associated with remote isolated areas. The negative relation between our variables SPARSVIL and WMPROP suggests that in these sparsely populated remote areas the proportion of wage labor in the agricultural work force tends to be low.

[19] Cohen's (1978) logical proposition that, if labor power is a commodity, production must serve the accumulation of capital, depends on the assumption that all markets are competitive. If there is territorial monopoly by landlords and village markets are isolated and fragmented, a system of surplus extraction from local wage labor may survive for a long time without being forced by competition to serve the accumulation of capital.

the five districts in India which have been resurveyed,[20] the hired proportion of total farm labor days went up from 32 to 55 percent in Ferozepur (Punjab) between 1956–57 and 1969–70, from 28 to 36 percent in Muzaffarnagar (western Uttar Pradesh) between 1956–57 and 1968–69, from 44 to 50 percent in Hooghly (West Bengal) between 1956–57 and 1970–71, from 25 to 82 percent in Coimbatore (Tamil Nadu) between 1956–57 and 1971–72, and from 30 to 32 percent in Ahmadnagar (Maharashtra) between 1956–57 and 1967–68. If one takes the agricultural labor households (i.e., those whose primary source of income is farm wage labor) as a proportion of total rural households, this proportion went up from 21.8 percent to 25.3 percent for India as a whole between 1964–65 and 1974–75, according to Rural Labor Enquiry Reports (although the rise in this proportion seems to be more in eastern and south India than in the highest-growth region, Punjab–Haryana, where it only went up from 14.3 to 15.8 percent).

Not all of this rise can be interpreted as an increase in proletarianization. To the extent that the rise in the number of agricultural labor households is due to eviction of erstwhile tenants and occupational shifts by non-agricultural rural laborers, this may just be a change in the *composition* of the rural proletariat (or semi-proletariat) rather than increased proletarianization as such. But to the extent that some of the erstwhile family farmers and self-employed artisans have been forced by economic circumstances (rise in the cost and credit intensity of cultivation in the case of farmers, fall in the demand for traditional crafts and disintegration of household industry in the case of artisans) to join the ranks of agricultural laborers, there has indeed been increased proletarianization. Evidence of the relative importance of the latter is somewhat fragmentary. The Rural Labor Enquiry Report indicates that, in the rise in the number of agricultural labor households between 1964–65 and 1974–75, the largest increase has been in the agricultural labor households *with land*. As pointed out at the end of chapter 3, according to NSS Land Holdings Survey data, in 1970–71 in Punjab (including Haryana) even though only 9 per cent of the rural households did not *own* any land, as many as 54 percent did not *operate* any land. The corresponding percentages in 1960–61 were 12 and 39, respectively. An analysis of the Farm Management Survey data for Ferozepur suggests that, while in 1956–57 62 percent of farms were predominantly family farms (i.e., depending on family labor for more than three-quarters of their annual labor use), in 1969–70 only 27 percent were predominantly family farms.

Apart from technological change with its associated change in the profile of resource constraints, the demographic-institutional factor of sub-division of holdings at the time of inheritance has a serious effect on the pace of proletarianization over time. As the average size of farm declines with

[20] On account of a change in sample stratification in the Farm Management Survey between the earlier and the resurvey periods, there are some problems of comparability of data here.

subdivision, some labor-hiring rich farmer households disintegrate into the family farmer class, and some of the latter into that of poor peasants: the former process lowering the demand for hired labor, the latter increasing its supply. Bhalla (1977), on the basis of her study of rural Haryana, has pointed out how the adoption of new technology has even accelerated the usual process of subdivision of family farms; by raising income from cultivation per acre it has removed an economic constraint previously binding the joint family together.

IV

What has certainly increased over time in many areas is the consciousness of class interests, even though they are still overlaid with various kinds of ascriptive and ethnic divisions. In an agrarian economy anchored firmly in its ecological and demographic framework, changes in the forces of production are usually rather slow, and the corresponding process of transformation of any "class-in-itself" into a "class-for-itself" is exasperatingly long, unless some exogenous shock (like a war or foreign invasion)[21] or organized political entrepreneurship intervenes and hastens the pace. Yet even in a rural society as proverbially timeless as that of India, the signs of stirring are quite visible, and the last two or three decades have seen some remarkable changes in the peoples' perception of their common class interests and even in their willingness and capacity for organized action to pursue them.

The degree of articulation and organization is, of course, much more advanced for the top layers of the class structure, even though factional rivalries and caste divisiveness afflict organizational activities at each stage. At the local village level there are frequent tacit, if not explicit, agreements of a collusive nature among the landlords and rich farmers (in setting the daily wage rate for a given agricultural operation, the leadership in some villages is taken by one dominant landlord, and the others follow); beyond the village, they sometimes pool their organizational resources to cultivate the outside world of politics and bureaucracy. In recent years they are increasingly working toward political aggregation at the state and national level so that they can be more vocal and effective in channeling the bureaucratic allocation of various subsidies and inputs in their favor. In this process caste affiliations are used more as a tool of political mobilization (and of building particularistic bridges with the corridors of power) than as ascriptions of ritual ranking.

The class of capitalist landlords and rich farmers in India today contains disparate elements evolving from *both* of what Lenin considered as two alternative historical forms of agrarian development (what he called the "American" and the "Prussian" paths): upwardly mobile peasant farmers

---

[21] For an analysis of the critical effect of the breakdown of a previously unified and centralized state on the success of peasant revolutions, see Skocpol (1979).

who have had a long history of direct cultivation (often as tenants) and now expanding through buying and leasing in land from absentee or small landowners; and erstwhile noncultivating landlords converting themselves—somewhat in Junker-style—into a group of active farmers as the new technology and pliant government policies (of low taxation, high support prices, and liberal provision of credit and subsidized inputs) have made cultivation a more profitable proposition than rack-renting. Many of the families of capitalist landlords and rich farmers have also branched out into money-lending, trading, transport, and other business and services. This aspect of portfolio diversification in these families has made them less susceptible to the vagaries of agricultural production, apart from strengthening their urban connections. There are some rural families which are specialized exclusively in occupations like money-lending, trading, etc. But they do not usually have antagonistic contradictions with the top layer of the agrarian class structure,[22] with whom they form natural alliances whenever there is any "trouble" with the lower classes.

[22] The possible conflicts of interests between the rural merchants and moneylenders on one side and the rich farmers on the other has sometimes been overplayed in the literature. Bhaduri (1981), for example, finds in these conflicts the root of differential agricultural growth performance between the eastern and northwestern parts of India. The main item of conflict emphasized in this context is that productive agricultural investment by rich farmers, by providing greater employment and income opportunities for poor peasants and laborers, weakens the latter's dependence on the professional moneylenders. Neither Bhaduri nor anyone else subscribing to this view has provided even the slightest piece of evidence that in recent years productive investment by rich farmers in East India has been resisted by professional moneylenders or merchants on this or any other ground, or that the former have been deterred by such resistance. (Even on the theoretical level it is not shown why the investing rich farmer cannot squeeze all the extra surplus generated from the poor peasant, so that the latter is left just as dependent on consumption loans as before.)

Besides, it is not entirely clear that the "grip" of professional moneylenders and traders is quantitatively that much more important in eastern than in the northwestern parts of India. If one takes the All-India Debt and Investment Survey data of the Reserve Bank of India for 1971, of the total cash debt incurred by cultivator and agricultural labor households, the percentage owed to professional moneylenders and traders is actually *lower* in Assam, Bihar, and Orissa than in Punjab, and the corresponding percentage in West Bengal is higher than that in Punjab but lower than that in Haryana. The historical as well as current evidence for the contrasting regions of western and eastern Uttar Pradesh indicates exactly the opposite of Bhaduri's presupposition. Let us quote, for example, from Stokes, who in discussing historically the origin of the regional variations in dynamism in Uttar Pradesh agriculture comments: "One fact seems clear. In the eastern districts landlords and superior agriculturists constituted the main source of agricultural credit, whereas in Meerut (the most thriving district of the western Uttar Pradesh) the professional moneylender and trader held a large share of the business" (1978:240). This is confirmed by the Reserve Bank data for western and eastern Uttar Pradesh in 1971.

That output-raising investments in agriculture are carried out less often in eastern than in northwestern India is not because of the fear that it will cut down on anyone's usury or speculative income (either of the rich farmer himself or of the professional lender and trader). It has more to do with the fact that the ecological-demographic-institutional framework in East India has kept both the amount of investable surplus and the rate of profitability in cultivation relatively low. The ecology of densely populated monsoon paddy agriculture,

More problematic is, of course, the state of development of class consciousness of the poor peasants and landless workers. Do they still represent, to use Marx's picturesque description of the French peasantry in the *Eighteenth Brumaire,* "the great mass ... formed by simple addition of homologous magnitudes, much as potatoes in a sack form a sack of potatoes?" There is a great deal of regional variations in this, but in general organized class action on the part of these groups is still highly fragmentary, localized, and infrequent. Even in cases of group action their solidarity has not always been principally based on a shared perception of their class positions. More frequent are cases of their involvement in large-scale rural movements where they have been mobilized and harnessed by richer farmers to serve primarily the latters' class interests (in agitations for lower taxes, higher prices, and better subsidies).

Yet there is no doubt that the moral and political environment of age-old deference to hierarchical norms is changing rapidly. Everywhere in India the poor have started questioning what has been one of history's most well-entrenched and ornately elaborate ideological systems for legitimizing inequality and exploitation. This questioning becomes more acute as, with the expansion of the market nexus, landlords renege on some of their traditional patronage functions and, with the periodic exigencies of electoral politics, the vote-mobilizing rhetoric of competing political notables escalates in radical populism. It is, of course, not at all clear whether the poor peasants' perception of exploitation is in terms of some abstract concept of egalitarian distribution of property (as in Roemer's counterfactual). Scott (1976) cites many examples from history of completely different moral principles on which their sense of exploitation, notion of injustice, and moral outrage are often based. In the Central Luzon haciendas of the Philippines, for example, the rebelling tenants, sparked by the landlord's refusal of previously customary grain loans, sometimes stormed his granary, but confiscated only the amount equivalent to their customary share.[23] Scott

---

accompanied by agricultural involution, dwarf holdings, and petty landlordism (nurtured for long by the particular land tenure under the colonial administration in this region) leave the generation of investable surplus per farm rather low in eastern India (as contrasted to the case in northwestern India of relatively large land holdings, a long tradition of direct cultivation, and, for Punjab, a larger income supplement from some members of the farmer family being in the army or other services in different parts of the country). Unlike in the case of wheat, the new technology is also more fragile for monsoon paddy, and public irrigation facilities and electricity to energize pumps are much more limited in eastern India. With the development of irrigation and public credit, there has been substantial progress in the production of wheat and summer paddy (both outside the monsoon season) in West Bengal in recent years, carried out mostly by the rich farmers. This shows that when the other conditions and forces of production are ripe, the alleged merchant-moneylender resistance is immaterial.

[23] Similar examples are available in studies of the moral economy of crowds in precapitalist England and France made by Thompson (1971) and Rudé (1964): when the price of bread and flour shot above tolerable levels for the working poor, an angry crowd often occupied the market, sold staples at what they considered the "just price", and occasionally even handed over the proceeds to the merchants.

comments: "Their action was designed to enact, unilaterally, a critical subsistence right which had been suddenly denied them. Their goal was not the elimination of landowners as a category but the restoration of more tolerable terms of exchange within the existing stratification" (1976:190).

Even when an individual peasant does not find the terms of exchange within the existing stratification tolerable and feels exploited, his sense of outrage usually takes on a social dimension only when he perceives it to be shared by the kinship or ethnic group with which he easily identifies. His sense of exploitation can thus be diffused by prospering, upwardly mobile members of his own caste, who sometimes offer him patronage on kinship lines. Clear cases of class confrontation in the Indian countryside, even those organized by the leftist parties, like the widely publicized ones of east Tanjore or the Kuttanad area, are usually also cases of clear demarcation of caste or ethnic homogeneity on each side of the opposing classes. The merging of class and caste in a bipolarized structure makes the conflict of interests in these cases much more transparent than is commonly observed elsewhere. Sometimes "negative class consciousness", to use Hilton's (1977) term, is forged on an unorganized group when it is treated as an undifferentiated group by its adversaries. As Breman (1974) notes, from his fieldwork in southern Gujarat, about the landless *Dubla* laborers: "Their awareness of unity is further stimulated from outside because *Anavils* (the landowning class) regard all the *Dublas* being cut from the same cloth." Beteille (1974) shows how, even on the landowners' side, the group known as *Jotedars* in West Bengal (who differ substantially among themselves in their economic as well as cultural features in different parts of the state) have been invested with a unity more by the political process (in which the leftist peasant movements brand them as an undifferentiated class enemy); in this context he quotes Sartre's statement that classes are not given, men make them ("les classes ne sont pas, on les fait").

Of course, men do not make them out of thin air. There is an underlying economic structure around which class conciousness crystallizes. But within that structure there are intraclass ambiguities which hinder the process, even apart from the diffusing effects of the cross-cutting cleavages of caste and ethnicity. A landlord who rotates his tenants not merely keeps them from acquiring occupancy rights on the land but also, by periodically giving the tenancy back to them, keeps them away from merging with the wage laborers in class solidarity.[24] Similarly, by hiring some attached laborers, giving them secured year-round employment (and other benefits), and rewarding them for loyalty and for reporting on delinquent casual workers, the landlord effectively separates the former from their fellow class members. As noted in chapter 5, we found in the Bardhan–Rudra 1979 survey of 110 sample villages in West Bengal that in villages where some form of group bargaining or labor agitation for agricultural wage increase took place, most of our tied-

---

[24] For an emphasis on the effect of tenant rotation on class formation, see Mencher (1974).

labor respondents reported nonparticipation in the movements, and the majority of them cited their ties with the landlord as the primary reason for their nonparticipation.

In general, personalized clientelization fragments the labor market, fractures the formation of class consciousness, and emasculates class organization. As noted before, such clientelization largely arises from the absence of credit and insurance markets. In such situations, party-based political entrepreneurship to mobilize poor peasants and laborers in consciousness-rousing protest movements or labor agitations may not be effective or sustained until and unless the organizational resources are also channeled toward building viable local community institutions providing alternative sources of credit and social insurance. Even in the cases of successful labor agitations resulting in a higher agricultural wage rate, their economic and organizational effects are often largely confined to an individual village or neighborhood, and the territorial affinities and moral boundaries of the latter effectively circumscribe class-based organization.

In the cases in which class action taken by poor peasants and laborers fails, the consequences in terms of exposure to insecurities and oppression are sometimes much worse than the status quo ante. It is the high risk of failure and deep doubts of organizational feasibility and sustainability of class action that get internalized in the peasant mind, and their behavioral expressions take forms that are often interpreted as quiescence, or false consciousness. The elaborate network of primordial loyalties and hierarchical norms in the peasant life that anthropologists often cite as evidence against his class consciousness is sometimes nothing more than forms of strategic behavior under the given constraints and manipulation of symbolic resources in his endless personal struggle to survive. In other cases, he may be trying to handle cognitive dissonance by adjusting his beliefs to the current capacity constraints of his class.[25] But in a situation of social and political flux like that of India today, such submergence of class tensions cannot remain deep for long, and all kinds of latent structural conflicts have started coming out into the open with increasing regularity.

---

[25] These indicate the problems of judging the empirical validity of class categories by trying to find out if the peasants themselves express their social divisions in these terms or not.

CHAPTER 14

Poverty of Agricultural Laborers and "Trickle-Down" in Rural India

I

For those who find radical institutional changes politically disturbing or unfeasible the so-called trickle-down effects of growth on poverty offer a comforting hypothesis. The evidence (mostly indirect) from rural India on this hypothesis is, however, mixed and not unambiguously comforting. This is particularly so for the case of agricultural laborers, who are usually among the poorest of the poor. Of course, in general, growth in agricultural output tends to generate some forces improving the income of wage laborers. Yield-increasing or land-improvement factors increase, as the statistical analysis in chapter 3 corroborates, the demand for hired labor, and this is, by and large, the case for the biochemical innovations which are part of the new agricultural technology. By shortening the duration of the crop cycle and increasing the importance of timeliness of each operation, the new technology also increases the bargaining power of wage laborers at some crucial points of time. In spite of all this, it is commonly observed that in India the new technology may have adversely affected the *relative* share of wage labor in output.[1] What is more controversial, however, is the question of absolute immiserization of agricultural laborers. Before turning to the evidence on this question, let us first enumerate the possible ways in which the income-generating forces mentioned above could have been counteracted and the trickle-down process of agricultural growth blocked, as far as agricultural wage laborers are concerned.

One possible way that can be immediately cited is the effect of adoption of labor-displacing machinery, which is considerable in some of the high-growth regions. A second factor may be that the new agricultural strategy has strengthened the political bargaining power of the rich farmers at the state and national level, which has resulted in higher administered prices of foodgrains (of which the agricultural laborers are net buyers), whereas typically wages lag behind the price rises (and as monetization of wage payments increases with agricultural progress, as noted in section VI of chapter 4). Third, and probably most significant in many regions, there may have been a heavy influx of labor suppliers in the agricultural labor

[1] See, for example, the studies by Parthasarathy and Prasad and Mellor and Lele, cited in the survey article by K. Bardhan (1977), on incremental share of hired labor with the switch to high-yielding varieties.

market, depressing wage income, partly as a result of the growth process itself.[2] One can think of several mechanisms at work here:

  a. increased profitability of self-cultivation by big landlords leading to eviction of small tenants;
  b. increased dependence of agriculture on purchased inputs and privately controlled irrigation driving some small farmers with limited access to resources and credit out of cultivation and into crowding the agricultural labor market;
  c. some small farmers being driven out of cultivation as pumpsets enable richer farmers to appropriate communal groundwater, resulting in a possible drop in water tables and making the traditional lift irrigation technology even less effective than before for poorer farmers without pumpsets, or with the big farmers having acquired their own irrigation equipment, the village leadership, largely dominated by them, is now less interested in the maintenance of old irrigation channels, hurting the poorer farmers who depend on them;
  d. a similar crowding of the agricultural labor market by displaced village artisans, as the demand pattern of the new rural rich shifts away from local handicrafts and services to mass-produced urban consumer goods and services; and
  e. growth-induced in-migration of agricultural labor from backward areas.[3]

Let us now turn to evidence on the question of absolute poverty of agricultural laborers. Unfortunately, there is a serious lack of time-series data on poverty of agricultural labor households. A major source of data is the periodic Rural Labor Enquiries. Their latest reports allow us to compare two points over the ten-year period, 1964–65 to 1974–75. According to this source, the average daily earnings in agricultural operations by men belonging to agricultural labor households, deflated by the consumer price index of agricultural laborers, *declined* by 12 percent over this ten-year period[4] for the whole of rural India; at the State level it declined in all the States, except Punjab–Haryana, Uttar Pradesh, and Jammu and Kashmir (where it rose) and Karnataka (where it stayed the

---

[2] This is apart from the usual demographic factors: natural growth in agricultural labor households; subdivision of farms driving more family farmers into the class of poor peasants; the shift in the age distribution over time in favor of the very young, raising the proportion of agricultural laborers (the Census data suggest that the proportion of agricultural laborers among male rural workers goes down with age), etc.

[3] It is often reported that in-migration of rural labor in Punjab from the backward districts of Bihar and eastern Uttar Pradesh has kept the growth of wage income in check. It is, however, doubtful that such in-migration is as yet substantial enough to have significant effects. A study of migration flows by Oberai and Singh (1980) shows that in a 1977 survey of 2,124 rural households in 26 villages in Ludhiana district in Punjab, there were in all 92 agricultural laborer in-migrants as opposed to 79 agricultural laborer out-migrants, so that there was net in-migration of only 13 agricultural laborers in the whole sample.

[4] The year 1974–75 is not a very good agricultural year. It should nevertheless be noted that, between 1964–65 and 1974–75, net production of foodgrains went up by 20 percent and net domestic product from agriculture (at 1960–61 prices) went up by 11 percent.

TABLE 14.1

Annual wage income per agricultural labor household

State	Y_w (Rs.) 1964–65	1974–75	1974–75 at 1964–65 Prices	ACPI with 1964–65 as 100	Col. 3 as % of Col. 1.
	(1)	(2)	(3)	(4)	(5)
Andhra Pradesh	434.97	999.43	387.38	258	0.89
Assam	987.27	1933.22	740.70	261	0.75
Bihar	475.76	1094.49	419.34	261	0.88
Gujarat	845.12	1495.65	623.19	240	0.74
Jammu and Kashmir	616.06	1414.30	559.01	253	0.91
Karnataka	506.40	1183.16	501.34	236	0.99
Kerala	664.41	1440.08	496.58	290	0.75
Madhya Pradesh	620.19	1152.14	385.33	299	0.62
Maharashtra	630.91	1214.01	503.74	241	0.80
Orissa	498.39	780.98	280.93	278	0.56
Punjab-Haryana	992.38	2146.00	886.78	242	0.89
Rajasthan	617.17	1552.13	554.33	280	0.90
Tamil Nadu	445.89	1005.58	343.20	293	0.77
Uttar Pradesh	385.12	1081.85	470.37	230	1.22
West Bengal	767.23	1252.32	502.94	249	0.66
All India	536.53	1164.59	453.15	257	0.84

SOURCE: For 1964–65, Labor Bureau, Rural Labor Enquiry (LBRLE), *Final Report, 1963–65*, tables 2.1, 2.6, 3.2, 3.3, 4.4, 8.4, 8.8, 9.4, 9.8, and appendix 5; for 1974–75. LBRLE, *Summary Report on Wages and Earning, 1974–75*, tables 2(a). 1, 3(a). 1.1, 3(a). 1.2, 3(a). 1.3, and LBRLE, *Final Report on Wages and Earnings, 1974–75*, table 2.9 (a).1; and for ACPI, the agricultural laborer consumer price index, base year as given in LBRLE, *Final Report on Wages and Earnings, 1974–75*, table 3.4.

NOTE: Y_w is the total annual wage income earned by all usually occupied workers (male, female, and child) in the agricultural labor household.

same). But, of course, one is more interested in the movements in total annual earnings of the agricultural labor households than in daily wage rates. The Rural Labor Enquiry Reports do not provide these estimates for this period. But scattered in different parts of these reports there is enough information on days of employment in different occupations, the average number of earners in each household, etc., from which to construct an estimate of the total annual *wage income*[5] (from both farm and nonfarm work) of all the earning members (men, women, and children) in an

[5] It excludes income from self-employment. Of the total employment of members of the average agricultural labor household, self-employment is, however, only a very small proportion.

average agricultural labor household—what we have called Y_w in table 14.1 and computed for each states. Using the consumer price index of agricultural laborers as a deflator, we find from column 5 in table 14.1 that between 1964–65 and 1974–75 annual wage income per agricultural labor household declined in all states (*including* the highest-growth region of Punjab–Haryana) except Uttar Pradesh; for rural India as a whole it declined by 16 percent over this period.

More recently, the NSS tabulation of the results of the Thirty-Second Round (1977–78) Employment and Unemployment Survey has provided some information on the distribution of agricultural labor households by expenditure classes (see table 14.2). The last such year for which this percentage distribution data are available is 1963–64, from the Rural Labor Enquiry Report. Using Rs. 15 at 1960–61 prices as the poverty line,[6] the agricultural labor consumer price index as the deflator (which went up from 118 in 1963–64 to 323 in 1977–78), and applying the standard linear interpolation method to find a point between two discrete expenditure group limits, our estimates suggest that between 1963–64 and 1977–78 the

TABLE 14.2

Percentage distribution of agricultural labor households by expenditure classes, rural India, 1963–64 and 1977–78

1963–64		1977–78	
Annual per capita expenditure classes in Rs. at current prices	Percentage of total number of agricultural labor households	Annual per capita expenditure classes in Rs. at current prices	Percentage of total number of agricultural labor households
0–50	0.32	0–119.9	0.16
51–100	5.19	120–239.9	2.36
101–150	18.98	240–359.9	13.49
151–200	23.17	360–479.9	22.41
201–250	17.59	480–599.9	20.34
251–300	13.02	600–839.9	23.68
301–350	6.78	840–1199.9	12.28
350+	14.95	1200–1799.9	4.09
		1800–2399.9	0.78
		2400 +	0.41

SOURCE: For 1963–64, LBRLE, *Final Report, 1963–65*; for 1977–78, NSS, Second Quinquennial Survey on Employment and Unemployment, 32nd Round, Draft Report no. 298, May 1981.

[6] This is the poverty line that I have used in Bardhan (1973), which provides detailed justification on the basis of nutritional norms for this line. Sukhatme (1978) has since pointed to problems of assuming average nutritional norms on account of interpersonal variability of nutritional needs and the existence of adaptive mechanisms over time. I should note, however, that the nutritional minimum used in Bardhan (1973) involved only 2,100 calories per day per *adult* unit, which is lower than what Sukhatme regards as the critical minimum threshold and certainly much lower than the FAO norms.

proportion of agricultural labor households below the poverty line for rural India as a whole increased somewhat, from 52 percent to 56 percent. Over this period net domestic product from agriculture (at 1960-61 prices) went up by about 43 percent.

II

One problem with the preceding discussion, as with most of the literature on the subject, is that it uses data at a much too aggregative level. What one really needs is an intensive micro-level analysis of the effects unleashed by various types of agricultural growth processes under different institutional settings. There are a few scattered micro-level village case studies on this question, but usually they are more descriptive than analytical. Besides, their extremely small-scale inhibits wider generalization.

Analytical studies of rural poverty in India which are sufficiently intensive at the micro-level and yet yield results that are statistically generalizable are clearly lacking. The rest of this chapter is a limited attempt to analyze the NSS cross-section data on rural poverty, but at a disaggregated level, and to explain variations in the extent of poverty in terms of a multivariate model. Since our variables are necessarily confined to those defined and collected by NSS (supplemented by other such secondary sources of data that were available), quite often they cannot capture the finer variations and intricacies in technological and institutional determinants of poverty, and the analysis has to make do with crude proxy variables and, on some key determinants, no variables at all. Since the analysis with NSS data in the literature so far has been mostly at an even cruder aggregative level and since for quite some time to come the NSS will not have a long enough time series on poverty, deeper probes into the disaggregated NSS cross-section data may still be highly worthwhile, in spite of the obvious constraints of the NSS data collection framework.

We analyze the NSS cross-section data at two different levels of disaggregation: first, at the detailed individual household level in about 550 sample villages of West Bengal in 1977-78, from the NSS Thirty-Second Round data; and second, at the level of the 55 NSS agroclimatic regions covering almost the whole of rural India in the beginning of the 1970s. The first set of data will be analyzed in this section, and the other will be taken up in the next.

Taking the West Bengal 1977-78 sample households, we first separate out the agricultural labor households. We shall again take the poverty line as given by a monthly per capita expenditure level of Rs. 15 at 1960 prices.[7] (How we have derived an approximate district-level price index to deflate the current-prices expenditure data is explained in the notes to table 14.3).

---

[7] Since the cost of living in rural West Bengal in 1960 was higher than that for rural India this poverty line is in effect lower than the all-India poverty line of Rs. 15 at 1960 prices.

As against this, the mean per capita monthly expenditure at 1960 prices (what we call PCEXPR) in the agricultural labor households in West Bengal 1977–78 was Rs. 12.54 (with a standard deviation of Rs. 5.66).

We then carried out a LOGIT analysis of the probability that an agricultural labor household falls below our poverty line, and the results are reported in table 14.3. The explanatory variables taken are of different kinds and are derived from the NSS as well as Census and State Statistical Bureau sources. Some of the variables are specific to each individual household—area cultivated (CULTIVAT), number of nonearning dependents (NDEP), number of men with above-primary education level in the 15–60 age group (EDM), number of men usually occupied in nonfarm work (NFM), whether the household belongs to scheduled castes (SCHCASTE), and the NSS subround in which the household was visited (SBRND). Some other variables are specific to the village where the household happens to be located—village male wage rate for farm work in the reference week (VWAGEM), village irrigation level (VILIRR), distance of the village from nearest town (DIST), and whether adult males in the village got any wage employment in public works in or near the village in the reference week (PUBWORKM). The other variables relate to the district in which the sample village happens to be located (in the absence of villagewise information on these)—normal annual rainfall (RAIN), level of nitrogeneous fertilizer use (NHA), and rate of growth of agricultural production (GROWTH).

Most of the variables have highly significant coefficients (except for PUBWORKM and SBRND 3, though they have expected signs). As expected, the probability of falling below the poverty line is lower for an agricultural labor household with a larger area to cultivate for its own, smaller number of dependents, larger participation in nonfarm work, and better education level (both increasing the nonagricultural opportunities available to the household), or if it belongs to a village where the wage rate is higher, the cultivated land in the village is in general more irrigated, there is better rainfall and fertilizer use, and there are alternative opportunities to work on public works programs. The probability of falling below the poverty line is larger if, again as expected, the village is remote (hence fewer alternative opportunities for the labor household), the household belongs to a scheduled caste (fewer "connections", larger deprivations in access to resources and job opportunities, and lower bargaining power), and the current period is in an agriculturally slack season (subround 3—January–March—is largely a slack period in most parts of West Bengal).

What, however, may not be so expected is the highly significant positive coefficient[8] of the variable GROWTH in table 14.3. *Other things remaining*

[8] As for any possible multicollinearity problem, with GROWTH being correlated to other independent variables, let me note here that the correlation coefficients of GROWTH with VILIRR and NHA are significant but not very high: 0.37 and 0.51, respectively; the correlation coefficient of GROWTH with VWAGEM is negative, although not significant.

TABLE 14.3

LOGIT analysis of the probability of an agricultural labor household falling below the poverty line, rural West Bengal, 1977–78

Explanatory Variables	Estimated Coefficient	Standard Error
CULTIVAT (area cultivated by household in acres)*	−0.6094	0.1113
NDEP (number of dependents in household)*	0.4005	0.0362
EDM (number of men with above-primary education level in 15–60 age group)*	−0.8066	0.1901
NFM (number of men in household usually occupied in nonfarm work)*	−0.6549	0.2142
DIST (distance of village from nearest town in km.)*	0.0085	0.0034
VILIRR (village irrigation level)†*	−0.1669	0.0565
VWAGEM (average daily wage rate in Rs. for male agricultural labor in village in reference week)*	−0.3041	0.0494
PUBWORKM (dummy for male wage employment in public works in or near the village)	−0.3753	0.2610
SBRND 3 (dummy for Jan.–March Quarter)	0.2727	0.1577
SCHCASTE (dummy for schedule caste)*	0.3073	0.1222
RAIN (normal annual rainfall in district in meters)*	−0.3005	0.0879
NHA (nitrogenous fertilizer in kg. used per hectare of area under foodgrains in district)*	−0.0485	0.0079
GROWTH (rate of growth in agricultural production in district)*	0.2804	0.0933

Likelihood ratio index = 0.3020; no. of observations = 2,127

SOURCE: Data for CULTIVAT, NDEP, EDM, NFM, VILIRR, VWAGEM, PUBWORKM, SBRND 3, and SCHCASTE are from the NSS, 32d Round, household-level data. Data for DIST are from the 1971 Census Village Directory. VWAGEM has been computed by taking the total wage earnings on casual male farm labor by all NSS sample households in the village divided by the corresponding total number of casual male farm labor days. The district-level variables, RAIN, NHA, and GROWTH are from various publications of the State Statistical Bureau of West Bengal. GROWTH has been estimated by fitting a regression line on the annual time-series data on agricultural production over a period of 18 years (1960–61 to 1977–78) for each of rural West Bengal's 15 districts.

NOTE: The poverty line has been assumed to be given by a monthly per capita expenditure level of Rs. 15 at 1960 prices. To find a suitable deflator to convert the current-prices expenditure data was a problem. As an approximation I have used the food price index for the bottom expenditure class of households (Rs. 1–100 per month *per household*) for different regional centers, as regularly published by the State

Statistical Bureau of West Bengal. I have taken simple averages over the price index figures of different regional centers within a district and used this district-average price index to deflate the consumption expenditure of a household located in that district.
†Represents four percentage levels of irrigation in the village: zero; positive but not over 10 percent; between 10 and 25 percent; and over 25 percent.
*Significant at less than 5 percent level.

the same, the probability of an agricultural labor household sliding below the poverty line seems to be higher if the household is located in a district where agricultural production has grown at a faster rate. How far this result is due to the various possible adverse effects of the agricultural growth process we have briefly referred to in Section I (particularly those due to the crowding of the agricultural labor market resulting from growth-induced tenant eviction and smaller farmers being driven out of cultivation by the increased costliness and credit intensity of cultivation) is difficult to say. It is certainly consistent with (1) the trend increase in general poverty in rural West Bengal in the NSS time series (Ahluwalia 1978), in spite of the states's having one of the better agricultural growth records in India, particularly in more recent years; (2) the significant rise in the proportion of agricultural labor households to total rural households in West Bengal between 1964–65 and 1974–75, according to the Rural Labor Enquiry Reports; and (3) a finding in a survey of 110 randomly selected villages in West Bengal in 1975–76, described in Bardhan and Rudra (1978), that 81 percent of the villages in the highly advanced areas reported an increase in tenant eviction as opposed to 19 percent in the backward areas.[9]

Table 14.4 presents results of an OLS analysis of variations in the per capita monthly expenditure at 1960 prices (PCEXPR) in the same agricultural labor households in West Bengal, with very similar results[10] to those of the LOGIT analysis, except that two variables, PUBWORKM and SBRND 3, which were not statistically significant in the latter are now quite significant in the OLS analysis. Again, the variable GROWTH seems to have a highly significant association with *lower* level of living in the agricultural labor household, other things remaining the same.

III

Let us now go to a different level of disaggregation, from the household to

[9] An alternative explanation of our result on the relationship between growth and poverty could be associated with a usual problem of deriving time-series conclusions from cross-section data. If the faster-growing districts in West Bengal also happened to be the ones with above-average poverty in the initial year and if their growth was not sufficient to offset those initial conditions, one could get such a relationship as ours. While this is technically possible, it is empirically a very unlikely explanation. Looking at the districtwise data it is clear that the growth rate has been faster in those districts (including the I.A.D.P. districts) which had been relatively better off right from the beginning (early '60s).

[10] Since the dependent variable is now the level of per capita expenditure rather than probability of poverty, the signs of the coefficients of all the variables are, of course, exactly reversed.

TABLE 14.4

Linear regression analysis of determinants of per capita monthly expenditure (at 1960 prices) of agricultural labor households, rural West Bengal, 1977-78

Dependent Variable:	PCEXPR (per capita monthly expenditure at 1960 prices)	
Mean:	Rs. 12.54	
Standard Deviation:	Rs. 5.66	

Explanatory Variables[†]	Regression Coefficient	Standard Error	Significant at Percent Level
CULTIVAT	1.9011	0.2294	0.0
NDEP	−1.0305	0.0641	0.0
EDM	2.3801	0.4123	0.0
NFM	2.3575	0.4689	0.0
DIST	−0.0183	0.0063	0.4
VILIRR	0.4429	0.1152	0.0
VWAGEM	0.7900	0.1008	0.0
PUBWORKM	1.2075	0.5360	2.4
SBRND 3	−0.6449	0.2587	1.3
SCHCASTE	−0.7436	0.2499	0.3
RAIN	0.6028	0.1810	0.1
NHA	0.1227	0.0155	0.0
GROWTH	−0.7602	0.1715	0.0
Constant term	9.8718	1.7585	0.0

$R^2 = 0.2013$; F = 29.5; no. of observations = 2,127

[†]See table 14.3

the more aggregative level of NSS regions, but now expanding our coverage beyond West Bengal to most of rural India. Out of the total NSS set there are 55 regions for which we have been able to get data for all our subsequent variables.[11]

A major problem in analyzing variations in poverty at the regional level is that we do not have data *at that level* on distribution of consumer expenditure for agricultural labor households or the consumer price index facing them. So we had to take the per capita monthly expenditure level of the noncultivating wage-earner households (estimated from NSS Twenty-Fifth Round data on the "weaker sections" of the rural population) as an indicator of the level of living of agricultural labor households. We take the per capita monthly expenditure level of noncultivating wage-earner households in each region in 1970-71 and deflate it by the consumer price

[11] The excluded regions are Manipur, Meghalaya, Nagaland, Tripura, Pondicherry, Goa, Daman and Diu, Himachal Pradesh, Chandigarh, and one (the mountainous) of the three regions in Jammu and Kashmir.

index of agricultural laborers (for the state as a whole where the region belongs) to convert it into 1960–61 prices[12] and call this expenditure level at constant prices EXPWR. For these 55 regions its mean value is Rs. 14.84, and standard deviation is Rs. 3.68. Table 14.5 presents the results of a linear regression analysis of the regional variations in EXPWR. As expected, it is higher in regions with better rainfall, more irrigation, greater importance of wells as a source of irrigation (possibly indicating the productivity impact of private controllability of irrigation), lower density of population (usually associated with less crowding in the rural labor market), a larger importance of workers in manufacturing (indicating alternative opportunities for farm workers), and a smaller proportion of scheduled caste and scheduled tribe households (suffering from special social disadvantages in access to opportunities).

Unlike the results relating to West Bengal in the previous section, GROWTH, the rate of growth of crop production in the region, seems to have a positive impact on the level of living of the wage-earning households. However, one should also note the *negative* coefficient of PUMHA, the number of oil engines and electric pumpsets per hectare of cropped area in a region. This may indicate possible adverse effects associated with certain types of growth.[13] In this connection, it is also noteworthy that the proportional importance of big farmers in the region has also a negative effect, as indicated by the negative coefficient of LFARMP.[14] Agricultural growth in general seems to be helpful, but big farmer–dominated growth dependent on private ownership of modern equipment need not be.

Summing up the results of (1) the two time-point comparisons of annual wage income or poverty of agricultural labor households; (2) the LOGIT and OLS analyses of household-level cross-section data for about 550 NSS sample villages in West Bengal in section II, and (3) the OLS analysis of cross-section data for 55 regions covering most of rural India, it seems possible to say that the evidence on trickle-down effects of growth on poverty of agricultural laborers are at best rather mixed, and occasionally

[12] I should note here that this ignores the problem of regionally different costs of living in 1960–61 itself.

[13] The correlation of PUMHA with the other irrigation variables is not high; in particular, the correlation coefficient between PUMHA and WELLIRR is only 0.27. So it seems the positive coefficient of WELLIRR indicates more the effect of mostly other kinds of wells, not necessarily fitted with pumps, which still predominate in the total number of wells. It is striking that in the whole of rural India, the use of pumpsets is heaviest in Tamil Nadu. It is with respect to a study of a Tamil Nadu district (North Arcot) that Chambers and Farmer (1977) noted the serious adverse effects of privately owned pumpset irrigation, lowering water tables for poorer farmers and sometimes driving their land out of irrigated cultivation.

[14] Of course, regional variations in the quality of land make the uniform cut-off line of 7.5 acres for defining large farms very arbitrary, but as the effect of LFARMP is considered, after controlling for regional variations in some of the irrigation variables, the distortion introduced by this arbitrariness may not be large.

Production Relations and Poverty

TABLE 14.5

Linear regression analysis of determinants of per capita monthly expenditure (at 1960–61 prices) of noncultivating wage-earner households in 55 regions, rural India, 1970–71

Dependent Variable:	EXPWR (per capita monthly expenditure at 1960–61 prices of noncultivating wage-earner households in 1970–71)		
Mean:	Rs. 14.84		
Standard Deviation:	Rs. 3.68		

Explanatory Variables	Regression Coefficient	Standard Error	Significant at Percent Level
NRAIN (annual normal rainfall in region in meters)	2.0369	0.7005	0.6
IRRP (percentage of area irrigated)	0.1058	0.0365	0.6
WELLIRR (area irrigated from wells as a proportion of total area irrigated)	0.0442	0.0187	2.3
GROWTH (average annual rate of growth of agricultural output)	0.4896	0.1436	0.1
PUMHA (electric pumpsets and oil engines used per hectare of cropped area)	−18.4153	10.9015	9.8
LFARMP (large farmer households as a proportion of total rural households)	−0.0921	0.0440	4.2
DENS (density of population per sq. km.)	−0.0207	0.0041	0.0
MSCASTE (proportion of male population belonging to scheduled castes)	−0.1045	0.0567	7.2
MSTRIBE (proportion of male population belonging to scheduled tribes)	−0.1051	0.0290	0.1
MFGP (proportion of working population in region in manufacturing, repairing, and services)	0.1111	0.0864	20.5
Constant term	15.7150	1.9398	0.0

$R^2 = 0.6207$; F = 7.2; no. of observations = 55

SOURCE: EXPWR is taken from NSS, 25th Round, data relating to "weaker sections" of the rural population for each region; the deflator used is the agricultural labor consumer price index for the state where the region is located. The region-level estimates for NRAIN and WELLIRR have been worked out after taking simple averages of district-level data given in the *Season and Crop Reports*. IRRP for each region is taken as the area of owned irrigated land as percentage of total owned land as of June 30, 1971, as reported by the All-India Debt and Investment Survey of the Reserve Bank of India. From the same source we have taken LFARMP, the proportion of total rural households operating land above 7.5 acres. The region-level estimate of GROWTH has been computed after taking simple averages of district-level data on annual compound growth rate of output of 19 major crops over the period of 1962–65 to 1970–73, as given in Bhalla and Alagh (1979). PUMHA has been estimated by taking the data on electric pumps and oil engines from the Livestock Census Report and using the Bhalla–Alagh estimates of area under 19 crops in each region. Data for DENS, MSCASTE, MSTRIBE, and MFGP are all from the 1971 Census.

quite negative. Agricultural growth and productivity improvements in general tend to help raise incomes all around, but certain types of growth processes generate negative forces for the poor, particularly in an institutional setting of highly unequal distribution of assets and access to resources. For fully tracing the specific impact of particular types of growth processes, however, one needs a sufficiently large number of intensive microstudies and good panel data. It is futile to attempt to settle the controversial issues of this literature at the level of aggregation on which most of the discussion has been conducted so far.

CHAPTER 15

On Life and Death Questions: Poverty and Child Mortality in Rural India

I

The relationship between household poverty and child mortality is quite complex. It is, of course, true that a child seriously underweight and malnourished because of deficiency either in its own diet or in that of its mother at pregnancy and lactation has much lower chances of survival than otherwise. But, as Sukhatme (1978) has stressed, the usual estimates of poverty can be quite misleading as indices of malnourishment.[1] Many of these estimates are based on *average* nutritional norms, and to take those who are poor by the criterion of such norms as malnourished is to ignore interpersonal variability of nutritional needs as well as the existence of self-regulatory and adaptive mechanisms in the human body. But there is a threshold value of calorie intake which may be regarded as a lower limit of homeostasis below which the self-regulatory mechanism governing energy balance breaks down and the risk of high morbidity and mortality increases very sharply. Sukhatme roughly estimates this threshold value for India to be 2,300 calories per consumer unit per day.

A special problem with the usual poverty estimates for indicating the nutrition and health status of children is that they are based on average *household* food consumption data. In the absence of information on intrafamily distribution of food, these estimates are likely to understate the extent of malnutrition among children; in much of India's food culture the allocation of food is biased in favor of adults (particularly males), and there is a relative lack of perception of the food needs of the nutritionally most vulnerable member of the family, namely, the weaned infant or, more generally, the preschool child.

But whatever adjustments one makes, in the light of these problems, in the poverty estimates there is no getting away from the fact that the poorest state in India in terms of calorie intake is Kerala.[2] Even the average calorie intake per capita in 1971–72 for the total rural population in Kerala (not to

---

[1] For other problems in these estimates not discussed here, such as those relating to the data base, choice of appropriate price index for the poor, and the norm for nonfood expenditure, see my survey article, Bardhan (1974).

[2] This is by and large true even if one allows for the probable underestimation in NSS data of the consumption in Kerala of items like tapioca or coconut.

speak of the very poor) was 1,610 calories per day, according to NSS estimate, a figure substantially below Sukhatme's critical minimum threshold value. Yet in terms of child mortality, as in most other vital rates, this state has the best performance in the whole of India. The data from the sample registration system (SRS) indicate that in the early 1970s the rural death rate in the age group 0–4 years was below 25 per thousand in Kerala; in the 25–45 range in Jammu and Kashmir, Karnataka, Maharashtra, Punjab, Haryana, Assam, and West Bengal; in the 45–60 range in Andhra Pradesh and Tamil Nadu; and above 60 in Gujarat, Madhya Pradesh, Orissa, Rajasthan, and Uttar Pradesh (see table 15.1). West Bengal is also among the poorest states in rural India (in 1971–72, its average calorie intake per capita was the lowest except for Kerala, and for quite some years it has had the highest percentage of rural population below the poverty line by most estimates), yet in 1970 it had the third lowest death rate in the 0–4 age group among all states. On the other side of the child mortality range, Rajasthan and Gujarat have proportions of poor people which are below average for rural India, yet they have among the worst records in child death rates.[3]

It is sometimes pointed out that part of the explanation of Kerala's better performance in child mortality as against, say, Uttar Pradesh lies in a better distribution of household consumption (even though the average consumption level is low) and the near–universal coverage of the school lunch program in Kerala. The evidence in favor of this argument is not overwhelming. Measures of inequality of household consumption expenditure as estimated from NSS data over the years uniformly show a *higher* inequality for Kerala than for Uttar Pradesh (for example, in 1973–74 the Gini coefficient of consumption expenditure was 0.32 for Kerala and 0.25 for Uttar Pradesh). As for school lunch programs, although the coverage of children is certainly much better in Kerala, it is doubtful whether this has had much of an impact on differential child mortality. For, as Sukhatme (1978) and others have pointed out, the maximum damage that undernutrition does is in the *preschool* child, between the time of weaning to about age three. After a child survives to school age, his body has already adapted to the surrounding conditions, and lunch programs are reported to make not much of an impact on height or weight (there are also reports of intrafamily substitution: when school provides lunch, the child is sometimes fed less at home).

All this suggests that factors other than poverty in terms of household consumption or nutritional inadequacy can be quite important in determining survival chances of children. The major killers of small children in

[3] In these rough and ready interstate comparisons I am, of course, ignoring the fact that the minimum calorie requirement in north India may be higher than the national average on account of climatic factors, etc. and that the same food basket may yield different amounts of nutrients with differences in types of storing, processing, and preparation of food in different regions.

TABLE 15.1

Interstate variations in nutritional, demographic, and medical factors, rural India, early 1970s

State	MCHMOR	FCMORP	CAL	UNPDRINK	UTBIRTHAT	FLIT	SPARSVIL
Andhra Pradesh	50.8	0.86	2118	26.95	85.9	18.32	19.66
Assam	43.4	0.99	2132	44.85	92.2	22.76	25.27
Gujarat	72.6	1.10	2295	15.95	90.2	29.00	11.24
Haryana	25.5	1.36	2874	17.31	91.5	17.77	9.18
Jammu and Kashmir	32.7	0.97	2793	77.37	n.a.	10.94	26.88
Karnataka	43.6	0.98	2054	27.86	81.3	24.55	18.41
Kerala	22.0	1.00	1610	9.53	40.8	62.53	0.16
Madhya Pradesh	64.8	0.93	2852	25.11	91.9	13.08	27.87
Maharashtra	41.6	1.02	2033	24.94	88.1	31.00	14.12
Orissa	64.0	0.86	2017	49.44	88.1	16.29	39.47
Punjab	32.1	1.47	2954	17.31	77.6	29.91	15.48
Rajasthan	64.2	1.23	2586	12.47	n.a.	10.06	26.34
Tamil Nadu	53.3	1.02	1910	22.26	70.6	30.92	6.28
Uttar Pradesh	68.6	1.37	2407	16.33	94.8	12.46	24.30
West Bengal	35.4	0.97	1860	10.39	n.a.	26.56	19.97

SOURCE: Data for MCHMOR and FCMORP from *Sample Registration Bulletin* of the Registrar General's Office; for CAL, from NSS, 26th Round; data for UNPDRINK, from NSS, 18th Round (unfortunately no data found for more recent year); for UTBIRTHAT, Swamy (1979); for FLIT and SPARSVIL, the 1971 Census.

NOTE: MCHMOR = death rate per thousand in the 0–4 age group for males in 1970.

FCMORP = the ratio of female to male death rate in the 0–4 age group in 1970.

CAL = average calorie intake per capita per day in 1971–72.

UNPDRINK = percentage of villages reporting tank, pond, river, lake, spring and other such unprotected sources of drinking water in 1963–64.

UTBIRTHAT = percentage of live births not attended by any trained medical practitioners (including trained *dai* or midwife) in 1971.

FLIT = percentage of female population (above 4 years) literate in 1971.

SPARSVIL = proportion of total inhabited villages where the population is less than 200 in 1971.

rural India are of three types: (a) premature birth and neonatal tetanus in infants below one year (when breast-feeding still provides a large measure of protection) and in children above that age, (b) largely water-borne gastrointestinal diseases (like dysentery and diarrhoea); and (c) respiratory infections (like pneumonia).[4] Of these, maternal malnutrition may be responsible for the birth of premature, underweight babies, but the toll of the killer diseases depends more directly on availability of public medical facilities, safe drinking water, and environmental sanitation. The (preliminary) Report of the Survey on Infant and Child Mortality carried out by the Office of the Registrar General of India suggests that in 1978 the death rate for children in the 1–5 age group was 22 percent higher in villages without a water supply within the limits of the village (such villages were three-quarters of all villages) than in other villages; it was 20 percent higher in villages without medical facilities within the limits of the village than in other villages.

Even where drinking water is available within the village, there are problems of protecting it from contamination, conditions of community hygiene and sanitation around the source of drinking water, accessibility for socially disadvantaged groups, and regular maintenance of wells and pumps.[5] According to NSS data for 1963–64, the proportion of villages reporting tanks, ponds, river, lakes, springs, and other such unprotected sources of drinking water in Kerala is the lowest in the country (i.e., the proportion of villages with taps, wells, and tubewells as sources is the highest in the country).

As for medical attention at the time of birth or death, the evidence reported in Swamy (1979) suggests that more than 80 percent of births and the cases of over two deaths out of three in rural India are not attended by any trained medical practitioner. There are again large inter-state variations in this. Table 15.1, column 6, shows that Kerala is the only state in rural India where the majority of births are supervised by trained medical practitioners (including trained village *dai* and midwife). This indicates a substantially better access to medical practitioners in this state, and not just at birth. It is, therefore, no accident that Kerala has the lowest infant as well as child mortality rate in rural India. Infant and child mortality rates are much above the national rural average in Gujarat, Madhya Pradesh, Orissa, Rajasthan, and Uttar Pradesh, and these are all states where attendance by trained practitioners at birth (and presumably at other occasions) is much below the national average. Child mortality in rural India is the highest in Uttar Pradesh (taking mortality for both male and female children), and again it is no accident that in terms of access to

[4] See, for example, the preliminary Report of the Survey on Infant and Child Mortality, 1979, issued by the Office of the Registrar General of India.

[5] See on this the evaluation study of the accessibility of the poor to rural water supply carried out in late 1978 by the Program Evaluation Organization of the Indian Planning Commission.

trained medical practitioners at birth it is the worst-off state: only 5 percent of total live births in the rural areas of this vast state are attended by any trained practitioner.

It is, of course, well known that Kerala has the highest literacy rate in the country. From the point of view of child health, the literacy rate of the adult females in the household is probably more important, and Kerala is the only state in the country where the majority of women are literate. A better educational status of the mother improves the child's survival chance, particularly through better awareness of the usefulness of cleaner health and sanitation practices, the nutritional value of diet items, earlier diagnosis of illnesses, and greater belief in preventive and curative medical treatment. Often neglected, but equally important, particularly in the context of areas like Kerala, is the effect of education on politicization and awareness of social rights: the poor in Kerala are more vocal in demanding access to public medical facilities and more vigilant in ensuring that they are run properly. Some of the high child-mortality states, like Rajasthan, Uttar Pradesh, Madhya Pradesh, and Orissa, are areas where the female literacy rate is the lowest in the country (see table 15.1).

Kerala also happens to be a State where the rural–urban distinction is largely blurred and the rural areas are in general well connected in terms of transport and communication. Some of the high child-mortality states, like Orissa, Madhya Pradesh, Rajasthan, and Uttar Pradesh have a very significant proportion of villages which are sparsely populated, remote and inaccessible (see table 15.1, last column); infrastructural facilities are usually poorer in these areas.

We shall now report on a statistical analysis of rural infant death rates at a level somewhat more disaggregated than the state: the level of NSS agroclimatic regions. The infant death rate (IDR) is taken from the *Vital Statistics of India*. For the 39 regions for which we have adequate data,[6] the mean value of IDR in 1973 is 57.9 per thousand births, and the standard deviation is 26.8. Table 15.2 presents the results of two alternative regression equations to explain the regional variations in IDR.

In the first equation, IDR is positively and significantly associated with POVP, the percentage of rural population below the poverty line[7] (i.e., other things remaining the same; infants die more in areas where there are more people in poverty); negatively and significantly with FLITP, the

[6] As explained in the notes to table 15.2, I had to exclude the IDR data for 5 major states where the coverage of the data was not regarded as adequate or reliable. Since some of these states are also those where infant mortality rates are high, this explains why our mean value of IDR is lower than the national average (apart from the fact that civil registration data usually underestimate all death rates).

[7] The poverty line defined as Rs. 15 at 1960–61 prices, with the Agricultural Laborer Consumer Price Index for the State as the deflator, ignores among other things, (1) differential nutritional requirements in different regions; (2) different cost of buying the minimum basket in 1960–61 in different areas; (3) any difference in the price rise for the rural poor from that for agricultural laborers; and (4) intrastate differences in price rises.

TABLE 15.2

Linear regression analysis of determinants of infant death rates in NSS regions, rural India

Dependent Variable:	IDR (number of infant deaths per thousand births in rural areas 'in 1973)
Mean:	57.93 [61.67]
Standard Deviation:	26.85 [27.92]

Explanatory Variables	Regression Coefficient	Standard Error	Significant at Percent Level
POVP (percentage of rural population below poverty line in the region)	0.5429 [0.8781]	0.2337 [0.2987]	2.6 [0.7]
SPARSVIL (proportion of sparsely populated villages in region)	0.5482 [0.4969]	0.4138 [0.4613]	19.4 [29.1]
FLITP (percentage of female population who are literate	−0.8144	0.3956	4.7
UTBIRTHAT (percentage of live births not attended by any trained medical practitioner in rural areas of state where region is located)	[1.0557]	[0.3449]	[0.5]
MSCASTE (proportion of scheduled castes in rural male population in region)	[1.0141]	[0.6382]	[12.4]
Constant term	39.3230 [−83.5702]	13.5912 [35.8407]	0.7 [2.7]

$R^2 = 0.3169$; F = 5.4; no. of observations = 39
[0.5222] [7.4] [32]

SOURCE: Data for IDR computed for each NSS region by averaging the civil registration data for each district given in *Vital Statistics of India, 1973*. Since coverage of civil registration records is not yet adequate for some states, IDR estimates for Assam, Bihar, Orissa, Rajasthan, and Uttar Pradesh have been excluded. Data for POVP is NSS, regional-level consumer expenditure data for 1972–73 (poverty line has been defined as Rs. 15 at 1960–61 prices, with the agricultural laborer consumer price index for each state used as a price deflater for all regions in that state). Data for SPARSVIL, FLITP, and MSCASTE from 1971 Census.

SPARSVIL = proportion of total number of inhabited villages where the population is less than 200.

UTBIRTHAT is as in table 15.1. In the absence of region-level data for this variable, I have used the **State-level** figure for all the regions in a state. UTBIRTHAT relates to the year 1971. Since I do not have data on UTBIRTHAT for Jammu and Kashmir and West Bengal, I had to exclude these two **States** in the regression that uses that variable.

NOTE: This table incorporates the results of *two* alternative regressions, with the same dependent variable, IDR: one with the independent variables POVP, SPARSVIL, and FLITP; the second with the independent variables POVP, SPARSVIL, UTBIRTHAT, and FLITP. The second regression results are denoted by square brackets.

percentage of female population who are literate (indicating the beneficial effects of female literacy on infant survival); and positively (though weakly) with SPARSVIL., the proportion of sparsely populated villages in the region. (indicating the effects of poor infrastructural facilities and inaccessibility). In this regression equation we also wanted to use UTBIRTHAT, the percentage of live births not attended by any trained medical practitioner, as an independent variable, but its correlation with another independent variable, FLITP, is so high (the correlation coefficient is about 0.8) that we decided to use these two variables alternatively. Hence the second alternative regression equation.

In this second equation UTBIRTHAT replaced FLITP and, as expected, has a highly significant positive association with IDR (indicating the effect of the type of access to medical facilities on infant mortality). In this equation the regression coefficient for POVP is still highly significant and positive; that for SPARSVIL is still (weakly) positive. IDR is now also positively associated with the numerical importance of scheduled castes in the population (indicating the special disadvantages these social groups have in their access to safe drinking water sources and other public facilities). On the whole, the statistical fit is better for the second equation.

All in all the regional cross-section data, with all their limitations (particularly those of registration data on infant death rates), confirm the expected effects on infant mortality of poverty, poor infrastructural facilities, lack of access to trained medical practitioners, special disadvantages of low-caste groups, and female literacy.

II

One of the most striking features of the child mortality data in rural India is the male–female differential. Table 15.1, column 3, shows that in 1970 the death rate of female children (in the 0–4 age group) was as much as 47 percent higher than that of males in Punjab, 37 percent higher in Uttar Pradesh, 36 percent higher in Haryana, 23 percent higher in Rajasthan, and 10 percent higher in Gujarat. By contrast, most states in east and south India have a female-to-male child death rate ratio that is below the average for rural India.

This differential mortality is also reflected in the remarkable regional differences in the sex ratio of the rural population. Figure 15.1, which is a district map of the sex ratio of the rural population under age 10 in 1961, reproduced from Sopher (1980),.makes the pattern of regional contrasts quite vivid.[8] The number of males per 1,000 females among the rural population under age 10 is the highest in northwest India, and it clearly

[8] Since the possible influence of sex-selective migration of children and of regional variation in the sex ratio at birth are minimal, differential mortality is the major explanation of the regional variation in the juvenile sex ratio. For an analysis of the sex ratio of the Indian population, see Visaria (1971).

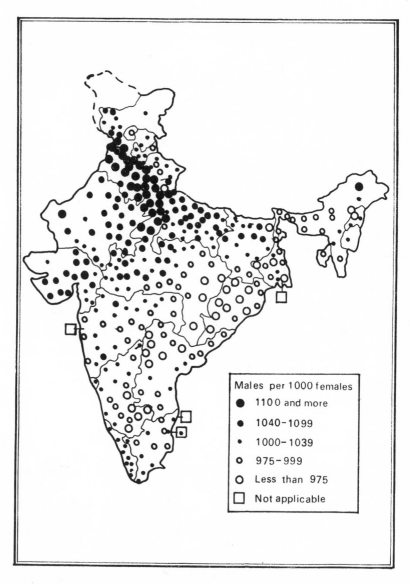

Figure 15.1 Rural Sex Ratio (masculinity): Children Under 10, 1961.

decreases as one moves south and east. Historically, the practice of female infanticide has been known to exist in north and northwest India. The 1911 Census Report points out that the practice "was found to be extremely prevalent in the United Provinces, the Punjab and Rajputana amongst various sections of the population before about the third quarter of the nineteenth century ".The practice has died out, but the long-run legacy of general neglect (conscious or unconscious) of girl children in terms of undernutrition, tardiness in cases of their illness in approaching medical facilities even when they are accessible, premature stopping of medical treatment, etc., may have persisted in this region to a larger extent than in east or south India.

The question remains as to why, historically, this general neglect of female children (including the extinct practice of female infanticide) came to be more prevalent in northwest India. This is obviously a complex subject in which historical, cultural, ecological, and sociological factors interact, and easy answers are not possible, nor is it within the scope of the present chapter. Let us nevertheless mention a factor or two at the level of sweeping generality.

It is often suggested that the north and northwestern parts of the Indian subcontinent are an extension of the broad cultural region of West Asia, and the impact of Islamic culture was consolidated there over the centuries of Muslim rule. This, allegedly, may have resulted in the lower status of women and the higher incidence of female child mortality. It is difficult to test this proposition rigorously, but one of the few countrywide surveys of infant mortality rates by religious groups in India does not seem to support the presumption of higher female-to-male infant mortality ratio among the Muslims. The NSS Nineteenth Round (1964–65) data have been tabulated (see NSS Report No. 177) to give us religious groupwise infant mortality rates. In fact, it seems from the data that the female-to-male infant mortality ratio is somewhat higher for the Hindus than for the Muslims in rural India. It is possible that underreporting of female infant deaths may vary across religious groups, but the presumption of a higher female-to-male infant mortality ratio among the Muslims has yet to be established. If one looks at the Census data on sex ratio of population by religious groups, one finds that the male bias in the sex ratio is more region-specific than religion-specific. For example, males per 1,000 females (of all ages) in 1971 was 1,123 in Uttar Pradesh and 972 in Kerala for the Hindu population; for the Muslim population it was 1,138 in Uttar Pradesh and 981 in Kerala.

Of course, the male child is a potential source of economic support and gets the lion's share of parental attention and nourishment compared with his sisters. But this should be true of all regions. If anything, the impact of male bias in intrafamily distribution of food on morbidity and mortality rates is likely to be more severe in areas where the per capita availability of food is less than where it is more. Where there is more food to go around in the family, the female may have better chances. But compared with most of east and south India, in north and northwest India the average per capita availability is in general higher even for the relatively poor households. (Table 15.1 shows that per capita calorie intake in north and northwest India is substantially higher than in east and south India.)

Why, then, do the female children suffer from special disadvantages in their chances of survival in north and northwest India compared with east and south India? Why is the male offspring more valued in the former region as against the latter? In Bardhan (1974), where we briefly considered this question, we offered a conjecture in terms of ecological variations in crop production and economic activity in general. In all the states of east and south India (except Karnataka) the predominant crop is paddy which—unlike wheat and dry-region crops—tends to be relatively'intensive in female labor.[9] Transplantation of paddy is an exclusively female job in many paddy areas; besides, female labor plays a very important role in weeding, harvesting, threshing, and various kinds of processing of paddy. By contrast, in dry cultivation and even in wheat cultivation under irrigation, the work involves more muscle power and less tedious, often back-breaking, but delicate, operations (of which trans- plantation is an example). Could it be that, in areas with paddy agri- culture, the economic value of a woman is more than in other areas—so that the female child is regarded less of a liability than in, say, north and northwest India?

Put more generally, the hypothesis relates the differential survival chances of the female child to the expected employment or earning opportunities of female adults. This hypothesis was recently put to test by Rosenzweig and Schultz (1982) with data from 1,334 rural households in India in 1971, collected by the National Council of Applied Economic Research. In their two-stage regression analysis, the first stage confirms that there is a significant positive correlation between normal (district- level) rainfall and the probability that a woman is employed in rural India (thus supporting our hunch about wet agriculture being relatively intensive in female labor), and the second stage confirms that the differential survival chance of the female child improves with higher female employment rate or with a lower male–female earning differential per day. If there is any validity to this, this means that expanding employment opportunities for women or lowering the male–female wage differential in rural India is not just another "feminist" cause: it may actually save the lives of many little girls in rural households.

While it is far from our intention to minimize the larger issues of cultural geography and anthropology involved here, it is perhaps permissible to hazard a guess that in general the social and economic value of the woman is likely to be related to the ecological conditions and production relations of a particular region and that the male offspring will be valued more in arid areas, where occupations like hunting, grazing, and dry cultivation are chief sources of livelihood, than in areas where female participation may be just as useful as male. It is worth investigating if the so-called West Asian culture syndrome of male dominance and virility (which may have infected

[9] Even in paddy areas, female participation rates in the usual data show rather low values (for example, in West Bengal or Bangladesh), except for tribal or scheduled-caste groups, to a large extent because they effectively exclude work on many of the postharvest operations involved in rice agriculture: threshing, dehusking, parboiling, drying, winnowing, making puffed rice, and so on.

the social mores of the north and northwestern part of the Indian sub-continent) has its origin in (pastoral or nomadic) production conditions, in which female labor was less useful.

The question of the economic value of a woman and regional variations in it is also linked with variations in the institution of dowry and marriage payments. Miller (1980) has suggested that the practice of systematic neglect of female children in north and northwest India is to be explained partly by the higher cost of marrying them off when they grow up in this region than in, say, south India. Putting together the results of a number of ethnographic studies in different parts of rural India, she comes to the conclusion that dowry (and in general the high cost of marriage for the bride's family) is most prevalent in north and northwest India (particularly among the propertied groups), whereas reciprocity characterizes marriages among many propertied groups in the South, and "negative dowry" or bridewealth is found most frequently among unpropertied groups in the South. Taking the unpropertied groups first (among whom any female neglect is likely to have more severe effects in terms of mortality), our hypothesis is that lower female participation in agriculture and other economic activities (conditioned partly by ecology) in the North than in the South lowers the economic value of the woman (and hence raises the compensating need for dowry) in the former region than in the latter. Even in the North, ethnic groups (like the tribals) among whom female participation is particularly high, usually have the practice of bridewealth or reciprocity.

Comparing the propertied and the unpropertied, dowry and marriage costs for the bride's family are usually higher among the former all over rural India, partly reflecting the lower female participation rates in the former groups. It also partly reflects the inheritance practices among the propertied: the female heir's share, particularly in north India, often takes the form of a claim on the movable property of the family, settled as a payment of dowry on her marriage. On these grounds, one would expect a larger degree of relative neglect of female children in propertied classes in rural India; on the other hand, this neglect is less likely to be fatal in these richer households compared with the poor. In the Rosenzweig–Schultz statistical analysis of the 1971 household data for rural India referred to above, the regression results suggest that an increase in the household ownership of land assets is associated with a larger survival prospect of female children, holding constant for predicted female employment rate. Thus the differential chance of survival of a female child will depend on a variety of related and economically important factors, such as the wealth position of the household, its inheritance and marriage payment practice, and female employment prospects, apart from the educational and caste status of the household, the degree of prevalence of hypergamy (usually involving large dowries), and the process of Sanskritization (through which the lower castes try to upgrade themselves by adopting upper-caste practices like the dowry and work taboo for women).

CHAPTER 16

Private Property as a Growth Constraint in a Hydraulic Economy

I

In countries like India, in many ways water is destiny. The life of most Indian peasants continues to be a precarious gamble on the rains, even apart from the fact that their children die by the millions every year from unsafe drinking water and largely water-borne diseases. Except for east India, the coastal rims of south and west India, and the Himalayan foothills, it is largely a semi-arid country with low and, more significantly, highly variable rainfall. In the high-rainfall areas, devastation by floods is a much too frequent calamity. Area under *assured* irrigation and even minimal drainage is relatively small, even though India has the second largest irrigated acreage in the whole world.

In 1853, when Marx and Engels first discussed, in correspondence, the problems of "Asiatic" societies, they immediately agreed on the particular importance of public irrigation works in these societies, necessitated by climatic aridity. In this emphasis on hydraulic agriculture, they carried forward one strand of European thinking on Asian history and society (particularly fostered by Adam Smith and John Stuart Mill).[1] But they looked upon this as the ecological basis of their vision of the centralized despotic state with a monopoly on land in Asia. In his June 10, 1853, *New York Daily Tribune* article on India, Marx explained:

> Climatic and territorial conditions, especially the vast tracts of desert, extending from the Sahara, through Arabia, Persia, India, and Tartary, to the most elevated Asiatic highlands, constituted artificial irrigation by canals and waterworks the basis of Oriental agriculture.... This prime necessity of an economical and common use of water, which in the Occident drove private enterprise to voluntary association, as in Flanders and Italy, necessitated in the Orient... the interference of the centralized power of Government.

It is now widely recognized that the historical basis of the idea of an absence of private property in land in Asia and that of the centralized hydraulic state with its agromanagerial bureaucracy exercising complete control over labor power, particularly as enunciated in the drastic generalizations of

---

[1] For an account of the roots of Marx's thinking on this question in earlier European tradition as well as a critique of the ingredients of the concept of "Asiatic mode of production", see Anderson (1974).

Wittfogel (1957), is highly dubious.[2] But the importance of hydraulic agriculture itself cannot be denied; more than that, there *is* a basic contradiction between agrarian development in a hydraulic economy and the untrammeled exercise of private property in land, which Marx may have hinted at.

Availability of irrigation clearly has been one of the crucial factors governing regional variations in agricultural productivity in India in recent years. In the Bhalla–Alagh (1979) districtwise study, the districts which showed a high level of crop output of Rs. 1,500 or above per hectare in 1970 -73 constituted only 14.5 percent of gross cropped area, but 34 percent of gross irrigated area; at the other end, the low-productivity districts (less than Rs. 700 of output per hectare) accounted for 31.7 percent of gross cropped area and only 11.8 percent of gross irrigated area. In the highest-growth area of Punjab, Haryana, and western Uttar Pradesh not merely is the major proportion of net sown area under irrigation, but even among different sources of irrigation there has been a phenomenal expansion in this area in privately controlled (and hence more secure, from the individual farmer's point of view) irrigation such as that from energized tubewells. The question therefore arises why this irrigation performance cannot be reproduced in other parts of India. This is a particularly relevant question in view of the fact that, unlike some other semi-arid zones of the world, large parts of India have a very substantial physical potential of surface and groundwater irrigation as yet unutilized.

Faced with this question economists often emphasize the need for the massive investments that such a vast program of irrigation and drainage entails and the problems of mobilizing resources to finance investments on such a scale, particularly when the beneficiary farmers are politically so difficult to tax. The political power of the rich farmers and their increasing ability to resist higher irrigation and power charges and betterment levies or repayment of subsidized loans from the state, of course, point to a constraint ultimately derived from private property rights in land, but in this chapter I wish to focus on the impact of these rights more on water management than on investment finance.

II

In surface irrigation the major modes of effective irrigation organization in India are those of the bureaucratically operated large canal systems. This is in some contrast to the much smaller-scale irrigation systems of East Asia. This contrast may have more to do with ecology than with differential

[2] On the lack of historical evidence on communal property in precolonial India, see Thorner (1966). On the relationship between irrigation and social and political organization, the anthropological literature is large. For a review of several case studies of local irrigation systems (but not any from the Indian subcontinent) as well as most of the relevant anthropological references to date, see Hunt and Hunt (1976).

adherence to ideas like "small is beautiful" in the two regions. Most parts of India have a more seasonally concentrated distribution of rainfall than most of East Asia (particularly, Japan, Korea, Taiwan, and the rice-producing regions of China). A more even seasonal distribution of rainfall leads to a more even seasonal distribution of river flows, which makes it possible in East Asia to supplement rainfall by relatively simple diversion-type works, tanks, lift irrigation, and other small-scale projects, instead of massive storage-based irrigation systems. Thus about 90 percent of the irrigated area in China is served by relatively small-scale works, whereas in India around 37 percent of the irrigated area is served by canals fed for the most part from medium and large storage works.[3] This difference in the scale of irrigation works also partly explains the traditionally different degree of local community participation in irrigation organization in the two regions.

The large irrigation systems in India are managed and maintained by the government down to the level of outlets serving areas of about 40 hectares, and development below that point has been usually left to the farmers;[4] in the rice areas of east and south India the common method used thereon is that of "field-to-field", so that water is allowed to flood over the whole area below the outlet, passing directly from one field to the next, whereas in the wheat areas water generally reaches the field by a network of watercourses along field boundaries, constructed by the farmers. While there are major problems with the management of the main systems, with the structure and practices of the irrigation bureaucracy and with their insensitivity to local needs,[5] I shall concentrate here more on the community-level action for the allocation of water, maintenance of distribuion structures, and resolution of conflicts below the outlet.

Private property rights in land and lack of community organization have played havoc with maintenance and water distribution in many parts of India's canal irrigation systems and have led to what Hart has described as the "anarchy syndrome" in the scramble for water. I will quote in detail from his account from a walk along one of the watercourses intended to feed 4,300 acres of canal-commanded land in Shirol, a tail-end village of Karnataka's Ghataprabha project:

> Of seven outlet gates at the lower end of the watercourse, six were ripped out of their concrete channels, bent, or otherwise prevented from closing. The seventh was intact, but so hopelessly blocked with sediment that water could never reach it. "It has been like this for three years", said the junior engineer. "The cultivators

---

[3] For a brief presentation of this argument as well as some intercountry evidence, see Vaidyanathan and Jose (1978).

[4] Only very recently the Command Area Development (CAD) program has been given some responsibility for land development even below the outlet level. The performance of this program so far has been rather disappointing.

[5] See Chambers and Wade (1980) for emphasizing that these problems of the main system may overshadow the problems below outlet level.

break the gates. They should be severely punished. But what can we do?"
The junior engineer, an exceptional officer, had in fact tried to do something. We saw the need for it, and the difficulties, two kilometers further down the watercourse. At this point water in the channel simply dried up, leaving the last four outlets useless.... [The irrigators on the middle reaches of the watercourse], having blocked closure of their outlet gates, had also headed up water into them by means of home-made barriers in the bed of the watercourse. This effectively preempted the already insufficient flows from reaching the tail. The junior engineer had instituted closure of all upper outlets of the watercourse... during half of every week, pushing water down to the tail. It was an improvised rotational delivery.

It was not, however, entirely successful. When water began reaching the tail for the first time in many years, part of it was illegally diverted by a large landowner having twenty acres *above* the watercourse. His land was designed to receive canal water from an entirely different channel higher up. But finding water available here he had headed up the little supply one or two feet, dug an entirely unauthorized ditch to his land, and appropriated what he needed. His illegal ditch stood as evidence that the Irrigation Department was impotent. (1978: A-125).

This is an account quite typical of many of India's watercourses under the canals. Apart from illegal diversions and misappropriation of water often by the wealthy and the powerful, tail-end farmers in general get too little water and too late.[6] This is partly because of the poor maintenance of ditches and field channels, and partly because of the chaotic procedures of water allocation. The need for maintenance of field channels is felt more acutely by the farmer at the tail end, but the work has to be done near the head on someone else's property, but the latter has less incentive to allow this. This incentive problem is even apart from the usual "free-rider problem" that afflicts individual incentives for all such maintenance work.[7] Besides, there is the additional problem that, with the rich farmers increasingly acquiring their own pumpsets for irrigation, the village leadership, largely dominated by them, is now less interested in the maintenance of old irrigation channels.

In water allocation the Central irrigation administration is trying to encourage adoption of rotational irrigation (like the method known as *warabandi*, best developed in the canal colonies of the Punjab at the turn of the century), under which farmers on the same watercourse or under the same outlet follow a prearranged roster of turns to take water. Obvious

[6] As a result the tail-end farmers are usually poorer. Vander Velde (1980) cites evidence from villages in Hissar district of Haryana about the more advantageous location of larger farmers. The latter may also have more political power to influence the original decision as to from where the watercourses will run.
[7] In this context, I believe that the "free rider" problem is less important than the other incentive problem. As Taylor (1976) has shown, in repetitive situations (i.e., in "supergames" as opposed to one-shot "prisoner's dilemma" situations), even rational selfish agents may choose to cooperate rather than act as free riders if they are in a small static community with mutual policing of behavior being feasible.

conflicts of interests under private cultivation have made it difficult to implement or enforce this in south or east or central India: if a farmer whose turn has passed believes his crop needs more water, he is strongly tempted to take some out of turn, depriving another of his share; if each farmer expects that others will disregard the roster, none will wait in line. As Wade (1980) points out, the introduction of rotational irrigation is especially difficult now because of the particular water requirements of the high-yielding varieties of seeds. If these varieties do not get water at certain critical periods, yields fall off dramatically; in contrast, the varieties which were prevalent in northwest India when rotational irrigation was institutionalized could withstand a wide range of variation in water supply without much effect on productivity.

Even where a fixed rotation is enforced, while it reduces uncertainty of water arrival for individual farmers compared with the continuous flow system, it is socially inefficient since it allows no adjustment to particular needs and variations in soil, environment, and field locations. While the rationing of water ensures some kind of equity, it serves the purpose more of protective irrigation by assuring a minimum supply of water; it is not well suited to productivity-maximizing allocation of water. Even on the question of equity, the standard policy in rotational irrigation of sharing the available water among farmers on the basis of their landholding size is essentially regressive, and it results in a multiplication of the existing inequalities on the basis of land. Of course, *warabandi* rotation is more equitable than the continuous flow irrigation of south India, or even the *osrabandi* system of parts of Uttar Pradesh where water is distributed to the *thoks* or blocks into which the command area is divided according to a predetermined roster but water to the farmers within each *thok* is distributed by the *thokdar* (an 'influential" cultivator nominated by the Irrigation Department) with obvious adverse consequences for smaller farmers.

Apart from maintenance of ditches and water allocation, land preparation for irrgation is also seriously affected by private property rights. The most comprehensive and, in the long run, effective land-shaping and leveling programs involve consolidation of land fragments and realignment of field boundaries. Land fragmentation is excessive in India,[8] particularly in the eastern regions, and the progress of consolidation, in spite of copious legislation, has been very poor (except in northwest India). Small farmers often strongly resist consolidation of holdings for various reasons: (a) fear (and distrust of officials) that in the process they may be cheated out of even their tiny amounts of land; (b) a similar fear of tenants that they will be evicted in the process; (c) since irrigation water delivery is good at some locations and bad at others, fragmentation is sometimes a

---

[8] According to NSS data, in 1960-61 the number of parcels per holding in rural India was on an average 5.7 and the average size per parcel was 1.15 acres.

way of reducing risks of water supply through location diversification; (d) in areas of shallow, variable soil, generations of work may have gone into building up soil fertility, which may be lost in the exchange process, and a farmer may end up with land of someone who cared less about its fertility than he (and his ancestors) did for the land he had to give away; (e) the related problem of arbitrariness in the administrative valuation of the quality of the land parcels exchanged. In the absence of land consolidation, field channels, even when constructed by the government or by the community, have to take long, circuitous routes leading to high costs of construction and maintenance. But, more importantly, the construction of field channels and drains and leveling of land by farmers themselves suffer in view of the conflict of interests (one or two recalcitrant landowners can frustrate the whole project) and the considerable externalities of such land development programs which cannot be internalized by individual farmers. The construction of drains is particularly important in the traditional rice-growing regions. In the monsoon season a farmer may find it impossible to drain his flooded fields if his neighbors' fields are also flooded. Even in other seasons or other regions, lack of proper drainage facilities leads to waterlogging and salinity in low-lying areas.

If we shift our attention from surface irrigation to groundwater (where the irrigation potential is supposed to be very high, particularly in the Gangetic plains), similar (and some special) conflicts of interest arising from private property rights loom large. Land-size and fragmentation disabilities afflict investment in private electric and diesel tubewells. East India, where the potential from tubewell irrigation is particularly high, is also the area with the most acute problem of fragmentation and where the size of holding for the overwhelming majority of farmers is below the minimum threshold size which makes investment in a tubewell privately profitable (apart from the problem of the requisite credit collateral). In fact, as noted in chapter 14, appropriation of groundwater by rich farmers, who are going for pumpsets and tubewells in a big way, results in a possible drop in water tables and makes the traditional lift irrigation technology even less effective than before for poorer farmers without pumpsets.[9]

In the case of state or community tubewells, problems very similar to those under canal irrigation have come up: misappropriation of water by the powerful, lack of repairs and maintenance of tubewells, field channels, etc.[10] In some cases, rich farmers owning private tubewells and selling some of the water at high rates have done their best to see that the existing public tubewells fail or that new projects for installing them get blocked.

III

Given the externalities of water management, one way of overcoming the

[9] See, for example, Chambers and Farmer (1977).
[10] For an account of these problems in Uttar Pradesh, see Ghate (1980).

constraints imposed by private property rights is to form cooperative water user associations. In the quotation cited in the beginning of this chapter from his article on India, Marx refers to voluntary associations in Flanders and Italy. Even in Oriental agriculture there are many current as well as past instances of such associations, particularly in East and Southeast Asia. Geertz (1980), for example, provides a detailed account of a *subak*, or irrigation society, in the Indonesian island of Bali which, among other things, plays a central role in the regulation of water supply to the community; as he puts it, "Theories of hydraulic despotism to the contrary notwithstanding, water control in Bali is an overwhelmingly local and intensely democratic matter." Similar examples of local irrigation organizations with highly collective responsibility are available from Japan and Taiwan.[11]

In India such local community organizations of water users are very rare, and, where they exist, are usually characterized by a relatively low level of organizational form. Wade (1979) provides a case study of a village committee referred to as *peddamanshula* in Andhra Pradesh which is involved in water allocation on a day-to-day basis and in appointment of sluice guards and field guards but not in maintenance of water courses. Jayaraman (1981) has two case studies from Gujarat where a village-level informal committee functions to maintain the irrigation system below the outlet level and to act as liaison between irrigation engineers and the farmers but not to distribute water. Hart (1978) refers to his observation of "pipe committees" (locally called *Kulaba samiti*) in Uttar Pradesh's Sarda–Sahayak command area, with responsibility of maintenance of field channels. In all these cases the functions of these committees are limited, their organization loose, and the method of election of members not always representative of all farmers. *Peddamanshula*, for example, literally and actually means "respected persons" or "gentlemen"; the members are not representatives in any formal sense. In fact, Wade refers to some feeling of antagonism between this committee and the *panchayat* (the statutory elected village council).

The more typical situation, of course, is of no local corporate body at all to look after common water management problems of farmers below the outlet level. In most villages, coordination is very low, and an anarchical water regime with inevitable dominance of the rich and powerful farmers prevails. Wade (1979) carries out a very useful comparative study of 24 villages located along two canals in a district in Andhra Pradesh, some with a corporate irrigation organization and some without, to highlight factors that facilitate the formation of such organization among cultivators in a village. One such facilitating factor operates when water supply from the canal system is a frequent problem for *all* irrigators in the village; a relatively high proportion of competition for water is then directed outside

[11] See, for example, Beardsley (1964) and Vander Meer (1980).

the village, toward getting more water "for the village" from other (usually upstream) villages, thus fostering village-wise cooperation and cohesion in some tail-end villages. If, on the other hand, intravillage conflicts of interest are too strong, the collective approach tends to break down.[12] As one of Wade's informants tells him: "In a (water) committee, if two members get water and the others don't, the committee breaks apart." In villages where the rich farmers are able to get enough water for their land without having to organize corporately and without having to incur large additional expenditures themselves since they own the land immediately below the outlets, they block the formation of a cooperative water control committee (which might curtail their own irrigation freedom) at the expense of the interests of the small cultivators lower down. Thus distribution of control over land in relation to proximity to the outlets strongly influences the nature of corporate response to a given water scarcity situation in a village.

The prospects of a substantial agricultural growth in India, particularly if it is to spread beyond the existing regional pockets (like those in the northwest), are crucially dependent on provision of controlled supply of water and a vast network of water management and distribution. The full growth potential cannot be realized, even if resources for the requisite massive investments can be mobilized, until local broad-based community organizations, which can rise above or supersede the private property interests of landlords and "water lords", are developed for the purpose of not merely maintenance of watercourses and drainage ditches and allocation of water but also for land preparation, consolidation, flood control, prevention of deforestation and soil erosion, etc. The primary bottleneck here, as with many other development problems in India, is organizational and political. Even the leftist parties in India, which in a few areas have some history of organizing peasants, are more oriented to price-tax-rent campaigns, limited land redistribution movements, and more recently to recording of rights of tenants and agitation for agricultural wage increases. Seldom is their attention directed toward developing productivity-oriented local cooperative organizations (for water management or for credit and social insurance). Even at the level of slogans the focus is on issues like "land to the tiller" (and hence a perpetuation of the private property system) and not on the need for building cooperative institutions. It is, of course, far easier to agitate against existing inequality and oppression than to build from the ground up viable community organizations and to sustain them. The latter require a completely different kind of organizational resources and political-entrepreneurial skills which the present leadership of these parties is often ill equipped to provide. Yet the need remains desperate.

[12] Jayaraman (1981) also notes that the relatively egalitarian structure of the community is an important factor in the farmers coming together in his Gujarat case studies.

Appendix Tables A to D

Here have been put together the values in the early 1970s, of various demographic environmental, agricultural, technological, economic, and institutional variables at the level of more than sixty agro-climatic regions in which almost the whole of India has been subdivided by the National Sample Survey Organization. The sources and definitions of the variables are explained at the end of each table. Apart from utilizing various surveys of the National Sample Survey Organization, we have collected materials for this purpose from the Census, Livestock Census, Season and Crop Reports, and All-India Debt and Investment Survey of the Reserve Bank of India.

Appendix Table A. Demographic Variables for NSS Regions

Case no.	State	Region	Name	WMPROP	IDR	FLIIP	MFGP	DENS	MSCASTE	MSTRIBE	SPARSVIL
1	Andhra Pradesh	Coastal		34.43	51.18	13.00	8.52	174.00	12.35	6.10	31.10
2		Inland	Northern	29.40	45.13	6.00	10.43	110.00	17.34	3.41	10.60
3		Inland	Southern	29.25	33.88	9.00	7.43	99.00	14.72	.03	6.10
4	Assam	Plains		14.56	—	16.00	4.42	205.00	6.27	10.04	21.40
5		Hills		2.26	—	10.00	1.07	20.00	2.14	57.69	66.10
6	Bihar	Southern		16.95	—	5.00	7.15	153.00	10.18	36.00	37.90
7		Northern		36.96	—	6.00	3.24	469.00	13.98	.81	12.80
8		Central		29.58	—	8.00	5.83	359.00	18.53	1.05	20.80
9	Gujarat	Eastern		20.56	36.81	16.00	9.59	115.00	5.37	39.47	13.50
10		Plains	Northern	24.63	48.44	22.00	16.12	163.00	8.30	3.48	6.70
11		Plains	Southern	26.39	32.57	18.00	10.73	203.00	3.99	48.69	13.00
12		Dry	Areas	21.94	56.96	16.00	9.37	51.00	9.31	2.35	10.50
13		Saurashtra		14.64	54.80	15.00	11.03	54.00	7.15	.22	7.90
14	Haryana	Eastern		10.37	51.62	11.00	11.58	223.00	20.23	0.00	11.20
15		Western		15.71	56.68	7.00	7.05	148.00	20.99	0.00	4.00
16	Himachal Pradesh	Mountainous		3.07	—	18.00	4.18	63.00	23.02	4.36	71.10
17	Jammu and Kashmir	Outer	Hills	5.56	47.69	12.00	7.58	138.00	30.81	0.00	32.50
18		Jhelum	Valley	.45	61.59	4.00	2.53	48.00	10.67	0.00	30.50
19	Karnatak	Coastal	Ghats	1.95	37.54	3.00	8.71	120.00	0.00	0.00	21.30
20		Inland	Eastern	23.20	29.47	29.00	17.09	122.00	5.25	2.81	26.20
21		Inland	Southern	32.36	49.32	21.00	6.26	101.00	16.09	1.56	26.90
22		Inland	Northern	23.85	44.03	12.00	11.54	155.00	19.19	.41	21.90
23	Kerala	Northern		29.15	61.59	11.00	8.78	105.00	12.94	.57	7.30
24		Southern		25.74	19.11	42.00	13.12	402.00	6.57	2.99	0.00
25	Madhya Pradesh	Eastern		23.96	13.14	60.00	17.36	538.00	10.45	.53	.30
26		Western		25.97	82.24	7.00	5.22	79.00	10.89	30.92	22.10
27		Inland	Eastern	22.45	106.11	6.00	7.05	80.00	9.73	31.51	33.30
28		Inland	Western	24.91	144.86	8.00	8.43	71.00	16.67	14.22	32.30

Appendix Table A (continued)

Case no.	State	Region	Name	WMPROP	IDR	FLITP	MFGP	DENS	MSCASTE	MSTRIBE	SPARSVIL
29		Western		17.81	96.90	5.00	8.00	85.00	14.67	23.77	27.10
30		Northern		10.15	59.08	5.00	5.66	81.00	20.30	4.55	27.00
31	Maharashtra	Coastal		18.70	88.04	23.00	27.76	150.50	1.68	16.52	5.90
32		Inland	Western	12.15	63.39	18.00	11.55	135.00	9.64	2.69	6.00
33		Inland	Northern	26.93	79.93	16.00	8.19	118.00	3.80	26.34	11.40
34		Inland	Central	24.72	73.79	10.00	4.65	109.00	10.22	1.94	7.70
35		Inland	Eastern	38.58	104.06	21.00	7.16	98.00	4.23	4.43	21.10
36		Eastern		31.90	103.53	15.00	12.30	83.00	4.62	8.07	23.00
37	Orissa	Coastal		27.59	—	17.00	5.61	260.00	17.28	5.75	32.90
38		Southern		34.63	—	6.00	3.69	91.00	15.80	34.54	55.80
39		Northern		29.81	—	9.00	11.44	112.00	13.07	37.26	31.70
40	Punjab	Northern		19.68	66.18	24.00	14.27	257.00	29.23	0.00	18.00
41		Southern		22.60	57.32	14.00	7.40	165.00	25.92	0.00	10.90
42	Rajasthan	Western		3.00	—	3.00	5.60	35.00	16.11	2.74	15.90
43		North	Eastern	4.53	—	4.00	7.60	96.00	19.26	9.58	25.20
44		Southern		5.96	—	4.00	5.03	97.00	7.66	49.06	31.60
45		South	Eastern	7.69	—	5.00	7.01	77.00	17.03	18.39	35.30
46	Tamil Nadu	Coastal	Northern	33.95	54.44	16.00	13.36	266.00	26.56	1.36	7.20
47		Coastal	Southern	32.11	57.57	26.00	13.25	246.00	19.85	.05	6.10
48		Inland		28.88	51.26	16.00	13.46	206.00	18.38	1.50	4.90
49	Tripura	Himalayan		27.12	—	17.00	3.52	—	13.11	31.80	63.40
50	Uttar Pradesh	Himalayan		5.12	—	12.00	3.66	64.00	17.69	4.51	63.70
51		Western		12.98	—	8.00	8.24	315.00	18.77	.04	12.80
52		Central		11.19	—	7.00	7.34	288.00	29.87	.14	10.90
53		Eastern		15.69	—	6.00	6.33	357.00	21.50	.05	23.70
54		Southern		12.61	—	6.00	5.00	125.00	26.18	0.00	17.20
55	West Bengal	Himalayan		32.20	36.02	11.00	4.28	279.00	37.31	15.14	11.50
56		Eastern	Plains	32.99	40.74	12.00	7.19	419.00	20.87	5.72	17.40

Appendix Table A (continued)

Case no.	State	Region	Name	WMPROP	IDR	FLITP	MFGP	DENS	MSCASTE	MSTRIBE	SPARSVIL
57		Central	Plains	34.82	27.61	19.00	22.94	493.00	27.81	3.68	5.10
58		West	Plains	30.84	34.66	15.00	5.71	318.00	17.46	11.20	31.10
59	Delhi			7.60	—	21.00	—	—	25.33	0.00	8.20
60	Goa, Daman, Diu			16.80	—	31.00	—	—	1.61	.96	16.10
61	Pondicherry			40.44	—	36.00	—	—	21.01	0.00	19.20

SOURCE: For WMPROP, National Sample Survey Organization, 27th Round, 1972–73; for IDR, *Vital Statistics of India, 1973*; for FLITP, MFGP, DENS, MSCASTE, MSTRIBE, and SPARSVIL, Census, 1971.

NOTE: Dash indicates data not available.

WMPROP — Proportion of farm wage laborers in rural labor force for males in the 15–59 age group in each region in 1972–73.

IDR — Number of infant deaths per thousand births in rural areas in each region, computed by averaging the civil registration data for each district. The dash for this variable also covers cases of regions in states where the civil registration records are not regarded as adequate or reliable by the Office of the Registrar General of India and hence excluded from this analysis.

FLITP — Proportion of literates among total female population.

MFGP — Proportion of working population in the region in manufacturing, repairing, and services.

DENS — Density of population per square kilometer in each region.

MASCASTE — Proportion of scheduled castes in total rural male population in each region.

MSTRIBE — Proportion of scheduled tribes in total rural male population in each region.

SPARSVIL — Proportion of total inhabited villages in each region having a population of less than 200.

224

Appendix Table B. Physical Variables for NSS Regions

Case no.	State	Region	Name	IRRP	NRAIN	RAINDEF	MONRAIN	WELLIRR	SOIL
1	Andhra Pradesh	Coastal		28.76	995.70	3.00	64.67	5.80	68.80
2		Inland	Northern	15.06	894.00	12.00	99.27	20.00	67.50
3		Inland	Southern	11.61	670.40	5.00	66.75	34.90	70.50
4	Assam	Plains		6.68	2161.30	−13.00	69.10	0.00	56.30
5		Hills		1.16	2244.62	7.00	69.10	0.00	56.60
6	Bihar	Southern		8.45	1376.38	−17.00	81.42	18.40	59.50
7		Northern		11.36	1319.83	8.00	84.52	38.40	55.40
8		Central		30.40	1127.62	5.00	85.19	24.00	54.20
9	Gujarat	Eastern		4.18	1127.65	35.00	98.57	75.50	47.30
10		Plains	Northern	18.93	739.73	62.00	92.59	78.80	44.50
11		Plains	Southern	10.37	1139.28	40.00	98.61	65.80	50.60
12		Dry	Areas	6.86	557.08	90.00	90.25	86.70	47.50
13		Saurashtra		14.51	607.84	76.00	84.96	85.60	57.60
14	Haryana	Eastern		42.04	622.98	13.00	82.63	60.30	66.70
15		Western		38.00	439.80	16.00	82.61	8.40	69.50
16	Himachal Pradesh			1.69	1708.20	−51.00	72.10	1.00	50.40
17	Jammu and Kashmir	Mountainous		12.43	1047.05	54.00	83.28	0.00	—
18		Outer	Hills	2.55	1302.07	−13.00	55.27	0.90	—
19		Jhelum	Valley	21.82	1050.95	−51.00	23.58	0.50	—
20	Karnatak	Coastal	Ghats	16.57	2929.45	26.00	100.00	46.20	72.70
21		Inland	Eastern	15.00	1381.98	−1.00	100.00	4.20	71.90
22		Inland	Southern	9.73	341.56	−23.00	100.00	40.50	72.00
23		Inland	Northern	4.69	443.81	23.00	100.00	36.20	63.20
24	Kerala	Northern		8.75	3119.37	10.00	76.59	1.40	59.00
25		Southern		9.76	2919.13	−5.00	62.48	1.40	54.50
26	Madhya Pradesh	Eastern		9.34	1480.17	9.00	87.69	12.20	63.60
27		Inland	Eastern	2.11	1320.33	−4.00	88.43	25.60	47.40
28		Inland	Western	5.53	1207.30	7.00	90.75	61.90	50.10

Appendix Table B (continued)

Case no.	State	Region	Name	IRRP	NRAIN	RAINDEF		WELLIRR	SOIL
29		Western		8.10	877.27	15.00	90.64	86.50	49.50
30		Northern		13.42	857.50	−14.00	91.25	49.40	57.50
31	Maharashtra	Coastal		1.31	2637.55	37.00	94.41	50.00	65.00
32		Inland	Western	13.52	945.48	19.00	80.79	62.40	58.30
33		Inland	Northern	10.77	812.23	22.00	87.58	74.20	51.20
34		Inland	Central	9.48	785.24	13.00	83.57	80.20	54.40
35		Inland	Eastern	4.70	964.08	20.00	85.61	75.60	67.50
36		Eastern		16.68	1422.00	−6.00	89.03	2.20	60.40
37	Orissa	Coastal		14.38	1453.50	10.00	69.70	2.20	55.30
38		Southern		5.61	1398.67	27.00	77.20	3.90	61.30
39		Northern		7.51	1537.17	3.00	82.45	4.60	64.90
40	Punjab	Northern		46.77	732.97	5.00	76.55	72.30	73.70
41		Southern		55.24	521.35	−19.00	77.42	43.30	74.80
42	Rajasthan	Western		1.03	341.13	27.00	94.54	96.30	58.40
43		North	Eastern	28.02	567.10	4.00	74.77	47.40	62.80
44		Southern		10.51	736.75	13.00	79.27	80.40	61.20
45		South	Eastern	25.61	751.63	7.00	100.00	43.50	63.00
46	Tamil Nadu	Coastal	Northern	33.92	1164.15	2.00	34.22	32.90	70.20
47		Coastal	Southern	35.36	1067.95	−6.00	26.39	11.10	70.20
48		Inland		22.36	1009.63	−8.00	41.71	46.80	71.80
49	Tripura	Himalayan		3.12	2026.00	3.00	61.11	0.00	0.00
50	Uttar Pradesh	Western		20.06	1853.95	34.00	95.16	5.90	80.80
51		Central		50.53	835.78	−6.00	86.55	55.00	62.80
52		Eastern		33.35	928.20	32.00	88.29	28.40	65.10
53		Southern		45.12	1087.34	23.00	87.78	67.00	61.60
54		Southern		15.82	864.65	15.00	90.27	11.80	59.20

			IRRP	NRAIN	RAINDEF	MONRAIN	WELLIRR	SOIL
55	West Bengal	Himalayan	.32	3513.67	−4.00	78.20	9.40	55.40
56		Eastern Plains	8.72	1454.60	14.00	76.90	0.00	53.00
57		Central Plains	14.16	1510.50	23.00	79.00	0.20	55.20
58		West Plains	3.91	1199.00	39.00	79.00	1.20	60.50
59	Delhi		13.93	—	—	—	72.70	—
60	Goa, Daman, Diu		—	3043.84	−15.00	91.81	0.00	—
61	Pondicherry		—	1827.25	4.00	56.44	37.70	—

SOURCE: For IRRP, Reserve Bank of India, All-India Debt and Investment Survey, 1971–72; for NRAIN, RAINDEF, MONRAIN, and WELLIRR, *Season and Crop Reports*; for SOIL, indices prepared by K. B. Shome and S. P. Raychaudhuri, reported and used in the district tables in *Reserve Bank of India Bulletin*, October 1969.

NOTE: IRRP= area of owned irrigated land as percentage of total owned land in each region as of June 30, 1971.

NRAIN= annual normal rainfall in the region in meters calculated as a simple average of district-level data. In the absence of requisite data, for Assam we have taken the average of actual rainfall in 1960–70 and for Purulia district in the western plains region of West Bengal the average of actual rainfall in 1965–74. For the Himalayan region of Uttar Pradesh normal rainfall data were available only for 2 out of 8 districts.

RAINDEF= percentage deficit of actual rainfall in 1970–71 from normal in the region, calculated as a simple average of district-level data. The nonzero negative figures indicate the cases of deficit, and the positive figures, cases of excess. For Assam, Gujarat, Jammu and Kashmir, Maharashtra, and Tripura, the actual rainfall figures relate to 1970, not to 1970–71. Data for one district in the northern plains district of Gujarat and 6 districts in the Himalayan region of Uttar Pradesh were not available. In some cases the data for a meteorological center located in a district have been taken as representative of the district as a whole.

MONRAIN= proportion of annual normal rainfall concentrated in the June–September monsoon. The normal monsoon rainfall figure was not available for Assam by district, so the same figure has been used for both its regions. For West Bengal, in the absence of normal monsoon rainfall data the average over 1965–74 has been used for each region. In the absence of data for some districts in Rajasthan, those for 4 districts have been take for its western region, 3 districts for its north eastern region, only 1 district for its southern region, and 2 districts for its southeastern region.

WELLIRR= area irrigated from wells and tubewells as a proportion of total net area irrigated in 1970–71. Figures for Haryana refer to 1971–72, Jammu and Kashmir to 1969–70, Rajasthan to 1971–72, Uttar Pradesh to 1966–67 and West Bengal to 1967–68. In the absence of data we had to use the same statewise figure for both regions of Assam and of Kerala. For the coastal region of Orissa we did not have data for 1 district, and for the southern region of Orissa we had to use 1959–60 figures for 2 districts.

Appendix Table C. Economic and Institutional Variables for NSS Regions

Case no.	State	Region	Name	ASTPOOR	LFARMP	CVLC	URR	ATTMP	EXPWR	POVP	LSPROP	CRLOP	WMR
1	Andhra Pradesh	Coastal		40.97	6.44	1.04	12.79	13.30	17.67	43.63	11.34	.7653	2.03
2		Inland	Northern	20.70	18.79	1.30	10.44	38.28	15.06	46.79	7.50	.7015	1.70
3		Inland	Southern	25.71	17.12	1.28	11.51	16.64	16.52	37.72	9.92	.7255	1.76
4	Assam	Plains		16.40	6.09	1.59	1.97	50.17	17.08	28.90	19.86	.5926	3.51
5		Hills		—	7.14	1.11	0.99	15.00	18.45	27.49	16.44	.4212	4.00
6	Bihar	Southern		10.58	6.40	1.33	8.24	28.51	10.33	64.28	5.60	.5285	1.74
7		Northern		23.55	6.15	1.31	9.45	21.72	11.82	54.41	17.97	.6668	2.01
8		Central		16.80	9.11	1.01	13.55	45.82	10.85	52.05	16.95	.6864	1.88
9		Eastern		17.86	15.01	1.06	7.67	21.88	16.68	60.51	1.78	.5356	2.33
10	Gujarat	Plains	Northern	10.45	15.22	0.83	5.50	17.63	16.21	28.67	9.30	.6733	2.43
11		Plains	Southern	29.45	9.45	1.19	4.55	35.33	15.56	26.83	3.38	.8042	2.14
12		Dry	Areas	9.54	51.04	1.12	5.93	35.46	16.08	37.89	3.91	.5778	2.75
13		Saurashtra		13.45	41.10	1.11	2.90	33.21	19.50	19.97	1.23	.6022	3.60
14	Haryana	Eastern		8.12	24.14	1.26	2.72	58.96	18.92	14.40	29.50	.7585	2.68
15		Western		7.00	36.59	1.21	3.05	53.77	15.16	9.75	20.94	.6426	3.95
16	Himachal Pradesh			1.91	9.65	0.99	0.42	51.18	40.26	10.66	10.20	.5174	—
17	Jammu and Kashmir	Mountainous		1.79	14.30	0.91	1.00	43.24	18.04	17.71	16.94	.4901	4.05
18	Kashmir	Outer	Hills	0.83	6.37	1.63	1.01	100.00	16.31	44.39	5.28	.3868	4.33
19		Jhelum	Valley	1.32	2.33	0.89	16.81	97.22	23.43	11.49	2.44	.3781	2.22
20	Karnatak	Coastal	Ghats	30.63	7.30	1.67	5.23	26.08	18.62	40.41	53.86	.7131	2.45
21		Inland	Eastern	28.45	15.37	1.61	5.60	28.07	14.66	36.78	8.08	.5453	2.32
22		Inland	Southern	24.12	10.17	0.97	8.08	24.18	13.06	34.56	9.54	.6127	1.67
23		Inland	Northern	16.94	36.81	1.17	11.03	18.34	14.68	47.62	17.01	.6465	1.73
24	Kerala	Northern		18.55	3.35	1.03	21.89	8.08	11.08	55.72	5.06	.6898	2.90
25		Southern		14.08	1.85	1.22	24.97	10.57	12.69	47.67	11.68	.6803	3.11

Case no.	State	Region	Name	ASTPOOR	LFARMP	CVLC	URR	ATTMP	EXPWR	POVP	LSPROP	CRLOP	WMR
26	Madhya Pradesh	Eastern		16.85	18.16	1.17	2.42	40.84	13.30	68.82	8.28	.6092	1.59
27		Inland	Eastern	18.23	24.39	1.12	3.23	44.09	10.70	67.61	6.27	.5922	1.24
28		Inland	Western	19.86	40.26	1.32	4.05	39.59	15.24	53.31	8.20	.6300	1.93
29		Western		11.06	43.82	1.28	6.26	29.59	14.33	48.81	6.57	.4880	1.56
30		Northern		10.23	30.13	1.10	1.98	43.80	13.06	40.25	8.17	.5599	2.05
31	Maharashtra	Coastal		22.10	9.44	0.98	6.01	28.32	20.18	59.33	9.78	.6506	2.61
32		Inland	Western	16.65	25.07	1.04	8.81	23.24	13.99	48.79	3.68	.6850	2.20
33		Inland	Northern	25.73	30.15	1.19	14.55	31.17	12.26	53.83	7.04	.6188	2.15
34		Inland	Central	20.74	41.69	1.10	7.13	34.91	13.16	54.57	7.25	.6472	1.97
35		Inland	Eastern	28.62	38.41	1.16	11.53	30.24	13.66	61.59	6.32	.6553	2.22
36		Eastern		14.35	12.60	0.95	14.66	29.29	17.35	60.44	8.71	.6233	1.98
37	Orissa	Coastal		17.47	4.87	1.04	17.07	21.07	11.55	53.71	18.63	.6352	2.04
38		Southern		33.40	11.04	1.21	5.28	21.19	6.93	83.95	13.01	.6055	1.65
39		Northern		23.34	10.88	1.14	10.72	23.54	9.50	80.00	9.19	.6029	1.81
40	Punjab	Northern		6.37	15.32	0.99	6.25	27.23	22.28	11.85	25.22	.7898	4.64
41		Southern		6.99	30.83	1.60	2.02	55.54	21.58	14.12	30.52	.6969	5.53
42	Rajasthan	Western		6.75	64.83	0.82	5.05	16.76	12.48	28.27	4.97	.5306	2.80
43		North	Eastern	6.67	34.44	1.06	3.21	29.08	16.67	28.74	5.92	.5688	2.62
44		Southern		5.75	12.89	1.11	1.10	65.15	9.60	78.94	2.47	.3911	2.08
45		South	Eastern	5.61	36.94	1.30	1.32	65.43	16.13	47.19	8.32	.5104	1.96
46	Tamil Nadu	Coastal	Northern	38.46	2.96	1.31	14.59	14.20	11.64	48.74	13.74	.6691	1.86
47		Coastal	Southern	38.75	5.45	0.95	14.49	9.16	15.84	38.52	17.04	.7363	2.63
48		Inland		37.57	6.43	1.13	9.50	18.01	13.87	41.10	10.60	.7394	1.98
49	Tripura			22.77	3.46	1.05	5.94	24.13	16.22	23.92		—	3.08
50	Uttar Pradesh	Himalayan		13.21	2.04	1.79	1.18	37.16	26.34	47.72	19.71	.7592	2.47
51		Western		9.48	10.94	0.96	2.76	18.95	14.36	45.34	12.71	.6096	2.64
52		Central		11.19	8.43	1.03	2.28	25.56	14.50	48.79	15.13	.5582	1.89
53		Eastern		8.52	6.61	1.14	4.56	39.22	13.80	46.62	10.15	.5669	1.59

Appendix Table C (continued)

Case no.	State	Region	Name	ASTPOOR	LFARMP	CVLC	URR	ATTMP	EXPWR	POVP	LSPROP	CRLOP	WMR
54		Southern		13.44	28.12	1.02	3.28	36.97	12.54	49.61	16.38	.6649	1.62
55	West Bengal	Himalayan		30.43	4.90	1.03	7.80	58.91	15.08	44.25	26.52	.5137	2.87
56		Eastern	Plains	32.85	6.39	0.97	11.37	25.08	11.15	59.53	17.14	.6130	2.26
57		Central	Plains	34.02	2.53	0.91	9.63	6.36	11.30	45.27	24.37	.7352	2.81
58		West	Plains	19.30	4.90	0.88	14.42	14.88	11.56	57.99	11.02	.5879	2.34
59	Delhi			12.51	12.00	0.88	3.17	16.13	28.58	—	—	—	3.00
60	Goa, Daman, Diu			—	—	—	20.96	0.00	—	—	—	—	4.10
61	Pondicherry			—	—	—	19.82	10.55	—	—	—	—	2.88

SOURCE: Data for ASTPOOR, LFARMP, and CVLC are from Reserve Bank of India, Debt and Investment Survey, 1971–72; for LSPROP and CRLOP, EXPWR, from NSS, 25th Round, 1970–71; for POVP, URR, and ATTMP, from NSS, 27th Round, 1972–73.

NOTE: ASTPOOR = proportion of rural households in each region that possess assets of Rs. 1,000 or less as of June 30, 1971.

LFARMP = proportion of total rural households operating land above 7.5 acres.

CVLC = coefficient of variation of land cultivated across size classes.

LSPROP = Proportion of cultivated area leased in each region.

CRLOP = Concentration ratio calculated of land operated.

WMR = average rate of earning per man-day of farm wage work for males in the 15–59 age group in rural noncultivating wage-earner households in 1970–71 at 1960–61 prices. The deflator used is the consumer price index of agricultural laborers (with 1960–61 as a base) of the State where the region belongs.

POVP = percentage of rural population in 1972–73 below a poverty line defined as Rs. 15 per capita per month at 1960–61 prices. The deflator for the poverty line is the consumer price index of agricultural laborers of the State where the region belongs. (The deflator for the region belongs. (These estimates were made available to me by S. D. Tendulkar.)

URR = average daily rural unemployment rate in the region.

ATTMP = regular (as opposed to casual) farm male laborers in the 15–59 age group as a proportion of total farm male laborers in that age group.

EXPWR = per capita monthly expenditure at 1960–61 prices of rural noncultivating wage-earner households in 1970–71. The deflator used is the consumer price index of agricultural laborers of the state where the region belongs.

Appendix Table D. Technological variables for NSS Regions

Case no.	State	Region	Name	PUMHA	OPH	GEMHA	FHA	GROWTH
1	Andhra Pradesh	Coastal		.02	1632.13	7.33	.05	.35
2		Inland	Northern	.03	652.90	4.40	.02	-1.70
3		Inland	Southern	.04	1019.22	15.22	.02	.01
4	Assam	Plains		.00	1215.05	4.60	.00	2.01
5		Hills		.00	1524.34	3.65	.00	5.81
6	Bihar	Southern		.00	865.67	4.10	.00	-.90
7		Northern		.01	967.38	7.06	.01	.20
8		Central		.02	1079.41	15.67	.02	.87
9	Gujarat	Eastern		.05	956.52	26.46	.02	-.06
10		Plains	Northern	.09	1821.12	77.15	.04	2.89
11		Plains	Southern	.08	1676.05	36.08	.03	-.49
12		Dry	Areas	.02	436.89	15.89	.01	3.28
13		Saurashtra		.04	832.01	59.95	.02	2.28
14	Haryana	Eastern		.04	1372.88	36.17	.03	6.00
15		Western		.01	911.52	24.83	.01	4.95
16	Himachal Pradesh			—	—	—	—	—
17	Jammu and Kashmir	Mountainous		—	520.79	—	—	5.67
18		Outer	Hills	.00	861.90	4.96	.00	5.67
19		Jehlum	Valley	.00	1506.04	13.63	.02	5.44
20	Karnatak	Coastal	Ghats	.09	1666.22	27.36	.01	-.66
21		Inland	Eastern	.01	1582.26	32.10	.05	2.29
22		Inland	Southern	.06	1409.64	31.24	.05	2.55
23		Inland	Northern	.02	713.65	12.98	.02	1.92
24	Kerala	Northern		.03	1735.88	9.43	.05	.71
25		Southern		.03	1800.30	41.37	.11	1.60
26	Madhya Pradesh	Eastern		.00	897.39	4.57	.01	1.37
27		Inland	Eastern	.00	592.47	3.80	.00	2.43
28		Inland	Western	.01	617.12	18.24	.01	1.30

Appendix Table D. (continued)

Case no.	State	Region	Name	PUMHA	OPH	GEMHA	FHA	GROWTH
29		Western		.02	628.49	11.81	.01	.41
30		Northern		.00	674.31	17.62	.01	1.95
31	Maharashtra	Coastal	Western	.01	1345.40	19.82	.02	-2.32
32		Inland	Northern	.04	632.37	137.03	.02	-4.25
33		Inland	Central	.04	496.06	30.49	.02	-5.39
34		Inland		.02	293.18	9.14	.01	-7.18
35		Inland	Eastern	.01	398.04	8.42	.01	-2.52
36		Eastern		.00	657.53	10.06	.01	-.48
37	Orissa	Coastal		.00	1067.21	3.99	.02	-.16
38		Southern		.00	974.92	2.62	.00	-.09
39		Northern		.00	1011.37	1.77	.01	-.44
40	Punjab	Northern		.08	1793.40	99.19	.08	8.02
41		Southern		.06	1734.64	38.06	.06	7.39
42	Rajasthan	Western		.00	225.82	5.65	.00	2.79
43		North	Eastern	.01	684.22	21.91	.01	4.97
44		Southern		.01	775.80	9.79	.00	2.10
45		South	Eastern	.01	705.27	9.99	.02	4.35
46	Tamil Nadu	Coastal	Northern	.20	2030.31	46.53	.05	3.24
47		Coastal	Southern	.06	1820.81	9.02	.05	2.74
48		Inland		.19	1562.85	18.34	.05	1.18
49	Tripura			—	—	—	—	—
50	Uttar Pradesh	Himalayan		.00	1034.90	9.59	.02	2.15
51		Western		.02	1345.06	30.43	.03	3.40
52		Central		.01	1015.15	18.16	.02	2.06
53		Eastern		.01	928.49	16.05	.03	1.54
54		Southern		.00	721.98	8.27	.01	2.46
55	West Bengal	Himalayan		.00	1323.11	6.89	.01	2.58
56		Eastern	Plains	.00	1372.15	5.87	.01	3.02
57		Central	Plains	.00	1609.14	18.07	.02	1.82

| 60 | Goa, Daman, Diu | — | — | — | — | — | — |
| 61 | Pondicherry | — | — | — | — | — | — |

SOURCE: data for PUMHA from Livestock Census; for OPH and GROWTH, from Bhalla and Alagh (1979); for GEMHA, from Reserve Bank of India, All-India Debt and Investment Survey, 1971–72; for FHA, from *Fertilizer Statistics* and Bhalla and Alagh (1979).

NOTE: PUMHA = number of electric pumpsets and oil engines used per hectare of cropped area in 1971.
OPH = value in Rs. of output per hectare of 19 major crops, averaged for the years 1970–71 to 1972–73.
GEMHA = gross capital expenditure in Rs. on agricultural implements, machinery, and transport equipment per hectare of 19 major crops.
FHA = value in Rs. of fertilizers used in 1970–71 per hectare of area under 19 major crops, averaged over districts in each region.
GROWTH = average of exponential annual rates of growth of output of 19 major crops of all districts in a region over the period 1962–65 to 1970–73. The estimated rate for the coastal region of Andhra Pradesh includes that for Kurnool District (while the latter is excluded from the southern region), that for Assam plains region includes the rate for Dibrugarh, that for northern Bihar includes the rate for Monghyr, that for central Bihar includes the rate for Saharsa, and that for the northern plains region of Gujarat excludes that for Gandhinagar. In the absence of breakdown in the data, the same rate has been used for the mountainous and the outer hills regions of Jammu and Kashmir.

Glossary of Variables

ABPRIMED	Dummy for education beyond primary level
ACTFEM	Number of economically active females in the household
ACTMALE	Number of economically active males in the household
ADA	Number of adult family workers per acre
ADCULT	Number of adult cultivators in the family
ADED	Number of adults in household having more than primary education
ADF	Number of adult workers in the family
ADWOMEN	Number of adult women in the household
AGDEV	Composite agricultural development index for the district
AGE	Age of the laborer in years
AGLABP	Percentage of agricultural labor households to all rural households
ASTPOOR	Proportion of rural households that are asset-poor
ATTMP	Regular farm male laborers in the 15–59 age group as a proportion of total farm male laborers in that age group
ATTP	Percentage of attached agricultural labor households to the total number of agricultural labor households
AWAYM	Dummy for some male member of the household gone away for work
BAB	Number of children in the 0–4 age group in the household
CAL	Average calorie intake per capita per day in 1971–72
CASTRIB	Dummy for scheduled caste or tribe
CBOR	Percentage of total annual borrowing by small cultivator households taken to meet household expenses
CENPL	Dummy for central plains region in West Bengal
CHDOM	Number of children in the household in the 5–14 age group who are currently in domestic work
CLFDAYS	Number of person-days each adult woman in the usual labor force spent in the current labor force in the reference week
CRLOP	Concentration ratio of land operated
CTIRRP	Percentage of area irrigated from canals and tubewells
CTIRLS	Percentage of leased-in area irrigated from canals and tubewells
CULTIVAT	Area cultivated by the household in acres
CURPCPF	Proportion of all usually active women in the household who are in the current labor force
CVLC	Coefficient of variation of cultivated land across size classes of land holdings
DEBTEMP	Percentage of total debt of an indebted labor household borrowed from employers
DENS	Density of population per square kilometer
DEP	Number of dependents as proportion of household size

DEPE	Number of dependents per earner in the labor household
DIST	Distance of the village from nearest town in kilometers
DUR	Duration for which the laborer has been available for work or additional work
EARNERM	Number of male earners in the household
EDF	Number of women with above-primary education level in the 15–60 age group
EDM	Number of men with above-primary education level in the 15–60 age group
EMDEBT	Dummy for indebtedness to employer
EJECTP	Percentage of leased-in area under contracts in which the tenant may be evicted at will
EXPWR	Per capita monthly expenditure at 1960–61 prices of rural non-cultivating wage-earner households in 1970–71
FCMORP	Ratio of female to male death rate in 0–4 age group in 1970
FDINDEX	Food cost-of-living index in 1977–78 in the district
FHA	Value in P.s. of fertilizers used per hectare of cropped area
FLIT	Percentage of female population above 4 years who are literate
FLITP	Percentage of female population who are literate
FMA	Value of fertilizers and manure per acre
FWAGE	Daily farm wage rate currently received by the casual laborer in the reference week
GEMHA	Gross capital expenditure on agricultural equipment per hectare of cropped area
GROWTH	Rate of growth in agricultural production in the district where the village is located
HARVPROP	Proportion of paddy-cropped area harvested
HARVW	Harvesting wage rate per day in annas for males in agricultural labor households in 1950–51
HARVWAGEM	Male daily wage rate for harvesting
HBKDA	Hired bullock labor days per acre
HI	Hiring in
HLDA	Hired man-days per year per acre of cultivated area
HLDAR	Hired farm labor days per acre in the reference week
HMUNOWN	Dummy for unowned homestead
HO	Hiring Out
HOUF	Number of farm labor days hired out on unemployed in the reference week for females in the 15–60 age group
HOUI	Number of farm labor days hired out or unemployed in the reference week
HOUM	Number of farm labor days hired out on unemployed in the reference week for males in the 15–60 age group
IDR	Number of infant deaths per thousand births in rural areas in 1973
IRRCULT	Percentage of cultivated area of the farm that is irrigated
IRRP	Percentage of area irrigated in the region
LABFORF	Number of adult women currently in the labor force
LABFORM	Number of adult men currently in the labor force

LFARMP	Large farmer households as a proportion of total rural households
LSPROP	Proportion of cultivated area leased in
MAXMINW	Maximum to minimum agricultural wage ratio across seasonal operations
MCHMOR	Death rate per thousand in 0–4 age group for males in 1970
MCI	Multiple cropping index
MECHSKILL	Dummy for laborers with special mechanical skills
MFGP	Proportion of working population in the region in manufacturing, repairing, and services
MONRAIN	Proportion of annual normal rainfall concentrated in the June–September monsoon
MSCASTE	Proportion of scheduled castes in total male population in the region
MSTRIBE	Proportion of scheduled tribes in total male population in the region
NDEP	Number of dependents in the household
NFFE	Dummy for women who are employed in nonfarm family enterprise
NFFP	Percentage of women in the usual labor force who are in nonfarm casual labor or family enterprise
NFM	Number of men in the household usually occupied in nonfarm work
NHA	Nitrogenous fertilizer in kilograms used per hectare of area under foodgrains in the district
NHI	Net hiring in
NMAR	Dummy for women who never married
NONAGMP	Proportion of nonagricultural male workers in the village
NRAIN	Normal annual rainfall in the region in meters
OBKPA	Owned bullock labor days used per acre of cultivated area under paddy
OPH	Agricultural output per hectare in Rs.
OWNED	Area owned by the household
PCEXPR	Mean per capita monthly expenditure
PCULTIVAT	Per capita land cultivated by the household to which the laborer belongs
PHARVW	Predicted harvesting wage rate
POVP	Percentage of rural population below the poverty line in the region
PRIMED	Dummy for education up to the primary level
PRINDEX	Index of land productivity
PUBWORKF	Dummy for female wage employment in public works in or near the village
PUBWORKM	Dummy for male wage employment in public works in or near the village
PUMHA	Electric pumpsets and oil engines used per hectare of cropped area
PUR	Potential underemployment

RAIN	Normal annual rainfall in the district in meters
RAINDEF	Percentage deficit in actual rainfall from normal in the district
REG	Dummy for women who have regular wage employment
REGP	Percentage of women in usual labor force who have regular wage employment
REGSAL	Monthly salary of regular farm laborers
RICEP	Proportion of cropped area under rice and other labor-intensive crops
SBRND 1	Dummy for July–September quarter
SBRND 2	Dummy for October–December quarter
SBRND 3	Dummy for January–March quarter
SBRND 4	Dummy for April–June quarter
SCHCASTE	Dummy for scheduled caste
SCHOOLCH	Number of school-going children in the household
SCHTRIBE	Dummy for scheduled tribe
SCVTLDF	Seasonal coefficient of variation in total labor days used on farm
SE	Self-employment
SEXF	Dummy to represent women
SHPROP	Area under sharecropping as percentage of area under sharecropping plus fixed-rent tenancy in 1953–54
SOIL	Index of soil rating of the land in the region
SPARSVIL	Proportion of sparsely populated villages in the region
UALABFORF	Number of adult women in the household participating in the labor force by usual status
UNEMD	Average number of days unemployed in the year for adult males in agricultural laborer household.
UNEMPM	Rate of unemployment of male members in the household
UNPDRINK	Percentage of villages reporting unprotected sources of drinking water in 1963–64
UNSKILL	Dummy for unskilled women
UR	Current rate of underemployment of the laborer in the reference week
URR	Average rural unemployment rate in the region
UTBIRTHAT	Percentage of live births not attended by any trained medical practitioner in the rural areas of the State where the region is located
VAR	Variation in agricultural output in the district
VILIRR	Village irrigation level
VILPOP	Village size in thousands of population in 1971
VIRR	Dummy for village irrigation
VMULCR	Dummy to represent whether most of the village land is cropped more than once a year
VUR	Unemployment rate in the village
VWAGE	Average farm wage rate in village
VWAGEF	Average daily wage rate in Rs. for female agricultural labor in the village in the reference week
VWAGEM	Average daily wage rate in Rs. for male agricultural labor in the village in the reference week

WAGEACPT	Acceptable wage rate reported by casual agricultural laborers for hypothetical wage employment inside the village
WELLIRR	Area irrigated from wells as a proportion of total area irrigated
WID	Dummy for widowed, divorced, and separated women
WMPROP	Proportion of farm wage laborers in rural labor force for males in 15–59 age group
WMR	Average rate of earning per man-day of farm wage work for males in the 15–59 age group in rural noncultivating wage-earner households in 1970–71 at 1960–61 prices
YHA	Yield in tons per hectare of foodgrains in the district

References

Government Sources

Agricultural Labor Enquiry Survey, Ministry of Labor, 1950–51 and 1956–57.
Census, various years. Carried out every ten years by Registrar General of India.
Farm Management Survey, Food and Agricultural Ministry, various states, various years.
Fertilizer Statistics. Fertilizer Corporation of India, various years.
First Agricultural Labor Enquiry. *Report.* Ministry of Labor.
Labor Bureau. Rural Labor Enquiry, 1963–64, 1964–65, and 1974–75.
Livestock Census. Department of Economics and Statistics.
NSS. National Sample Survey Organization. Employment and Unemployment Survey, 27th Round, 1972–73; 32d Round, 1977–78.
—— Land Holdings Survey. 8th Round, 1953–54; 26th Round, 1971–72.
Registrar General. Census, various years.
—— Report of the Survey on Infant and Child Mortality, 1978.
Reserve Bank of India. All-India Debt and Investment Survey, 1971–72.
—— All-India Rural Credit Survey, 1951–52.
—— *Bulletin*, October 1969.
Season and Crop Reports. Various states, various years.
Statistical Abstract of India. Central Statistical Organization, various years.
Statistical Abstract of West Bengal. Government of West Bengal, various years.
Vital Statistics of India. Registrar General of India, various years.

Secondary Sources

Adams, D. W. and N. Rask. 1968. "Economics of Cost-Share Leases in Less-Developed Countries." *American Journal of Agricultural Economics* (November), vol. 15.
Adams, W. and J. Yellen. 1976. "Commodity Bundling and the Burden of Monopoly." *Quarterly Journal of Economics* (August), vol. 90.
Ahluwalia, M. S. 1978. "Rural Poverty and Agricultural Performance in India." *Journal of Development Studies* (April), vol. 14.
Akerlof, G. A. 1970. "The Market for 'Lemons': Qualitative Uncertainty and the Market Mechanism." *Quarterly Journal of Economics* (August), vol. 84.
Alavi, H. 1973. "Peasants and Revolution." Reprinted in A. R. Desai, ed., *Peasant Struggles in India.* Bombay: Oxford University Press, 1979.
Anderson, P. 1974. *Lineages of the Absolutist State.* London: NLB.
Arrow, K. J. 1971. *Essays in the Theory of Risk-Bearing.* Chicago: Markham.
Bailey, F. G. 1971. "The Peasant View of the Bad Life." In T. Shanin, ed., *Peasants and Peasant Societies.* Middlesex: Penguin Books.
Bardhan, K. 1977. "Rural Employment, Wages, and Labor Markets in India: A Survey of Research." *Economic and Political Weekly* (June 25, July 2, and July 9), vol. 12.
Bardhan, P. 1973a. "Size, Productivity, and Returns to Scale: An Analysis of

Farm-level Data in Indian Agriculture." *Journal of Political Economy*, (November–December), vol. 81.

—— 1973 b. "On the Incidence of Poverty in Rural India in the Sixties." *Economic and Political Weekly* (February), vol. 8. Reprinted in T. N. Srinivasan and P. Bardhan, eds., *Poverty and Income Distribution in India.* Calcutta: Statistical Publishing Society.

—— 1974. "On Life and Death Questions." *Economic and Political Weekly* (August),   vol. 9.

—— 1978. "On Measuring Rural Unemployment." *Journal of Development Studies* (April), vol. 14.

—— 1979. "Labor Supply functions in a Poor Agrarian Economy." *American Economic Review* (March), vol. 69.

Bardhan, P. and A. Rudra. 1978. "Interlinkage of Land, Labour, and Credit Relations: An analysis of Village Survey Data in East India." *Economic and Political Weekly* (February), vol. 13.

—— 1981. "Terms and Conditions of Labour Contracts in Agriculture: Results of a Survey in West Bengal 1979." *Oxford Bulletin of Economics and Statistics* (February), vol. 43.

Bardhan, P. et al. 1978. *Labor Absorption in Indian Agriculture: Some Exploratory Investigations. Bangkok:* ARTEP, *International Labour Organisation.*

Barnum H. N. and L. Squire. 1979. "An Econometric Application of the Theory of the Farm-Household." *Journal of Development Economics* (March), vol. 6.

Beardsley. R. 1964. "Ecological and Social Parallels Between Rice-Growing Communities of Japan and Spain." In V. Garfield and E. Friedl, eds., *Symposium on Community Studies in Anthropology.* Seattle: University of Washington Press.

Bell, C. 1976. "Production Conditions, Innovation, and Choice of Lease in Agriculture." *Sankhya* (December), series C, vol. 38.

—— 1977. "Alternative Theories of Sharecropping: Some Tests Using Evidence from North-East India." *Journal of Development Studies* (July), vol. 13.

Bell, C. and P. Zusman. 1976. "A Bargaining Theoretic Approach to Crop-sharing Contracts." *American Economic Review* (September), vol. 66.

—— 1979. "New Approaches to the Theory of Rental Contracts in Agriculture." Washington D.C.: World Bank.

Beteille, A. 1974. *Studies in Agrarian Social Structure* Delhi: Oxford University Press.

Bhaduri, A. 1973. "Agricultural Backwardness Under Semi-Feudalism." *Economic Journal* (March), vol. 88.

—— 1977. "On the Formation of Usurious Interest Rates in Backward Agriculture." *Cambridge Journal of Economics* (March), vol. 5.

—— 1981. "Class Relations and the Pattern of Accumulation in an Agrarian Economy." *Cambridge Journal of Economics* (March), vol. 5.

Bhalla, G. S. and Y. K. Alagh. 1979. *Performance of Indian Agriculture: A Districtwise Study.* New Delhi: Sterling.

Bhalla, S. 1976. "New Relations of Production in Haryana Agriculture." *Economic and Political Weekly* (March), vol. 11.

—— 1977. "Changes in Acreage and Tenure Structure of Land Holdings in Haryana, 1962–72." *Economic and Political Weekly* (March), vol. 12.

Bharadwaj, K. 1974. *Production Conditions in Indian Agriculture.* Cambridge:

Cambridge University Press.

Bhardwaj, K. and P. Das. 1975. "Tenurial Conditions and Mode of Exploitation: A Study of Some Villages in Orissa." *Economic and Political Weekly* (February 6 and 7), vol. 10.

Binswanger, H. P. 1977. *The Economics of Tractors in the Indian Subcontinent: An Analytical Review*. Hyderabad: ICRISAT.

—— 1981. "Attitude Toward Risk: Theoretical Implications of an Experiment in Rural India." *Economic Journal* (December), vol. 91.

Binswanger, H. P. et al. 1981., "Common Features and Contrasts in Labor Relations in the Semi-Arid Tropics of India." In H. P. Binswanger and M. Rosenzweig, eds., *Contractual Arrangements, Employment, and Wages in Rural Labor Markets in Asia*. New Haven: Yale University Press.

Bliss, C. J. and N. H. Stern. 1978. "Productivity, Wages and Nutrition" parts 1 and 2. *Journal of Development Economics* (December), vol. 5.

—— 1982. *Palanpur: Studies in the Economy of a North Indian Village*. London: Oxford University Press.

Bohannan, P. and G. Dalton, eds. 1962. *Markets in Africa*. Evanston: Northwestern University Press.

Boserup, E. 1970. *Woman's Role in Economic Development*. London: Allen and Unwin.

Braverman, A. and T. N. Srinivasan. 1981. "Agrarian Reforms in Developing Rural Economies Characterized by Interlinked Credit and Tenancy Markets." In H. P. Binswanger and M. Rosenzweig, eds., *Contractual Arrangements, Employment, and Wages in Rural Labor Market in Asia*. New Haven: Yale University Press.

Braverman, A. and J. Stiglitz. 1981a. "Landlords, Tenants, and Technological Innovations." (January). Washington, D. C.: World Bank.

—— 1981b. "Cost Sharing Arrangements Under Sharecropping: A Multi-dimensional Incentive Problem." (May). Washington, D. C.: World Bank.

—— 1981c. "Sharecropping and the Interlinking of Agrarian Markets." (May). Washington, D. C.: World Bank.

Breman, J. 1974. *Patronage and Exploitation: Changing Agrarian Relations in South Gujarat*. Berkeley: University of California Press.

Chambers, R. and B. H. Farmer. 1977. "Perceptions, Technology and the Future." In B. H. Farmer, ed., *Green Revolution: Technology and Change in Rice Growing Areas of Tamil Nadu and Sri Lanka*. London: Macmillan.

Chambers, R. and R. Wade. 1980. "Managing the Main System: Canal Irrigation's Blind Spot." *Economic and Political Weekly* (September), vol. 15.

Chayanov, A. V. 1966. *The Theory of Peasant Economy*. Homewood, Ill.: Irwin.

Cohen, G. A. 1978. *Karl Marx's Theory of History: A Defence*. Princeton: Princeton University Press.

Coward, E. W., Jr., ed. 1980. *Irrigation and Agricultural Development in Asia*. Ithaca: Cornell University Press.

Datta, S. K. and J. B. Nugent. 1981. "Tenancy Choice and Contractual Terms in a Competitive Framework." (April). Los Angeles: University of Southern California.

Day, R. H. 1967. "The Economics of Technological Change and the Demise of the Share-Cropper." *American Economic Review* (June), vol. 57.

Dewey, A. 1962. *Peasant Marketing in Java*. New York: Free Press of Glencoe.

Djurfeldt, G. and S. Lindberg. 1975. *Behind Poverty: The Social Formation in a Tamil Village.* Lund/London: Curzon Press.

Elster, J. 1979. *Ulysses and the Sirens: Studies in Rationality and Irrationality.* Cambridge: Cambridge University Press.

Eriksson, I. and J. Rogers. 1978. *Rural Labour and Population Change: Social and Demographic Developments in East-Central Sweden During the Nineteenth Century.* Uppsala: Almqvist and Wiksell.

Geertz, C. 1973. "Thick Description: Toward an Interpretive Theory of Culture." In *The Interpretation of Cultures: Selected Essays.* New York: Basic Books.

—— 1978. "The Bazaar Economy: Information and Search in Peasant Marketing." *American Economic Review* (May), vol. 68.

—— 1980. "Organization of the Balinese Subak." In E. W. Coward, Jr, ed., *Irrigation and Agricultural Development in Asia.* Ithaca: Cornell University Press.

Ghate, P. G. 1980. "Irrigation for Very Small Farmers: Appropriate Technology or Appropriate Organization?" *Economic and Political Weekly* (December 27), vol. 15.

Ghose, A. K. and A. Saith. 1976. "Indebtedness, Tenancy, and the Adoption of New Technology in Semi-Feudal Agriculture." *World Development* (April), vol. 4.

Gough, K. 1969. "Peasant Resistance and Revolt in South India." Reprinted in A. R. Desai, ed., *Peansant Struggle in India.* Bombay: Oxford University Press, 1979.

Griffin, K. 1974. *The Political Economy of Agrarian Change.* London: Macmillan.

Habib, I. 1969. "Problems of Marxist Historical Analysis." *Enquiry*, vol. 8. (Monsoon).

Hallagan, W. 1978. "Self-Selection by Contractual Choice and the Theory of Sharecropping." *Bell Journal of Economics* (Autumn), vol. 9.

Hansen, B. 1971. "Employment and Rural Wages in Egypt: A Reinterpretation." *American Economic Review* (June), vol. 61.

Hanson, J. A. 1971. "Employment and Rural Wages in Egypt: A Reinterpretation." *American Economic Review* (june), vol. 61.

Harris, M. 1979. *Cultural Materialism: The Struggle for a Science of Culture.* New York: Random House.

Hart, H. C. 1978. "Anarchy, Paternalism, or Collective Responsibility Under the Canals?" *Economic and Political Weekly* (December 23–30), vol. 13.

Hauser, P. M. 1974. "The Measurement of Labor Utilization." *Malayan Economic Review* (April), vol. 19.

Hayami, Y. and V. W. Ruttan. 1971. *Agricultural Development: An International Perspective.* Baltimore: Johns Hopkins University Press.

Hicks, J. R. 1969. *A Theory of Economic History.* Oxford: Clarendon Press.

Hilton, R. 1977. *Bond Men Made Free.* London: Methuen.

Hunt, R. and E. Hunt. 1976. "Canal Irrigation and Local Social Organization." *Current Anthropology* (September), vol. 17.

International Labor Organization. 1974. "Measuring the Adequacy of Employment in Developing Countries." *Journal of Development Planning,* vol. 5.

Ishikawa, S. 1967, *Economic Development in Asian Perspective.* Tokyo: Hitotsubashi University.

Jayaraman, T. K. 1981. "Farmers' Organizations in Surface Irrigation Projects:

Two Empirical Studies from Gujarat." *Economic and Political Weekly.* (September 26), vol. 16.

Jodha, N. S. 1981. "Agricultural Tenancy: Fresh Evidence from Dryland Areas in India." *Economic and Political Weekly* (December 26), vol. 16.

Johnson, D. G. 1950. "Resource Allocation Under Share Contracts." *Journal of Political Economy* (April), vol. 58.

Joshi, P. C. 1981. "Fieldwork Experience, Relived and Reconsidered: The Agrarian Society of Uttar Pradesh." *Journal of Peasant Studies* (July), vol. 8.

Kalecki, M., 1943. "Political Aspects of Full Employment", *Political Quarterly* (October–December), vol. 14.

Kotwal, A. 1981. "The Impact of Green Revolution on Labor Contracts and Rural Poverty" (August) Vancouver: University of British Columbia.

Krishna, R. 1976. *Rural Unemployment: A Survey of Concepts and Estimates for India.* Washington, D. C.: World Bank.

Krishnaji, N. 1980. "Agrarian Structure and Family Formation." *Economic and Political Weekly* (March 29), vol. 15.

Layard, R., M. Barton and A. Zabalza. 1980. "Married Women's Participation and Hours." *Economica* (February), vol. 47.

Leibenstein, H. 1957. *Economic Backwardness and Economic Growth: Studies in the Theory of Economic Development.* New York: Wiley.

Levine, A. and E.O. Wright., 1980. "Rationality and Class Struggle." *New Left Review* (September–October), no. 123.

Lucas, R. E. B. 1979. "Sharing, Monitoring, and Incentives: Marshallian Misallocation Reassessed." *Journal of Political Economy* (June), vol. 87.

Mazumdar, D. 1959. "The Marginal Productivity Theory of Wages and Disguised Unemployment." *Review of Economic Studies* (June), vol. 26.

—— 1965. "Size of Farm and Productivity: A Problem of Indian Peasant Agriculture." *Economica* (May), vol. 32.

Mencher, J. 1974. "Problems in Analysing Rural Class Structures." *Economic and Political Weekly* (August 31), vol. 9.

Miller, B. D. 1980. "Female Neglect and the Costs of Marriage in Rural India." *Contributions to Indian Sociology* (February), vol. 14.

Mintz, S. W. 1959. "Internal Market Systems as Mechanics of Social Articulation." In *Proceedings of the 1959 Annual Spring Meetings of the American Ethnological Society.* Seattle: University of Washington Press.

—— 1961. "Pratik: Haitian Personal Economic Relationships." In *Proceedings of the 1961 Annual Spring Meeting of the American Ethnological Society.* Seattle: University of Washington Press.

Mirrlees, J. 1975. "A Pure Theory of Underdeveloped Economies." In L. Reynolds, ed., *Agriculture in Development Theory.* New Haven: Yale University Press.

Mukhia, H. 1981. "Was There Feudalism in Indian History?" *Journal of Peasant Studies.* (April), vol. 8.

Newbery, D. M. G. 1975. "Tenurial Obstacles to Innovation." *Journal of Development Economics* (July), vol. 11.

—— 1977. "Risk-Sharing, Sharecropping and Uncertain Labour Markets." *Review of Economic Studies* (October), vol. 44.

Newbery, D. M. G. and J. E. Stiglitz. 1979. "Sharecropping, Risk-sharing, and the Importance of Imperfect Information." In J. A. Roumasset et al., eds., *Risk,*

Uncertainty, and Agricultural Development. New York: Agricultural Development Council.

Oberai, A. S. and H. K. Manmohan Singh. 1980. "Migration Flows in Punjab's Green Revolution Belt." *Economic and Political Weekly* (March 29), vol. 15.

Okun, A. M. 1975. "Inflation: Its Mechanics and Welfare Costs." *Brookings Papers on Economic Activity.*

Ostroy, J. M. and R. Starr. 1974. "Money and the Decentralization of Exchange." *Econometrica* (November), vol. 42.

Parthasarathy, G. 1975. "West Godavari, Andhra Pradesh." In *Changes in Rice Farming in Selected Areas of Asia.* Philippines: IRRI.

Parthasarathy, G. and D. S. Prasad. 1974. "Response to and Impact of HYV Rice by Size and Tenure in a Delta Village, Andhra Pradesh, India." *Developing Economies* (June).

Polanyi, K. *The Great Transformation.* 1944. New York: Farrar and Rhinehart.

Popkin, S. L. 1979. *The Rational Peasant: The Political Economy of Rural Society in Vietnam.* Berkeley: University of California Press.

Radner, R. 1981. "Monitoring Cooperative Agreements in a Repeated Principal–Agent Relationship." *Econometrica* (September), vol. 49.

Ransom, R. L. and R. Sutch. 1977. *One Kind of Freedom: The Economic Consequences of Emancipation.* New York: Cambridge University Press.

Rao, C. H. H. 1975. *Technological Change and Distribution of Gains in Indian Agriculture.* Delhi: Institute of Economic Growth.

Reid, J. D. 1973. "Sharecropping as an Understandable Market Response in the Postbellum South." *Journal of Economic History* (March), vol. 33.

Richards, A. 1979. "The Political Economy of Gutswirtschaft: A Comparative Analysis of East Elbian Germany, Egypt and Chile." *Comparative Studies in Society and History* (October), vol. 21.

Rodgers, G. B. 1975. "Nutritionally Based Wage Determination in the Low Income Labor Market." *Oxford Economic Papers* (March), vol. 27.

Roemer, J. 1982. *A General Theory of Exploitation and Class.* Cambridge: Harvard University Press.

Rosenzweig, M. R. 1980. "Neo-Classical Theory and the Optimizing Peasant: An Econometric Analysis of Market Family Labor Supply in a Developing Country." *Quarterly Journal of Economics.* (February), vol. 94.

Rosenzweig, M.R. and T. P. Schultz. 1982. "Market Opportunities, Genetic Endowments, and the Intra-family Distribution of Resources: Child Survival in Rural India." *American Economic Review* (June), vol. 72.

Rothschild, M. and J. E. Stiglitz. 1971. "Increasing Risk: Its Economic Consequences." *Journal of Economic Theory* (March), vol. 3.

Rude, E. 1964. *The Crowd in History: A Study of Popular Disturbances in France and England, 1730–1848.* New York: Wiley.

Rudra, A. 1971. "Employment Patterns in Large Farms of Punjab." *Economic and Political Weekly* (June 26), vol. 6.

—— 1978. "Class Relations in Indian Agriculture." *Economic and Political Weekly* (June 3, 10, and 17), vol. 16.

—— 1981. "Local Power and Farm Level Decision Making." New York: Social Science Research Council.

Sandmo, A. 1970. "The Effect of Uncertainty on Saving Decisions." *Review of Economic Studies* (July), vol. 37.

Scott, J. C. 1976. *The Moral Economy of the Peasant: Rebellion and Subsistence in Southeast Asia.* New Haven: Yale University Press.

Sen, A. K. 1962. "An Aspect of Indian Agriculture." *Economic Weekly* (February), vol. 14.

—— 1975. *Employment, Technology, and Development.* Oxford: Clarendon Press.

—— 1980. "Levels of Poverty: Policy and Change." World Bank Staff Working Paper, no. 401.

Sharma, P. S. 1973. *Agricultural Reorganization of India.* New Delhi: Allied.

Skoepol, T. 1979. *States and Social Revolutions.* Cambridge: Cambridge University Press.

Smith, J. P., ed., 1980. *Female Labor Supply: Theory and Estimation.* Princeton: Princeton University Press.

Sopher, D. E. 1980. "The Geographical Patterning of Culture in India." In D. E. Sopher, ed., *An Exploration of India: Geographical Perspectives on Society and Culture.* Ithaca: Cornell University Press.

Srinivasan, T. N. 1979a. "Bonded Labor Contracts and Incentives To Adopt Yield Raising Innovations in Semi-feudal Agriculture." Washington, D. C.: World Bank.

—— 1979b. "Agricultural Backwardness Under Semi-feudalism—Comment." *Economic Journal* (June), vol. 89.

Srinivasan, T. N., and P. Bardhan. 1974. *Poverty and Income Distribution in India.* Calcutta: Statistical Publishing Society.

Stiglitz, J. E. 1974. "Incentives and Risk Sharing in Sharecropping." *Review of Economic Studies* (April), vol. 41.

—— 1976. "The Efficiency Wage Hypothesis, Surplus Labor, and the Distribution of Income in L. D. C.s." *Oxford Economic Papers* (July), vol. 28.

Stokes, E. 1978. *The Peasant and the Raj.* Cambridge: Cambridge University Press.

Sukhatme, P.V. 1978. "Assessment of Adequacy of Diets of Different Income Levels." *Economic and Political Weekly* (August), special no.

Swamy, V. S. 1979. "Some Aspects of Child Mortality: A Profile." New Delhi: Office of the Registrar General, India.

Taylor, M. 1976 *Anarchy and Cooperation.* Chichester: Wiley.

Terray, E. 1975. "Classes and Class Consciousness in the Abron Kingdom of Gyaman." In M. Bloch, ed., *Marxist Analysis and Social Anthropology.* London: Malaby Press.

Thompson, E. P. 1971. "The Moral Economy of the English Crowd in the Eighteenth Century." *Past and Present* (February), vol. 50.

Thorner, D. 1966. "Marx on India and the Asiatic Mode of Production." *Contributions to Indian Sociology* (December), vol. 9.

Thorner, D. and A. Thorner. 1962. *Land and Labor in India.* New York: Asia Publishing House.

Vaidyanathan, A. and A. V. Jose, 1978. "Absorption of Human Labour in Agriculture: A Comparative Study of Some Asian Countries." In P. Bardhan et al. *Labor Absorption in Indian Agriculture: Some Exploratory Investigations.* Bangkok: ARTEP, International Labor Organization.

Vander Meer, C. 1980. "Changing Local Patterns in a Taiwanese Irrigation System." In E. W. Coward, Jr., ed., *Irrigation and Agricultural Development in*

Asia. Ithaca: Cornell University Press.

Vander Velde, E. J. 1980. "Local Consequences of a Large-Scale Irrigation System in India." In E. W. Coward, Jr., ed., *Irrigation and Agricultural Development in Asia.* Ithaca: Cornell University Press.

Visaria, P. M. 1971. *The Sex Ratio of the Population of India,* Census of India, 1961, Monograph no. 10. New Delhi.

Wade, R. 1979. "The Social Response to Irrigation: An Indian Case Study." *Journal of Development Studies* (October), vol. 16.

—— 1980. "India's Changing Strategy of Irrigation Development." In E. W. Coward, Jr., ed., *Irrigation and Agricultural Development in Asia.* Ithaca: Cornell University Press.

Wharton, C. R. 1962. "Marketing, Merchandising and Money Lending: A Note on Middleman Monopsony in Malaya." *Malayan Economic Review* (October), vol. 7.

White, B. and Makali. 1979. "Wage Labor and Wage Relations in Javanese Agriculture: Some Preliminary Notes from the Agro-Economic Survey."

Williamson, O. E. et al. 1975. "Understanding the Employment Relation: The Analysis of Idiosyncratic Exchange." *Bell Journal of Economics* (Spring), vol. 6.

Wittfogel, K. 1957. *Oriental Despotism.* New Haven: Yale University Press.

Wolf, E. 1969. *Peasant Wars of the Twentieth Century.* New York: Harper & Row.

Author Index

Subject Index

ATE DUE

DEC			
AUG			

DEMCO NO. 38-298